Cameron Hardiman joined the eighteen and served over thirty Most of his time with Victoria Police was as an air observer with the Air Wing. He eventually joined the Australian Federal Police and served on overseas missions that included the Solomon Islands and Timor-Leste. He then transferred into an investigations role, focusing first on general crime, then people smuggling operations and counterterrorism.

TEN FEET TALL
AND NOT QUITE
BULLETPROOF

DRUG BUSTS AND HELICOPTER RESCUES:
ONE COP'S EXTRAORDINARY TRUE STORY

CAMERON HARDIMAN

hachette
AUSTRALIA

Published in Australia and New Zealand in 2020
by Hachette Australia
(an imprint of Hachette Australia Pty Limited)
Level 17, 207 Kent Street, Sydney NSW 2000
www.hachette.com.au

10 9 8 7 6 5 4 3 2 1

 A catalogue record for this
NATIONAL book is available from the
LIBRARY National Library of Australia
OF AUSTRALIA

ISBN: 978 0 7336 4239 5

Cover design by Luke Causby, Blue Cork
Cover photographs courtesy of Ryan Mason/*Collective Magazine*, Fabrique Imagique/Adobe Stock, andrej pol/Adobe Stock
Text design by Kirby Jones
Typeset in Sabon by Kirby Jones
Printed and bound in Australia by McPherson's Printing Group

To Susan, Louis and Adele –
this book is really meant for you

I am glad of what
I have accomplished.
I have endured hardship,
trauma, pain and loss;
I have done so voluntarily;
I am not a victim,
I am a survivor.

Exit Wounds,
Major General John Cantwell AO DSC

CONTENTS

NOTE TO READERS

Readers are advised that this book contains graphic scenes of physical trauma, domestic violence and suicide, and detailed descriptions of the symptoms and lived-experience of post-traumatic stress disorder (PTSD).

1

BASS STRAIT

3 February 2005 – 0600 hours

I timed my mornings for maximum sleep, skipping breakfast, which I thought was for the weak. The shower did its best to wake me up and I stepped out feeling almost human.

My partner, Susan, was still in bed of course – she enjoyed her sleep as much as I did. We had met a few years before through work friends and had recently moved in together, into a comfortable flat in East Hawthorn.

Pulling away from the curb in my VW Golf, which was much cooler in my imagination than in reality, I cranked up the radio and surfed between stations to find something I liked, something I could sing along to out loud. I gave the weather little more than a glance. There was low cloud blanketing the city and the roads were wet from the night's rain. It was not typical summer weather for Melbourne, even though the city was known for experiencing sweltering heat in the morning and rain in the afternoon. Creedence's 'Bad Moon Rising' blared out of my speakers. I happily sang along and tapped out the drum beat on my steering wheel, totally oblivious to the warning of hurricanes and flooding in the song's chorus. Looking back, I had been warned.

When the music stopped on the half hour a weather report covered news of widespread storm damage around Melbourne and the coast. The *Spirit of Tasmania* had turned back to port, damaged in Bass Strait by twenty-metre-high waves. Windows were smashed, the deck flooded and passengers were injured. I shuddered. I had experience with Bass Strait and knew how unforgiving her waters were. In normal seas with deep water, swells build up over distance and roll as they move, eventually breaking into waves when they hit shallow water. In Bass Strait things were different. It wasn't that deep, and in high winds waves appeared out of nowhere and just smashed into each other. It was a wild stretch of water.

•

I walked through the front doors of our hangar. It was tucked away in a secluded part of Essendon Airport, twenty minutes' drive north of the city. The hangar lacked the typical blue and white signage that marked other police buildings around the state, not for reasons of disguise but simply because the general public never needed to knock on our door seeking help.

The metal door on my locker made its usual screech as I opened it. I took my keys out of my pocket and threw them onto the top shelf before getting undressed. Putting on the navy-blue flight suit was like putting on a suit of armour – I was ten feet tall and bulletproof when I was wearing it. The suit satisfied the ego all aircrew shared but didn't confess to. In 1992 when I was a General Duties copper attending a hold-up alarm at Melbourne Airport, three aircrew approached my divisional van wearing flight suits, blue leather bomber jackets and black suede zip-up boots. They looked like my childhood heroes from World War II – modern day versions of Douglas Bader and Guy Gibson – and having the opportunity to talk to these guys left me buzzing with excitement. That feeling remained with me every time I donned the navy-blue flight suit.

Now dressed, I started to fill my pockets. While I wasn't particular about much, I had a thing about folding my Nomex flight gloves so that they were perfectly flat before tucking them neatly into my left thigh pocket. Next, I put my mobile phone in my left breast pocket. I saved my lucky Cuban cigar for last. Most of us had a talisman of some sort – mine was the Cuban cigar in its battered aluminium tube. I slipped it into the narrow leg pocket just above my right ankle, saving it for celebrating that one job that was somehow going to be bigger than all the rest. Bigger also meant more dangerous, but I suppose I should have been careful about what I wished for.

Just as I closed the door on my locker that morning I caught a glimpse of a broken winch cable I kept at the back of the top shelf. The twisted section of cable had broken strands sticking out of it like tiny barbs. Winch cables never broke. But this one had. It was more than ten years ago that I had been hanging from it one hundred feet in the air during training over Port Phillip Bay. It started pinging as each fine strand of wire snapped, one at a time. I could feel something was wrong and there was absolutely nothing I could do about it, not from one hundred feet above the water anyway. I could only hope that the crew in the helicopter picked up on the problem. They did. The helicopter's nose tilted and dived towards the water. I pulled my emergency quick release and dropped into the waves, where I was picked up by a safety boat and taken to shore. I had only fallen about thirty feet, but I knew that I had dodged a bullet. The pinging I felt through the cable as each of the wire strands snapped was something that I will never forget. I kept the broken winch cable, not as a reminder of my lucky escape, but as a badge of honour.

All suited up, I strolled back across the hangar. Two helicopters sat parked along one side – the Air Ambulance and the police helicopter. I could have been rostered to work on either one of them, but today I was working on the police helicopter.

I tossed my flight helmet and leather jacket into the helicopter and headed to the mess room. I continued with my morning ritual by sorting through the pile of stained coffee mugs, trying to find one not growing mould. A spoonful of Nescafé, instant hot water from the electric urn, a splash of milk and I was good to go. With hands wrapped around my mug I walked towards the helicopter. Already loading our gear into the cabin, my fellow observer Brendan Francis informed me that we were on standby to search for a distress beacon activated in Bass Strait fifty miles south of the Mornington Peninsula. It was the perfect time to decide who would be the lucky one to go down on the winch cable if we had to perform a rescue during the shift.

'I'll do it,' I said without any thought. I probably shouldn't have volunteered so quickly, considering the way the weather was.

Brendan was a lot younger than me and had been at the Air Wing a few years. Although the weather was bad, he was a good winch operator so I wasn't worried about being on the end of the winch cable with him at the controls. Together we inspected the rescue winch and took a quick inventory of our equipment. We were ready.

An amplified ring sounded out of the small speaker in the hangar, signalling a call from D24 – our police communications centre. Someone reported seeing a fourteen-year-old boy washed over a bridge and into the swollen Skeleton Creek at Hoppers Crossing – a suburb on the western outskirts of Melbourne.

The hangar doors rattled open and Brendan fired up the tractor to tow the helicopter outside onto the tarmac. Our pilot, Ray Pitts, hurried out from the mess room wiping the last hurried sip of his coffee from his mouth. He joined me in the middle of the hangar and we both followed the helicopter out through the hangar doors.

With his slicked-back rocker hairstyle and sideburns, Ray looked more like a skinny Elvis than a pilot. I half expected him to pull out a pocket comb, reach over his head and glide it through his hair. More often than not he could be found in front of the hangar doors hunched against the wind, sucking deep on a cigarette to draw every last grain of tobacco out of it before grinding the butt into the tarmac with the heel of his flying boot.

Jumping into the rear cabin and starting to put a harness on, I recited the start-up procedure in my head – every step, every sound. The date was an odd number, so I knew Ray would start the left engine first. This ensured that neither engine was overburdened mechanically.

Through the earphones in my flight helmet I heard the buzz as the helicopter's batteries came on. At the press of a button, fuel was pumped into the turbine engine and ignited. I could feel the gentle rocking as the rotors began to turn, slowly at first, then gathered speed. The sound of the Dauphin's signature tail fan overtook the noise of the rotors, producing that unmistakeable high-pitched whine. Ray started the right engine and the rotor blades soon hit top speed. The rocking stopped and the helicopter settled.

Ray radioed the control tower for clearance so we could avoid air traffic arriving into nearby Melbourne Airport, only a few miles north of us. Brendan was up front next to the pilot. Today, he would be navigating and I would operate the thermal camera if needed. Brendan flicked through the *Melway Street Directory* and quickly located the ominously named Skeleton Creek. He pointed Ray in the right direction and we were cleared to take off.

Ten minutes later, we approached the search area. Ray slowed the helicopter down and I sank into my seat with the rapid decrease in speed and height. We entered a right-hand turn and continued to descend then steadied at our search height – not much higher than the spire on St Paul's Cathedral in the city.

I moved from my seat and into the rear cabin where I clipped my harness into an anchor point on the floor. As I slid the cabin door open, a blast of cold air shot under my helmet. For a split second the wind opened my microphone and the sound from outside roared into my earphones so I quickly adjusted my intercom. I would now have to press the transmit button at the end of my flight helmet lead to talk. I shuffled to the edge of the doorway, my feet dangling below the aircraft. I had the perfect panoramic view of Skeleton Creek, snaking its way between vacant land, housing and a large industrial area.

The brackish brown floodwater was dangerously close to houses. I could see a stranded school bus stuck on a road on a raised island, surrounded by the swollen creek. Further south the water was trying its hardest to flow down towards Port Phillip Bay. Water swirled violently beneath the bridge – the one the fourteen-year-old boy was reported to have been swept off. Large eddies formed downstream where obstructions each created their own whirlpool, sucking in all the debris as it washed past.

I scanned the floodwater, immediately fearing that a kid would not survive long in it. I mentally divided the area into sections, scanning each one in a pattern to ensure I covered every square metre of ground. In my mind I pictured what I was looking for – something appearing out of place, a colour or a shape that stood out or didn't belong. Every round or solid floating object got a closer look. Best-case scenario was that we would find the teenager stranded on high ground waving for help. But more than likely he would be found floating face down in the water, arms and legs fanned out from his body. Best-case scenarios didn't happen very often in our job.

After three solid sweeps of the area, doubt began to creep in. I leant back into the helicopter and flicked on my mic. 'Brendan, how many calls did they get about this kid?'

'Just the one.'

'Has anyone reported a kid missing?'

'Not yet.' Brendan was clearly thinking along the same lines as me, I could hear it in his voice – it could have been a hoax call.

Before we had the chance to discuss whether we should call off the search another job came through, an urgent one. A flurry of radio communications arranged our Air Ambulance helicopter to come and take over the search for the missing teenager while we headed back to base to be briefed on the new job. A lone yachtsman was in trouble and needed rescuing.

I looked over the horizon towards the south. All I could see was a mass of dark cloud looming over Bass Strait.

2

SURFBOARDS AND PINBALL MACHINES

My dad was a Royal Australian Air Force (RAAF) policeman, so I spent my early years growing up around RAAF bases. The most memorable was RAAF Base Edinburgh in South Australia during the mid-1970s when I was ten years old. I loved riding to the base in the back of Dad's old lime green Kingswood station wagon with my two brothers, Allister and Scott, seeing who could spot the first plane on the tarmac as we approached. It was hardly a competition: they were always parked in the same place. If Dad had to go to his office to pick something up, or to just say hello to the guys, I would eagerly tag along – especially if it meant getting to see the planes.

Then there were outings to the base movie hall. Mum and Dad would drop us off at the makeshift movie cinema – a hall packed with uncomfortable steel fold-out chairs and a hundred or so other Air Force brats. None of us were particularly interested in the evening's feature – what kid would be remotely interested in *Raid on Entebbe*? This was more of an opportunity to wreak havoc away from the watchful eyes of our parents.

The highlight of growing up near an Air Force base was the flying displays. Caribou cargo aircraft, Neptune Bombers and F-111 jets put on shows that would impress any kid. The Caribou's short take-off and landing, and the Neptune's explosive strike on a black cardboard submarine were always impressive, but they could never outdo the F-111 lighting up its afterburners. The only thing that could top that for me was a flying demonstration from my favourite – the UH-1 Iroquois helicopter that had flown down from the base in New South Wales. It beat afterburners and cardboard submarines hands down.

My obsession with helicopters was sealed one summer's day in the mid-1970s while I was involved in a battle with Scott in our front yard, both of us armed with old fence palings that our imaginations had turned into guns. The sound was faint at first, but it was unmistakeable. The beat of massive rotor blades chopping through the air. I threw down my gun and surrendered. An Iroquois was coming.

The beat got louder. Any minute the chopper would show itself. I searched the horizon, waited and listened. Then, there it was like a giant insect on the hunt, its nose down sniffing out prey. It was coming straight for me. The massive two-piece windscreen became eyes on top of a black painted nose. Large dark rotor blades spun in a blur like dragonfly wings. It was fast, skimming low over the rooftops like in the television coverage of Vietnam.

The chopper flew right over me, the beat of the blades drowned out by the scream of the turbine engine. It banked over the top of my house. Its side doors were open, pushed back alongside the body. Someone dressed in a green flight suit and helmet with a dark visor was sitting in the open cabin. I would have given anything to be just like him. I waved madly, desperate to get his attention. I was a soldier stranded in a jungle and this helicopter was my only chance of rescue.

Then it happened. He waved back. I couldn't believe it. He waved at me.

•

My transient Air Force education gave me some unexpected skills. On my first day at each new school I would become the class comedian, joking around and acting up in front of the teacher while on the lookout for anyone who thought I was funny. At break time I'd make a beeline for them. Jokes and laughter became a way of concealing the fact that I was uncomfortable, nervous or sometimes even scared. This was an approach I would use throughout my adult life.

Sport was an entree into social groups too, although I avoided the popular sports like rugby union because it was played by the most popular kids. And I thought the class comedian wouldn't stand a chance breaking into the tight-knit group formed by a sport like rugby. I would play whatever sport came a close second – usually baseball or hockey, which were played by casual knockabouts; they were my kind of people. Soon I would move schools again and start over.

Dad eventually retired from the military after twenty-eight years' service and we packed up and moved to Melbourne. For a while Dad worked as an insurance investigator but it wasn't long before he was back in uniform again, this time as a prison officer at Pentridge Prison.

My schooling concluded at the local high school in Gladstone Park, a working-class suburb only a stone's throw from Melbourne Airport. The school never appeared on the end-of-year list of top performing schools, but it was close to home and I made a bunch of friends there. I learned I had artistic flair but no academic ability and my report cards reflected that, with variations on the popular statements: *Cameron could do so much better if he only applied himself more* and *Cameron is easily distracted*. The only things that changed on my report cards were the dates and the teachers' names. With great enthusiasm and no appreciation of my limited academic ability, I commenced my last year of school in 1983, sailing confidently into HSC maths, physics, graphic art and English.

In my final exam, maths, I did not get much beyond writing my name on the front page of the paper before coughing a prearranged code to my mate Karl. He replied in kind, whereupon we both stood and walked out. My maths teacher explained my final mark: I was given 1 per cent for every class I attended. I could have sworn I turned up more than fourteen times.

Karl and I discussed our futures later on in his rumpus room as we dived into white paper parcels of fish and chips.

In the end, I did what I thought every eighteen-year-old kid who failed his HSC should do – I applied for the dole and went surfing. Mum and Dad weren't pleased.

I invested a large sum of my fortnightly dole payments in the pinball machines, video games and strong Turkish coffee at a dingy little Turkish cafe near the dole office. It was more of an illegal gambling den than a cafe and was always occupied by the same group of old men smoking rollies, playing poker and keeping coded notes on their winnings in case the local coppers walked in. The old men left me alone to play the machines and drink my coffee, and I left them to their game. Not that it was difficult: they didn't speak a word of English and I had no idea what language they were speaking.

A couple of times a month I would drive along the coast in search of the perfect wave. For me, surfing was a dangerous activity – the nomadic RAAF lifestyle meant I escaped any kind of swimming lessons as a youngster and therefore wasn't a particularly confident swimmer. But I never let my lack of experience stop me from seeking out the thrill of big waves. At the height of my post-school surfing binge I headed for the big waves near Warrnambool, three hours' drive east of Melbourne. The weather that day was horrendous. Clouds swirled overhead, threatening a show of lightning and thunder, and a bitterly cold offshore wind that must have come straight off the ice in Antarctica blew hard. It explained the lack of other surfers in the water. My school friend who'd come with me wasn't keen on tackling the huge waves forming offshore, but I was. Perhaps a little too confident.

I paddled out to meet the incoming swell, picking the perfect spot to wait just beyond the break. Sitting up on my board, the sets rolled underneath me.

It wasn't long before the sea morphed into three perfectly formed waves. I paddled out a little further to meet them head on. I rolled over the first wave, then, as I turned around, the second one barrelled towards me. It was massive – the biggest wave I had ever seen – and it was all mine. When I felt my board climb up the wall of water, I jumped to my feet and shot down the front of the wave, but it was far too powerful. I fell headfirst over the front of my board and disappeared underwater. I was trapped beneath the surface in the wave's turbulence as it rolled over the top of me, pummelling me like I was in a boxing ring. When I finally broke the surface I was dazed. My leg rope had snapped and my board was nowhere to be seen. I tried desperately to swim back to shore but with each stroke it seemed further and further away. It wasn't long before I had used every ounce of strength I had.

Wave after wave forced me back underwater until I gave up the fight. I rolled over onto my back and waited for the next wave to hit. I was a goner, for sure. I took a deep breath and accepted that it would be my last. But, suddenly, my body pumped with adrenaline and I started swimming. When the waves rolled through I let them take me under without a fight. When I burst back on the surface, I'd swim for it. Eventually, I made it back to shallow water. My friend, who was standing on the beach the whole time, hadn't seen a thing.

For most people, being seconds away from drowning would be enough to make them reconsider the wisdom of surfing. It might have been resilience, perhaps stupidity, but by the time my feet hit the beach I had put the experience behind me and was already planning my next big wave.

•

Although all my friends went to university, that wasn't an option for me. I had been living a life of surfing, pinball machines and lounging around the house, getting under Mum's feet for the last twelve months, when one day I saw a recruitment ad for Victoria Police on television. There was a police car with flashing blue lights and a police dog on the scent of a bad guy. The ad promised an exciting career, and excitement was what I was after. Dad was full of support, seeing as he had considered a career with Victoria Police prior to joining the RAAF. As for Mum, the first words out of her mouth said it all.

'I'm not ironing any more blue uniform shirts!'

Not long after at the Westmeadows Police Station, the closest police station to home, I spoke to a copper for the first time in my life. The crusty old station sergeant told me that, in his opinion, I was too young to join the Force, that I should probably get some life experience first, but that he would submit my application anyway. I didn't really know what life experience was – I had just turned eighteen. I surfed and I could play a mean round of pinball. What more did he want?

After this lacklustre response, I was surprised when four weeks later I received a letter from Victoria Police recruiting asking me to sit the Police entrance exam. I hit the shops and bought my very first suit – a double-breasted light grey Italian number – as well as a very fashionable thin leather tie. I sat the entrance exam – a mix of English, mathematics and IQ testing. Not the type of examination someone with my academic skills would find easy. I was shitting my pants.

Somehow, though, I managed to pass the exam. Then there was an interview – more like an inquisition. Three coppers sat behind a long table and asked what I would do if … I bumbled my way through the answers and talked about my goals. I was then asked to wait outside. There were probably a dozen reasons why I was asked to wait, but the only reason I could think of is that they wanted to tell me in person that I didn't make the grade, saving them the trouble of typing a letter of rejection and paying for a stamp. Minutes later – although it felt like an hour – one of the interviewers came out, shook my hand and handed me a letter of offer. Someone must have thought I would make a good copper. I quickly signed on the dotted line before they could change their minds.

•

High on the hill in Glen Waverley, the Police Academy overlooks most of the eastern suburbs of Melbourne. It used to be a Catholic seminary until the police bought it in the 1970s. Its domed chapel and marble altar were immaculately maintained and are still used, mainly for police weddings and funerals. Neither of which I had any plans to attend. At eighteen I was the youngest recruit in my squad. Everyone else who started the eighteen weeks of training had come from other jobs. Some even had families. It felt just like the first day at a new school.

I expected the hard physical work, but I didn't realise how military-like it would be. I wasn't prepared for the random room inspections where our housekeeping skills were scrutinised to a point just shy of bouncing a coin on our beds to check how tightly we'd tucked in our sheets. Nor the uniform inspections where our shirts and pants were examined for any unapproved-of creases and our drill boots for a lack of mirror-like spit polish.

I still recall my squad's very first uniform inspection. It was on the morning of our third day in the Academy and we had only just been issued our uniforms. It was like leading lambs to the slaughter. The drill sergeant, who was a cranky old bastard, stood in front of me with his nose inches from mine.

'When was the last time you shaved, Hardiman?' he yelled.

'I have never shaved, sir.'

More yelling and abuse followed. I wish I could remember what he said, but the words blended into one loud indecipherable noise.

I was determined not to be berated by the drill sergeant again. Considering that it was only day three, I had some work to do. That night I drove to the local shopping centre and got an extra short haircut that would last me a month of inspections and I bought a bulk pack of disposable razors. I've shaved every morning since.

Every day in the Academy was the same as the previous one. Each morning we'd get out of bed, shave, shower, then put on our two-piece grey cover-alls and do 'morning fatigues' – chores that had to be completed before breakfast. My chore was to sweep a step at the back of the main building. Every morning for the entire eighteen weeks I swept the same step whether it needed it or not. It was then time to get dressed into our police uniform for breakfast. I would grab a blue police shirt from the closet and carefully remove it from its hanger, having spent most of the previous night ironing it. The only crease in each shirt was a strategically placed line across the shoulderblades – an indisputable sign that it had been well ironed. After breakfast the squad would form into three rows and march down to the parade ground at the back of the main building for rollcall and uniform inspections, then we'd march back to the main building to start our lectures.

Lectures covered criminal law, police procedure, state legislation and police powers. We also took part in physical training, swimming and drill (marching). We even did role plays. Our instructors would play the part of a criminal. We would approach them in pairs, determine if the suspect had committed a crime and if need be we would arrest and process them. Later on in our training we gave evidence against our instructor in a faux courtroom.

Each month we sat law examinations. The standard was quite high – an 80 per cent pass mark. I never liked examinations – in fact, I'd much prefer gouging my eyes out – but I found that criminal law and police procedure were far more interesting than high school English and maths. At the Academy, studying actually came easily to me and I discovered that doing well in an examination felt good.

We had a few dropouts, not because of their academic ability but because they had come to the realisation that policing was just not for them.

The Wheelers Hill Hotel, our local watering hole, provided a place and means to unwind within staggering distance from the Academy most Wednesday nights. Up until I joined the Academy I barely drank alcohol but I took to it like a fish to water. A bunch of us missed curfew a couple of nights and had to jump the front fence and sneak in past the security guard. Getting pissed was half the fun. The other half was getting away with it.

In our last week of training we had a mandatory visit to the Coroners Court to view an autopsy, in preparation for what we would see once we were out on the streets. The banter started immediately. Who would handle the blood and guts and who wouldn't? No one wanted to be the one who lost their shit and freaked out, calling into question their suitability to be a copper.

The Coroners Court sat at the dingy western end of Flinders Street in Melbourne. Not allowed to wear police uniforms outside the Academy until graduation day, we were dressed in our Sunday best. I wore the only piece of clothing I had that looked half respectable: my grey Italian-made suit.

The smell inside the autopsy room was like nothing I had ever experienced before. It was overpowering and smelt of … cold – the way I imagined freezing gas would smell. I was a bit nervous but trusted my own bravado. Everyone had their tough-faces on.

A female cadaver lay on a long stainless-steel tray. She was around forty years old, although it was hard to tell with her wax-like skin a dull blue–grey colour. One by one we stepped cautiously closer. The pathologist got straight to work, taking a scalpel and making an incision along the bottom of each breast. He removed the cadaver's breast implants, checking them for leaks or infections before holding them out at arm's length for all of us to see. He then made a single incision across the top of her head and folded the scalp back to reveal the skull. I watched in fascinated horror. He took a stainless-steel electric saw with a circular cutting blade and ran it across the skull. It had the familiar sound of a dentist's drill. I marvelled at his speed. After removing a section of skull, he removed the brain, weighed it and described it for the record. He then went on to remove all the other vital organs, weighing each of them, recording their description and explaining every move to us as he worked.

One of my squad mates, Deb Merryfull, suddenly turned around and ran out of the room. No one knew it at the time but Deb's aunt had recently died unexpectedly and an autopsy was performed to determine the cause of death. I suppose Deb will forever associate what she had just witnessed with the death of her aunt. I was surprised that she endured the autopsy for as long as she did.

Afterwards, the ride back to the Police Academy was a quiet one. I sat there in communal silence, reflecting on what I had just witnessed and trying to work out how I would get the smell of cold out of my suit.

I graduated along with my squad on 12 July 1985, marching out in front of our family and friends. Our marching routine was well-practised. In three rows we marched in both quick and slow time around the Academy's grass parade ground while the Victoria Police Pipe Band played. One by one we presented ourselves to the Chief Commissioner of Police, Sinclair Imrie Miller, or, as he was better known, 'Mick'. We greeted him with a salute and a handshake before he presented us with our certificates. At the end of the ceremony our squad was marched off the parade ground out of sight of the crowd. On the call of *fall out* we all turned and threw our police caps into the air.

I had just turned nineteen.

•

Fresh out of the Police Academy I arrived at Avondale Heights, my first training station, reluctantly displaying my P-plates on my car. I didn't want to get in trouble with the police on my very first day. It took only minutes for someone to spot them and it quickly became the station joke. I laughed along with everyone, of course – I was the class clown again trying to make friends and fit in.

There was a guy at the station who was a little older than me and a little different to everyone else. He looked like he would have been more comfortable working as a bank teller. I watched my new colleagues turn on him like wolves, always trying to set him up. One night, he came across a house fire on his way home from work. He called the fire brigade and asked around the neighbourhood to find out if anyone was living inside the house. The next day he arrived at work and was told that a TV crew would be coming to interview him about the story. The producer had asked, he was told, for him to apply make-up beforehand to save some time. There was no TV crew, just a bunch of laughing coppers making him feel stupid in his mother's foundation. If you fit in, things like this didn't happen to you.

I was assigned a training sergeant, Bob Croxford. Bob was an ex-homicide detective, which for a young copper like me was as impressive as it got. Bob had a perfectly manicured moustache and crystal blue eyes that bored like drills into probationary constables. Bob was a perfectionist in everything from the pressing of his uniform to his handwriting and magnificent signature.

At first, I was shit scared of him. I thought I'd never meet his high standards, especially with my paperwork. I would wait until he was on a day off before I put it in the sergeant's in-tray for checking. But all the other sergeants knew what I was up to and left it for Bob's return. I'd be called in to see him next time we were rostered on together and he would go through my work in meticulous detail. By the time Bob had finished, every page was covered in bright red corrections – immaculately written, of course. It was moments like these when the words of my high school teachers echoed: I should have applied myself more.

Joining the Police Force was like joining a secret club. Before you were accepted you had to prove yourself. You had to prove that you were worthy of wearing the uniform by lifting your weight at major jobs.

I was referred to as the 'new guy' or the 'trainee' until I had an opportunity to prove myself. Until then I did what I was told. I still remember the first words a street-hardened senior constable said to me on my very first shift on the road as I sat in the police car's passenger seat. 'Sit there and shut up. And don't touch the police radio unless I tell you to.' Needless to say, I was keen to shake off that title.

With a grand total of four weeks' operational experience I still hadn't shaken it, but things seemed to change quickly in this job. One day, it was close to three o'clock and my partner and I had almost made it back to the police station to knock off when D24 gave us one last job. Someone in Airport West had reported hearing an explosion in their garage. It wasn't the type of job we could just hand over to the replacement shift, plus any job with the word 'explosion' in it was an opportunity to finally prove myself.

On the way to the house I thought of all sorts of possible causes for the explosion – a gas bottle could have exploded while someone was welding; perhaps a car's leaking fuel tank ignited; or maybe a couple of kids had been trying to make a homemade bomb.

The home was typical for the suburb of Airport West – a postwar weatherboard. It was exceptionally maintained and the lawn was meticulously manicured. There were only a few shrubs in the garden, all pruned to within an inch of their lives.

Just as I stepped out of the divisional van an elderly European lady ran from out behind the house and down the driveway. She was crying for help and reciting prayers, all in broken English.

'Please, calm down. Calm down,' I said as I held my open hands up in front of her. 'Calm down. Calm down.' In the wailing I managed to understand two words: husband and garage.

The garage, made from yellow 1970s brick that indicated it was a late addition to the house, sat at the end of a long driveway. Its large wood-panelled front door was closed. I checked the latch and it was locked. The only other entrance was through a wooden door with a small window halfway along the side. My partner stayed with the lady while I approached the door.

I tried to peer through the window but it was pitch-black inside. The door handle was old and brittle, attached with a few tiny brass screws, all close to falling out. The door handle creaked as it turned.

'Hello?' I said. There was no answer. I stepped inside.

I didn't bother looking for a light switch just in case flicking it ignited something in the air. I took another step. In the dark I could just make out the shape of large work bench and some tools hanging from a pegboard behind it. Then a car. A few more steps and I could see an old green Toyota sedan. A coating of grime on the other side of the windows made it difficult to see through. I could only just make out a dark silhouette of something in the back seat.

I slid two fingers under the back passenger door handle, careful not to spread my fingerprints all over it. I pulled on the handle and the door clicked open. A man was sitting in the back seat, his left hand gripping the barrel of a shotgun and the thumb of his other hand against the trigger. The top of his head was missing, its contents the grime covering the windows.

I closed the door and walked out of the garage.

All I could think of was the need to isolate the scene, notify the sergeant and call the local detectives – just like

I had been taught in the Police Academy. But first I had to speak to the dead man's wife. I had always wondered what it would be like to tell someone that the one they loved was dead. And the seconds it took me to walk from the garage to the lady were not long enough to work it out. Perhaps I should have given it a little more consideration, but I thought it best to just get it over with. Not for my sake, but for hers.

I got my partner's attention and gave a subtle shake of my head, left to right – the signal that things were not okay and to prepare for a reaction. I stood before the lady and looked her in the eyes, careful not to show any expression that could be misunderstood.

'I am sorry, but your husband is dead.'

Even with the language barrier, she knew what I was saying. She started pounding on my chest with her fists then slowly fell to the ground, sobbing and wailing uncontrollably. I was expecting the sobbing, even the wailing, but not the beating on my chest – then I remembered being told during training that people handle grief in different ways.

The afternoon shift soon arrived at the house to take over. They had plenty of work ahead of them. Detectives would later arrive to make sure there were no suspicious circumstances, as would forensics and crime scene specialists to gather evidence just in case there were. When we arrived back at the station everyone rostered with me on the day shift, including the supervising sergeant, was heading to the local hotel at Keilor for drinks. I was expected to go. I went along, keen not to let anyone down. At the hotel, we all sat at a table tucked away in a quiet corner. A couple of drinks turned into many. Fresh beers appeared in front of me just as I was finishing the one I had in my hand, like magic. The flow never seemed to end, nor did the stories. Everyone shared tales about their worst jobs. When it was my turn that day, I had something to talk about. And when I spoke, everyone was keen to listen.

This wasn't a competition to see who had the worst story to tell. Aided by alcohol, it was a way of debriefing, of encouraging everyone to talk. After that day, I was no longer the trainee. I had proven myself at a major job and at the bar. I was now in the club, and telling the stories of traumatic jobs over alcohol was the way we decompressed. It was assumed that all we needed to do was collectively rid ourselves of bad memories over a good drink. Sharing them in any other forum was just not acceptable to my work colleagues. And it was these guys who I needed on my side the most.

3

RUSSELL STREET

Wearing long white gloves and directing traffic in front of the iconic Young & Jackson's Hotel on the corner of Swanston and Flinders streets in Melbourne's CBD was almost mandatory for every copper who joined Victoria Police.

After six months at Avondale Heights, I transferred to City Traffic for four weeks. As part of our training we had to do six months' worth of short assignments at a number of specialist policing areas, including D24, fingerprints and the Information Bureau, or Police Records. City Traffic was first on the list.

When I wasn't waving at traffic with long white gloves (which, to my disappointment, were not long gloves at all but cheap short woollen gloves with a cloth half-sleeve pinned to your jacket) I would find a quiet cafe to enjoy a coffee. Sometimes I teamed up with whoever was working the next intersection and snuck into the back of a movie cinema to catch a scene or two of the latest blockbuster – I could watch the whole movie over a week or two if I timed it right.

I had finished directing traffic through the Swanston and Bourke streets intersection and was taking a toilet break at the movie cinemas in Russell Street. (Cinema toilets were always clean and beat the hell out of being hassled by some weirdo who wanted to touch my clean white gloves in one of Melbourne's grubby underground public toilets.)

It was around 1 p.m. when I walked out of the toilets and heard an almighty explosion somewhere outside. It sounded like a major gas line had erupted beneath the city buildings. The ground shook underneath my feet.

I turned up the volume of my police radio and listened. The airwaves were chaos – every copper in town must have been transmitting at the same time. Through all the yelling I could just make out the words 'explosion' ... 'Russell Street' ... 'headquarters'. I burst out onto Russell Street, almost taking the cinema's glass entry door off its hinges. Our headquarters were only two city blocks away.

People had stopped dead in their tracks, looking up Russell Street in the direction of the blast. I ran through them all and out onto the road. I'm not sure how long it took me to cover the two city blocks, but I pushed myself so hard I started to dry retch. I ignored the feeling and kept running until I made it to headquarters.

I don't recall seeing the blackened and mangled wreck of a car parked outside the front door of our headquarters, blown apart after being packed with explosives, even though I stood only twenty or so metres from it. I don't remember seeing the street filled with a cloud of black smoke, or the road covered in pieces of shredded metal and shattered glass. Nor do I remember hearing the secondary explosions and watching people duck and run for cover. I had no idea that two young coppers, Angela Taylor and Carl Donadio, had been critically injured in the blast.

The next thing I knew it was 6 p.m. and I was taking part in a search for evidence in the streets surrounding headquarters. I joined twenty other coppers, forming a single line that stretched from footpath to footpath. We were all spaced at arm's length while we slowly moved forwards and searched the ground. But my mind wasn't on the job. I just followed the movement of the light blue shirts on either side of me, wondering if anyone else was missing five hours of that day.

A chunk of metal about the size of a clenched fist was just enough to grab my attention. I crouched down to get a closer look. Perhaps a piece of a car's engine block. The explosion had blown it sixteen storeys over the top of headquarters and into La Trobe Street, more than two hundred metres away. I called over a forensics expert who drew a circle around it with a piece of chalk. I then returned to walking with the line and wondering, *Does my missing chunk of memory make me the odd one out?*

It was 9 p.m. when I was finally relieved of duty. I went back to the City Traffic office and changed before heading home. I walked to the closest tram, which was already packed tight with passengers when it pulled up at the stop. I managed to squeeze myself on board, right next to the centre doors. I reached up to hold on to the overhead handle, steadying myself as the tram sped off down Elizabeth Street and onto Flemington Road.

Suddenly everything went blurry. My heart rate increased. I could no longer hear the tram gliding along the steel tracks or the whine of its electric motors. My body trembled and my knees went weak. I blacked out. I woke up lying head down in the tram's door well. The tram had stopped. The folding doors were trying to open and were pushing me against the steps, their sharp metal edges cutting into my back. People were yelling at the driver to close the doors. Dazed and a little embarrassed, I was helped to my feet by two passengers who told me that I had collapsed and was unconscious for thirty seconds. Someone offered me a seat, which I declined. I stood in the same spot as before, pretending nothing had happened.

I arrived home and staggered into my bedroom sometime before midnight, collapsing onto my bed. I was asleep within minutes. I returned to work the next day for a busy shift dealing with the fallout from the bombing. I didn't ever question again why I was missing a five-hour chunk of memory, or why I blacked out on the tram. Perhaps I should have. But I was back at work and I simply put that five-hour blank behind me. Constable Angela Taylor died in hospital a few weeks later. Constable Carl Donadio eventually returned to work and went on to serve a total of fifteen years with Victoria Police.

4

ACID-WASH JEANS

After I had completed my six months touring the specialist policing areas, I was transferred back to Avondale Heights Police Station to continue my training. I couldn't believe I was going back there when my squad mates were all heading to new stations.

Bob Croxford was my training sergeant again and, as I walked through the back door of the station to start my first shift, he greeted me with those crystal blue eyes. They drilled right through me. Nothing had changed with Bob. I had been shit scared of him when I left Avondale Heights six months ago, and I still was.

The allocation of training stations was determined by the Police Academy. So me being transferred back to Avondale Heights was either a mistake or whoever assigned us had it in for me, knowing that Bob Croxford had the unique ability to scare young coppers out of their skins.

The next six months were full of firsts for me – catching my first burglar on the run, attending my first drug overdose, my first court appearance, and my first fatal car accident. Fatal accidents were a test of mental fortitude and were the worst that policing could throw your way. The injuries that can be inflicted upon the human body during a car accident are unspeakable, and the scene of twisted metal car bodies, shattered glass and pieces of plastic is warlike. And, just like the autopsy viewing at the Coroners Court, my colleagues thought that if you couldn't handle all that, then you were weak and not worthy of wearing the police uniform.

Late one night I received a call from D24 to attend a four-car pile-up on the Calder Highway near Keilor, the next suburb north of Avondale Heights. There were reports of people seriously injured. My partner and I arrived to see a battle scene. Wrecked cars and debris were spread over a five-hundred-metre stretch of highway, the aftermath of two separate accidents. Two cars had collided while merging and had come to a stop in the middle of the highway, just over the crest of a hill. A young man, let's call him Adrian, was driving behind and saw the accident unfold. He pulled over into the emergency lane, got out of his car and went to help one of the drivers who was trapped in their car. A few minutes later, a third car came over the hill. Its driver didn't see the collision until too late. He slammed on his brakes, skidded straight into Adrian and dragged him and the car he was standing next to along the highway before eventually coming to a stop with Adrian wedged underneath the front bumper.

The ambulance crew had arrived before we had and were already treating Adrian. I opened the ambulance's back door, expecting to see a pile of body parts on a stretcher. I couldn't believe my eyes when I saw Adrian sitting upright, sucking madly on a Penthrane stick (a green plastic tube that looks like a whistle and contains a strong analgesic). His dark curly hair was matted together by a combination of road dirt and dried blood from a cut on the side of his head. A broken bone was penetrating through the skin on his right leg, which was in a pneumatic splint after the paramedics had cut off what was left of his jeans.

'Adrian, can you remember what happened?' I said.

He reluctantly removed the Penthrane stick from his mouth.

'I was just helping someone out who was stuck in their car when I was hit. I didn't see it coming,' he replied, wasting no time to put the Penthrane back in his mouth and sucking in a deep breath.

'Okay, mate, I'll contact you in a few days and arrange a time to get a statement from you, if that's okay?'

'Yeah, sure.'

I turned to walk away, stopping after a few steps to turn back and say, 'Adrian?'

'Yeah.'

'I reckon you would have to be luckiest man on earth.'

'Don't I know it.'

There wasn't much else for my partner and me to do at the accident scene, apart from getting the details of all those involved and clearing the highway so traffic could flow again.

The following morning, I walked into the office ready to finish off the paperwork for the accident. I checked the message book like I did at the start of every shift.

Cam. Adrian, the young guy from last night's accident, died overnight in hospital.

At first I thought the guys at the station were playing some morbid joke on me, but no one was laughing. A blood clot had formed in Adrian's leg and had broken away before lodging in his brain and killing him instantly. It's hard to describe the feeling of finding out that someone you spoke to only hours ago, and who was relatively healthy, was now dead. The only word that comes to mind is 'surreal'.

I attended many more fatal car accidents over the next few months. There was an expectation both within the Police Force and from the public that coppers were able to handle all the carnage associated with fatal accidents. And who doesn't want to live up to expectations?

One of those accidents was on the Calder Highway, not far from where Adrian had been hit. A car had collided at high speed with the back of another car that had been abandoned in the emergency lane. We were the first to arrive at the scene. The female driver was trapped in her car, pinned down by the dashboard and steering wheel. She had a major head injury after hitting the windscreen and her face and chest were covered in bright red blood. I was certain she had a spinal injury as well.

'An ambulance is on its way,' I said.

She looked up at me, struggling to keep her eyes from closing. She managed to choke out a grunt in reply.

'I'll stay with you until it arrives.'

I heard another grunt.

I grabbed hold of a T-shirt that was lying on the back seat of her car, opened the driver's door and leant inside.

With one hand I pressed the shirt against her head in an attempt to stop the flow of blood. I expected to feel some resistance as I applied pressure – instead her head felt soft and spongy underneath. I used my other hand to stop her head falling forwards and blocking her airway, or making any spinal injury worse.

I felt the need to talk to her but struggled to find a topic, any topic that would keep her conscious and thinking about anything other than her injuries. Conversation about family and friends was out of bounds, especially if she was worrying about whether or not she was ever going to see them again. Even asking where she was driving to when the accident happened was risky in case she was on the way home to see her kids. I quickly realised that there were no safe topics.

The shirt was soon soaked in blood. There was nothing else within arm's reach that I could use and eventually the blood seeped through and started covering my hands. It was warm and viscous at first, but soon turned cold and sticky as parts started to dry. I felt like I was holding weights above my head and my forearms started to burn. I was surprised how heavy a person's head can get after only a few minutes. But the burning disappeared the second I heard the faint wail of ambulance sirens in the distance.

'I can hear the ambulance now. It will be here soon,' I said.

Her grunts were now weak.

The ambulance couldn't come fast enough. I knew they were going as fast as they could, but to me it felt like they were crawling their way towards us. When they arrived, two paramedics rushed straight over to the car and swarmed over her. My hands were quickly replaced with layers of gauze padding and a plastic cervical collar.

I stood back and finally had a chance to take a deep breath. She was in far better hands now. I sat still in the police car on the way back to the station, while my partner drove. I was careful not to touch anything and spread the blood that covered my hands and shirt. I walked straight into the police station's bathroom, quickly removed my bloodied shirt, placed it in a plastic bag and dumped it in the rubbish bin. I had begun to wash my arms and hands when there was a knock at the door. It was our watch-house keeper with news that the Ambulance Service had called the station to let us know that the driver had died in the back of the ambulance. I left the station knowing that there would be another trip to the hotel in Keilor this week, where I could tell everyone about the lady in the car.

After three fatal accidents in as many months I became the subject of a few joking remarks around the station. I was now known, as every copper is for a period, as the 'Shit Magnet' for attracting bad jobs. I happily accepted it, regardless of what it took to earn it, and the nickname made me walk a little taller around the station.

•

Eighteen months after graduation, I returned to the Police Academy with the rest of my squad for the final phase of our training – a four-week retention course focused on revising and retaining all the knowledge acquired over the eighteen months of training. After this, I would no longer be on probation. The physical aspect was scaled back and was replaced with law and procedures. It was a relief to those of us who had lost the physical conditioning we had at graduation, which was not easy to maintain on a police officer's diet of fast food on the run and beers after work.

The new recruits could pick us easily. Our police shirts had lost their brand-new look and our boots were lucky to have seen Kiwi or Nugget polish or a brush in months. They treated us like royalty, moving aside and giving us room as we walked past them in the hallway, through a doorway or up a flight of stairs. I can't remember ever doing this when I was in their shoes. Maybe because at the time I was a teenager overwhelmed by exams and drill sessions and just didn't notice.

As the course came to an end, we were asked to nominate two police stations to be transferred to, where we would remain on permanent roster. We would only get our preference if the station was short staffed, so I was confident I would be placed at either Sunshine or Broadmeadows. Both were understaffed and overworked – and close to home. Really, I would have been happy with any station as long as it wasn't Avondale Heights. I wanted a little more action than it provided.

A few days before the end of the course a transfer list was pinned to the classroom noticeboard. Everybody rushed over and crowded around to search the list for their names. Being allocated a good station was like winning the lottery. There were cheers and fist pumps from some, while others walked away disappointed that they were heading to a station far from home or, worse, a quiet one where police calls were few and far between. As for me, I couldn't believe it. I was going back to Avondale Heights. Someone definitely had it in for me.

·

I walked, once again, through the back door of the Avondale Heights Police Station and past my old correspondence locker, the label with my surname printed on it still stuck to the door. I put all my files back into the locker, having only cleaned it out four weeks ago, thinking that I'd never return. I headed upstairs to the mess room – the same faces around the table having their morning tea and cake.

Bob Croxford stood up immediately and welcomed me back with a strong handshake.

'Glad to have you back, Cam,' he said.

'Thanks, Sergeant.'

'Sergeant? Bob will do. Sit down, Cam. Want some cake?' Bob's crystal blue eyes no longer drilled through me. I was not one of his trainees anymore.

Over the coming weeks I became confident enough to put my paperwork in Bob's in-tray and started to see fewer and fewer of his red corrections. When we were working the same shift I'd spend time with him in the sergeant's office while he told stories about his policing days in the seventies. Of course, there was a lesson in every one of them and I was keen to hear them all, including the one where he got shot by a crook in a dark cobblestone laneway in Richmond. The lesson: don't follow crooks down dark laneways.

A couple of months after I had walked back through the doors at Avondale Heights, Bob called me into his office for a quiet chat.

'Cam, I know you are disappointed that you haven't been sent to any other stations.'

I shrugged it off and pretended that it wasn't that big a deal.

'Well, I actually asked the Academy to send you back here,' he confessed, 'only because I reckon you would make a good detective one day and I want to make sure you get there.'

'Shit, Bob! I thought someone at the Academy had it in for me.'

We both laughed it off. I was relieved that the Academy wasn't against me and it was a huge boost to my confidence to know that Bob saw something in me.

A little more confidence made working the divisional van at Avondale Heights more enjoyable. There was no second guessing of my decisions or worrying about someone watching over my shoulder.

In 1988 I was allowed to sit the promotional exams to the rank of Senior Constable – two two-hour examinations held at Melbourne University in the city, one covering law and legislation, the other police procedure. You only got three attempts to pass the examinations, after that you were destined to be a constable for the rest of your career. I passed both examinations on my first attempt, but the rules didn't allow me to be promoted until I had accumulated five years of service, which by that time was two years away. I was allowed, though, to apply for a transfer to another station. Finally, I had a chance to leave Avondale Heights.

•

For most young coppers, interviewing a crook, processing their bail, then typing out a brief of evidence for prosecution is a daunting task. There would be far less headache in avoiding the arrest altogether. But if you're going to catch crooks you can't avoid it.

With Bob's help I had become reasonably confident in conducting interviews and all the paperwork that came with it. As a result, I was seconded to a plain clothes unit that worked the north-eastern suburbs of Melbourne. The unit was seen as a stepping stone for anyone wanting to become a detective – secondments there were hotly contested and rarely went to someone as junior in rank as I was at the time, so I put my plans to transfer out of Avondale Heights on hold while I worked with the plain clothes guys.

I had come across them a few times a month while out on patrol. They could often be found meeting up in a deserted shopping centre car park somewhere in the police district, standing around their cars with a couple of open pizza boxes on one of the bonnets, stuffing their faces. They dressed in scruffy clothes, with guns and handcuffs hidden under their jackets, and drove around in unmarked cars, complete with a blue light they pulled out from underneath the dashboard and stuck to the car roof when needed. They were today's version of Starsky and Hutch, only their cars weren't fancy red Ford Gran Torinos but far less impressive Toyota Corollas.

I heard all the stories of their late-night antics and close calls, and there was one story that seemed to get mentioned more than others. While executing a search warrant on a drug dealer's house, one of the plain clothes coppers got into a scuffle with a crook in a bedroom. During the fight the crook managed to get the revolver out of the copper's holster, pointed it at the copper's chest and pulled the trigger. Luckily the copper grabbed the barrel of the revolver, placing the webbing between his thumb and his forefinger in between the firing pin and the primer on the round. It never went off. The small hole in the webbing of his hand was far better than a gaping bullet wound in his chest.

I couldn't wait to start working with these guys. The unit mainly focused on drug offences. We also dabbled in investigating illegal gambling and stolen motor vehicle chop shops where stolen cars were reborn after being broken up and put back together with parts (and the identification numbers) of an old wreck. We worked office hours early in the week, pumping out evidence briefs on the crooks we caught in the previous month. By the weekend we were working nights, picking up any other crime we could get our hands on while patrolling the back lanes and hot spots around the police district. At the end of each month, we would execute a search warrant or two on a drug dealer's house or vehicle chop shop. The unit ran like a well-oiled machine.

When it came to executing search warrants I was always assigned the escape routes – the back door or side windows. If a crook decided to run out the back door or jump out a window, I would have to chase them down. As the youngest and most agile of the crew, the running always seemed to be left to me. I also had to be ready to smash a window and jump inside if need be. I didn't have to do it that often, but it was exhilarating smashing the glass out of a window with an old baseball bat and jumping inside, revolver drawn, to stop a dealer from flushing their product – our evidence – down the toilet. Search warrants kept everyone on their toes. They taught me to always expect the unexpected.

One night our unit had a search warrant for a suspected drug dealer's house in the northern suburb of Dallas. Under the cover of darkness, a couple of the guys and I crept along a damp drainage ditch that ran through some vacant land opposite his house until we reached a spot that gave us a perfect view of the front door. The rest of our unit were parked around the corner, waiting for the call to execute the warrant.

We watched customers walk up to the front door of the house, do their deals under its bright orange porch light, then walk off with their night's purchase. We couldn't approach the house while a deal was going down because they would see us coming from a mile away and the drugs would disappear down the toilet soon after. So we waited.

After an hour of lying in the freezing cold drainage ditch, we saw the orange porch light switch off. An approaching customer saw it too and stopped, paused, then turned around and walked away. The light must have been the sign that business was open. It was our chance to strike. The command to go came over the radio. I ran across the road and headed down the side of the house towards the back door. I heard some of our guys smash through the front door, then storm the house.

'Police! Get down!' they yelled.

Conveniently, the back door was left wide open, so I ran straight inside.

There were people scattering in every direction, looking for an exit or a place to hide. Some looked like they had never been to the house before and had no idea which way to turn. Rounding them all up was like trying to corral chickens. Once all the action had settled, we found a dozen one-kilogram bags of compressed cannabis on the lounge room coffee table plus more in the kitchen, and around ten thousand dollars in cash, tightly rolled into thousand-dollar lots.

All the occupants were split up and put into separate rooms then questioned in an attempt to figure out who was dealing, who was helping, and who was just an unlucky visitor. I remained in the kitchen with the rest of our guys recording the bags of cannabis and rolls of cash. Someone in our unit decided to turn the orange porch light back on, just to confirm whether it was the dealer's 'open for business' sign or not. It only took ten minutes before there was a knock at the front door.

I was sent to answer the door. Probably because I was the same age as everyone in the house, and I also dressed the same – in acid-wash denim jeans and a surfing brand T-shirt. I opened the front door to a young lad, not much younger than me, standing on the porch, already holding out a wad of cash ready to exchange for a deal bag of cannabis. I asked him inside the house to do business, telling him that you never know who's watching. He stepped inside, and got a lot more for his money than he expected.

As always, we celebrated our successes in a tiny evidence room in our office, playing darts for cans of Victoria Bitter until morning when the cleaner arrived and kicked us out. The following Monday we returned to the office to start a new week, typing out evidence briefs on our government-issued typewriters. I was twenty-one years old and living a life that most kids would only dream of.

•

Years later, on a Saturday morning, my boss and mentor with the striking blue eyes mowed his lawns at home just like he did every weekend. When Bob finished, he pushed his lawnmower into the garden shed, grabbed a piece of rope and hung himself with it.

No one ever knew why Bob did it.

5

A TASTE FOR CRIME

After nearly twelve months working at the plain clothes unit, I returned to Avondale Heights.

I started reading the *Police Gazette* – a fortnightly printed publication that listed all the vacant and filled positions around the state. I completed transfer applications for any stations in the western suburbs of Melbourne and eventually I was successful in getting a transfer to St Albans Police Station.

Geographically, St Albans was only a stone's throw across the Maribyrnong River from Avondale Heights, but it might as well have been on another planet. The area's claim to fame was that it had the highest rate of homicides in Melbourne and there were no signs of it losing its top ranking anytime soon. Its second most popular activity was domestic violence, homicide's closest relation, driven by alcohol or drugs. Most of the time it was both.

I knew St Albans pretty well, having responded to jobs while their crews were tied up. I also knew most of the coppers who worked at the station, having shared beers with them at nightshift barbecues – which were almost a religious ritual held at the end of each week of nightshift. We shared ours with the St Albans coppers and held them under the old Calder Highway Bridge that bordered the two districts.

I was looking forward to working there and couldn't wait to get my hands dirty.

•

Late 1980s St Albans was a suburb of high unemployment and a melting pot of cultures – Chinese, Maltese, Croatian and Serbian to name a few. Some of the ethnic groups carried a hatred for each other that began in their homelands centuries before they came to Australia. Late-night brawls between bored ethnic teens were more common than minor car accidents or petty shoplifting. But the most common violence of all was the domestic kind and it took up most of our time.

An unwritten course of action played out in response to a domestic violence call-out. If there was an act of violence we would charge the offender and make them leave the house – if we didn't arrest them on the spot – and then convince the victim to make a formal statement and consider taking out a restraining order. Every few weeks I would dress in my uniform tunic with its polished silver buttons, don my white police cap, then cram myself into the back of a police car with a bunch of other coppers from the station and drive off to our local court to give evidence against the offenders we had charged. That's if the victim hadn't rekindled their relationship with the offending party and refused to follow through on making a formal statement. Even if the victim had gone through with the statement, the offender would, more often than not, manage to excuse their actions because of the shitty card that life had dealt them. They'd receive a slap on the wrist and be back home before court had even closed. It was a merry-go-round of domestic violence.

There were only so many times I could go through the rigorous process of arresting, charging, bailing, taking statements, preparing briefs and attending court, only to have the whole case dropped like it never even happened. There was nothing more frustrating, and the feeling of sheer pointlessness made it increasingly difficult to do the right thing when attending domestic violence calls. After twelve months I thought I had seen it all. Battered wives and partners with injuries comparable to car accidents, houses damaged like they had endured a natural disaster after booze-fuelled arguments.

But every so often St Albans threw me a curve ball. One stinking hot afternoon I got into the divisional van, which the previous crew had only just returned to the station by the 3 o'clock knock-off time after a busy shift. As I got in the driver's side I caught the smell of hot oil and grease; they had pushed it hard. Tim Lewczuk, my partner for the afternoon, sat in the passenger seat. No one could really pronounce his surname properly nor could they get a nickname from it, so we just called him Tim. The van's inside was littered with remnants of discarded paperwork covered with hand-scribbled notes. Durable standard police issue vinyl and thick rubber matting replaced the usual factory cloth door linings and carpet flooring. I inched the van forwards out of the parking bay. Stopping at the edge of the roadway, I wondered what job we would get first. Before long, among the police radio chatter, we heard our call sign. Tim answered.

It was a domestic dispute, but this time gunshots had been heard coming from the house. A police unit from Sunshine called the radio operator and volunteered to back us up. Our flashing blue and red lights danced on house windows and street signs. Some cars swerved to get out of our way, some pulled over. People froze and stared at our car, a light show of human misery. I put my foot down and the engine roared. Dust that had collected in the unused centre of the road turned to a cloud of grey behind us. I weaved in and out of the traffic. Houses, cars and streets all a blur as we raced past them.

I can still remember the first time I ever drove to a job at the speed of light down a main road while dodging cars. I thought my head was going to explode with all the excitement. But I eventually became immune to it. By now, it had become no more exciting than driving to the local supermarket to do the weekly shopping.

Red traffic lights appeared ahead and approached fast. Maybe I could time it just right. I slowed down but only a little. We were so close. Please change to green. Tim got ready to hit the siren and I the brakes. We waited until the very last second. Tim looked to our left at the oncoming traffic.

'Clear left, Cam.'

We were almost at the point of no return. We wouldn't be able to stop. Fortune did favour the bold and the lights changed to green. Tim gave me one last 'clear left' while I checked for cars on my right who might try to beat the red lights. We sailed through. A feeling of weightlessness hit us as the van flew over the tiny rise in the middle of the intersection.

I could see the house up ahead. With the flashing lights now off, I started to slow. I stopped the van just short of the house. No one could see us approach from here. There was a faint click as I gently pushed my door closed. Tim followed. We crept up to the house, keeping tight against the fence. When we got to the house, I unclipped my holster and pulled out my revolver. Tim did the same, looking in through the front windows as we walked past them. There was no movement inside. We stopped near the front door and listened. Silence.

The fly-screen door was ajar and the front door behind it open. I could see a flicker of colour reflected on the walls from a television but there was no sound. Had someone left here in a hurry? Or maybe someone was waiting inside – for us. Tim gently pulled back on the fly-screen door. I pushed my revolver through the gap then slid in behind it. I was inside.

Sitting on a lounge chair was a lean, fit-looking man with deeply tanned skin. Michael Grech. He had an empty look on his face. He sat without saying a word, waiting for us to make the first move.

'Who else is in the house?' Tim asked him.

'My wife.'

'Where is she now?' I asked.

He didn't answer.

I saw a small crease slowly develop at the side of his mouth. A smirk.

'I'll check the house, Tim.' I left the room and walked cautiously through the house. The back door was open. I saw her as soon as I stepped into the backyard.

Roberta Grech was lying on her back in the middle of the yard. Red shotgun shells were scattered around her and a pump action shotgun was lying nearby. Her body was eaten away by its blasts. Her life most likely ended with a final shot to the head. She must have suffered before she died, one painful shot at a time.

I stepped back inside and closed the door behind me. No one else needed to go back there.

'She's dead,' I said.

Tim holstered his revolver, then stepped towards the man, grabbed one of his arms and pulled him to his feet. I watched his every move with my revolver trained on the centre of his chest. I was secretly hoping for the slightest hint that he was going to make one last stand. I have never hated anyone as much as I did this man. Tim handcuffed him and gave him his caution and rights. Only then did I lower my revolver and return it to its holster. Tim sat him back on the lounge and stood guard over him while I called D24, letting them know that our backup could slow down. There was no hurry anymore.

I heard a faint knock at the front door. Then another. The second louder and more hurried than the first. I opened the door to an older gentleman standing there. He looked as surprised as I was.

'My daughter Roberta, where is she? She just called me. She said, "Dad, I'm scared. Please hurry." I have come to get her. Where is Roberta? What is going on?'

It wasn't that long ago I had to tell a young man that both his parents had been killed in a car accident while returning from their holiday in Adelaide. But there was time to prepare for that message. What I would have given for a little time now.

There is never a nice way to tell someone that their child is dead, and this occasion was no exception. Roberta's father broke down, begging me to let him see his daughter. I stepped out into the front yard with him, the door slightly open so I could see Tim inside. I put one hand on his shoulder and told him that it would be best that he did not go into the house. A barrage of questions flowed, all of them understandable, none easy to answer.

Our backup soon arrived, followed by Homicide Squad detectives and the forensics team. I spent the next few hours sitting in the divisional van with Roberta's father, taking his statement for the detectives while Tim canvassed the neighbourhood for witnesses and Homicide detectives took Grech away to be for interviewed for murder.

It had started to rain lightly – a summer sprinkling. The smell of wet grass from the freshly mown paddock nearly enveloped the van. The sun was about to set and the backyard where Roberta's body lay was now covered in a blue tarpaulin, glowing from the spotlights underneath. It was erected to provide lighting for the forensics team and to keep the weather off the crime scene. A fine mist of rain droplets covered the van's windscreen. Roberta's father sat quietly in the passenger seat, slumped forwards, his head in his hands. Every now and then he would look out of the window and stare at the blue glow, knowing his daughter lay on the ground there.

I asked him a series of questions, writing his answers down as a formal statement. Each question was another reminder of his daughter.

'When was the last time you saw your daughter Roberta alive? Where was she and what was she doing? When was the last time you talked to Roberta? Had Roberta ever told you of any violence towards her from Michael?'

He answered every question the best he could, but each answer came with a bout of uncontrollable sobbing.

Weeks later, I was working behind the police station counter and the evening rush of people reporting on bail had started. As part of their bail conditions, some had to attend the station between 9 a.m. and 6 p.m. and sign their name in the bail book. A copper would then place the date, time and their signature next to their entry.

As I finished signing off one entry I looked up from the counter and at the queue of people waiting to report. There he was, Michael Grech, waiting in line for his turn to report in on bail. He was out on bail, free to come and go as he pleased as long as he reported to the police station on time. The merry-go-round operating at its best.

It was the fourth homicide I had been to in as many years. All of them had started out as domestic disputes. But Roberta's murder was the most brutal of them all. That's if there is such a thing as a less-brutal homicide. Before her murder the title went to a Vietnamese lady who had staggered around her house, spraying blood all over the walls, after her throat had been cut. She eventually bled out, dying on her front doorstep.

Michael Grech was eventually convicted for the murder of his wife and was sentenced to eighteen years in jail. He later appealed the severity of his sentence, which was then reduced to fifteen years, with a non-parole period of twelve years. Grech's low sentence was a serious blow to my belief that our justice system punished based on the seriousness of the crime and public expectation, which would have included my expectations. It made me question if I could remain a General Duties copper for the rest of my policing career.

Tim and I worked together for another two years and became good friends. Some years later, in 1997, he was working an evening shift when he and his partner pulled over a speeding car on the Western Ring Road in the suburb of Sunshine. The driver stopped their car on the crest of the bridge that crossed the Western Highway. Tim got out of his car and approached the driver. I imagine that his first words would have been to tell the driver to move their car forwards a little and get off the bridge, probably with some colourful language for effect. But then a third car travelling on the Ring Road failed to see the police car and ran into the back of it, pushing it forwards and hitting Tim, throwing him over the bridge and onto the busy Western Highway, fifteen metres below, killing him instantly.

I like to think that he never saw it coming and died before he left that bridge, but Tim's death shook me. More than ever, his death hammered home the inherent, inevitable dangers of policing.

6

CROSSROADS

By 1992 I had already found myself at a crossroads in my police career, and I was only twenty-five. I had had enough of the merry-go-round of domestic violence and pathetic court sentences, and Michael Grech's lenient sentence for killing his wife, Roberta, was the last straw. I needed a change from General Duties policing but there weren't too many options. Eventually I'd be eligible to sit the sergeant examinations, but that didn't appeal much to me – as you climb the ranks you also remove yourself from the frontline, where all the action is. I could apply to become a detective, working on drugs or major crimes. Applications were only called for once a year, but it would be the quickest way out of General Duties.

To become a detective I had to appear before a board of three senior detectives and present a portfolio of my previous six months of operational work. The portfolio had to include a sample of some of my briefs of evidence that had been to court and a summary of the jobs I had attended, the number of people I charged and for what offences. Even speeding tickets were counted. I would answer a bunch of questions and the panel would rate me before placing me into one of three groups – those free to apply for detective positions straightaway, those who could try again at the next board, and those who would make great traffic coppers.

Rumours soon started to circulate that the detective boards were approaching. It marked the start of the silly season – a mad frenzy where every detective hopeful scrambled to attend every job they could, and I was no different. If someone made an arrest within earshot of me I would offer to do the interview, charge the crook and type up the brief for them, as long as my name was on it – there wasn't a copper alive who would turn down that offer. Eventually my correspondence locker was overflowing with paperwork. I would regularly request a shift inside the station so I could catch up on the backlog, but one shift a week was never enough.

Despite being behind on my paperwork, my detective portfolio was looking impressive. I had a good mix of crime and traffic offences – exactly what the board was looking for. Everything got a mention, from failing to indicate while driving, to aggravated assault. I was confident that I had enough to get me through.

On one shift I was partnered with a copper called Roy Baker. (Roy's real name was actually Robert but we renamed him after Roy Baker, a character from the 1970s Australian television drama *Cop Shop*. Over the life of the TV series, Roy Baker never got promoted past the rank of

Senior Constable. Neither did our Roy Baker. Roy didn't mind the nickname, though – he actually answered to Roy more than he did Robert.) Near the end of the shift we were heading back to the station when we saw an old Holden Torana coming straight for us on the wrong side of the road to pass a long line of traffic stopped at the nearby railway gates. We were seconds off a head-on crash so Roy swung the van towards the kerb.

The Torana cut through a small gap in the traffic, mounted the kerb and drove along the grass median strip until the driver found a gap in the row of cars. He pulled into the gap and sat there patiently waiting for the railway gates to open just like everyone else, as if nothing had ever happened.

I figured this would be an easy way to get another statistic added to my detective portfolio. I turned on our flashing lights and Roy spun the van around 180 degrees. I grabbed the police radio hand piece and held it up to my mouth, ready to transmit in case the Torana driver decided to make a run for it.

Roy drove down the centre of the road and pulled up alongside the Torana. I got the driver's attention with a short burst of the siren. He turned back to me with a look that said 'You mean me?' I motioned for him to pull over. He mouthed a few obscenities, put on his left-hand indicator and looked behind him for oncoming traffic. Then, just like a responsible driver, he slowly moved over to the kerb. This guy was a dill. Roy broke through the line of traffic and pulled in behind him. The driver stepped out onto the road and stood beside his car, waiting for me to approach him. He looked as though he had just rolled out of bed after an all-night bender. His long black hair was all matted together on one side of his head and sticking out on the other. His wrists were heavily wrapped in leather bindings and his fingers were covered in chunky silver eagles and skulls. His ripped black denim jeans, chain-link belt and heavy metal T-shirt spoke volumes. He looked a little on edge, I thought he was probably high on drugs. He was certainly not happy we had pulled him over.

Before I said a word to him I saw a dark flash to my left. A clenched fist in full swing struck me in the jaw. My head spun around and I heard a sharp ring in my left ear. When I looked back I saw the driver shaping up to throw another punch. I grabbed hold of his shirt and pulled his body in close to mine so he couldn't swing his arms. There was another dark flash. This time it was Roy's long baton. But he wasn't holding on to it. I ducked as it flew past me, missing my head by millimetres. (Roy later told me that he saw the punch, grabbed the long baton from its holder on the inside of the police car's door, ran up behind me and took a swing at the driver. It slipped out of his hand.) The driver broke free of my grip and ran across the road, weaving through the traffic. I took off after him, gaining ground when he started to slow. He stopped in his tracks, turned around and shaped up for another punch.

In the meantime, Roy had managed to retrieve his baton and I could see him running towards us from the other side of the road.

'Mate, this isn't going to end nicely for you,' I said. 'Why don't you put your hands down and turn around for me?'

He looked confused, as if he was trying to process my instructions, trying to work out whether to follow them or not. Maybe he just couldn't understand English.

His expression changed. He had made a decision.

He took a swing.

I stepped back and he missed. Without a long baton and no other equipment on me but a revolver and a set of handcuffs, I had no option but to make a stand. I certainly couldn't walk away.

Round two was about to start when Roy stepped in between us and in one giant swing of the baton managed to wipe out both of the driver's clenched fists. His leather wristbands did little to protect them. He dropped to his knees with his arms folded across his chest. Even while screaming in pain, he managed to call us a few animal names and yell obscenities, some combinations of which I'd never heard before.

I walked over to him and leant in close. 'Told you so,' I whispered, as I took hold of his limp wrists and snapped my handcuffs around them. Roy searched him and found what was fuelling his fight – a small clear plastic deal bag with three white pills inside.

When the driver appeared in court a few weeks later he pleaded with the court for a light sentence. He claimed that it was the drugs that caused his violent behaviour and he was trying his hardest to get himself clean. His sob story worked. He was given a gentle smack on the wrist and a small fine, no more than the cost of his next score. I left the courtroom shaking my head in disgust and wondering what

I would have received if I'd punched him in the face when he got out of his car.

The day after I was back in the van, complaining to Roy about how much my jaw hurt and how little it was worth when a call for a hold-up alarm came over the police radio. It was at the Ansett Air Freight depot at Melbourne Airport and we were only a couple of minutes away. This time I was driving. I took a shortcut along a dirt road that led to the airport, avoiding the Tullamarine freeway and all its traffic. As I turned into the freight area of the airport I was stopped by a barrier of chequered police crime scene tape strung across the road. It looked as though we were the last to arrive.

There had been an armed hold-up, like something straight out of *Point Break*. Except these robbers were wearing rubber Michael Jackson masks instead of US presidents and they didn't get away. Norman Leung Lee, one of the state's most notorious armed robbers, had been shot by the Special Operations Group (SOG) and lay dead on the road. Another robber was seriously wounded. The third lay face down on the grass median strip in the centre of the road next to his getaway car, which the SOG had rammed with their four-wheel drive. A member of the SOG, dressed in his signature black overalls, was standing over him, his pump-action shotgun against his shoulder and the barrel pointing at the crook.

I wondered how everyone beat us here; even the detectives had arrived before us. Usually the divisional van would be the first to turn up to these sorts of calls and everyone else would follow. But I soon found out that it was the end of a four-month operation targeting this band of robbers. And everyone had been waiting nearby, ready to pounce when they entered the depot. We had missed out on the fun.

Another uniformed police unit arrived shortly after us and was already directing traffic around the crime scene. I reckoned it wouldn't be too long before we were asked to spend the next few hours taking witness statements for the detectives. Witness statements didn't count towards my detective portfolio, so I decided it was time to sneak away. Before I got a chance to drive off, three uniformed coppers swaggered up to our divisional van. Wearing navy-blue military-style flight suits and heavy blue leather jackets emblazoned on the left breast with a police badge with wings, flight gloves and black zip-up suede boots, their uniform was so different to ours. One was a pilot with the full wings, the other two had the air observer's half-wing, just like those worn by aircrew in World War II. These guys were the crew from the police helicopter.

I had heard the police helicopter on the radio before and they had even assisted us on some jobs, but I had never seen any of the crew before. They were like mythical beings that you only ever heard of, but never got to see. They told us how they were flying circles close to the airport waiting to be called in. As the heist went down they arrived overhead. Two robbers ran out of the freight depot with their bounty of cash in one hand and sawn-off shotguns in the other. They threw the cash into the back of a waiting Ford panel van before jumping in themselves. The helicopter swooped, ready for a chase. As the van accelerated away, the two robbers in the back tumbled out and onto the road. The heavily armed SOG officers pounced. The robbers stood up and decided to make a stand – all hell broke loose and the bullets started flying. The getaway car continued to drive off with the cash in the back and the police helicopter sat right over the top of it. Some SOG guys in a four-wheel drive rammed the van, jumped out and pulled the driver out, forcing him to the ground.

After the action was over, the helicopter landed on the airport tarmac and the crew decided to walk over to check out the crime scene before heading back to base.

'You guys aren't hanging around to take a few witness statements, are you?' I asked.

'What are they?' one of them replied, laughing.

Apart from their senses of humour there was something about these men that was different to the other coppers I had met over the years. They had a look about them, one of confidence built on harsh experience. It was in their faces, their uniforms and even the way they walked. Their black suede boots were worn down to bare leather, their leather jackets were covered in grazes, and the embroidered police patches on their sleeves were so filthy they were hardly recognisable. I knew I wasn't looking at the uniforms of men who just flew around all day.

Seeing them had woken up the little kid in me, the one who had his war interrupted by the Iroquois helicopter all those years ago. The kid who would have given anything to be just like the RAAF guy who waved to him from the helicopter. Suddenly, being promoted to sergeant or becoming a detective were no longer options. I was going to chase my childhood dream. I was going to be that guy.

7

BASS STRAIT

3 February 2005 – 0924 hours

We landed at Essendon Airport in preparation for the rescue job in Bass Strait. Our wheels touched the tarmac and the helicopter's engines idled for two minutes before they were shut down. Before we took off again we needed a briefing, an equipment check and a flight plan. We also had to locate a refuelling point – we couldn't do a winch sixty-five miles out to sea without topping up the tanks.

The rescue briefing was basic, covering only the minimum details we needed before getting airborne. A 71-year-old yachtsman, Ron Palmer, had used the satellite phone on board his yacht to contact the State Rescue Coordination Centre at the Water Police base. Palmer, a resident of Canada, was halfway through his solo around-the-world journey when he ran into the storm over Bass Strait. His yacht's mast had snapped in rough weather and now *Ron's Endeavour* was floundering in heavy seas, sixty-five nautical miles off the Gippsland coast. Brendan took notes. I looked over his shoulder to check the yacht's coordinates. Our pilot, Ray, and I moved over to the map table. Underneath a sheet of well-worn clear perspex was a large map covering Victoria, Bass Strait and the top of Tasmania.

'I reckon we could get out there in one go,' Ray said, tapping the location on the map. 'We'll winch him off and we can refuel at Latrobe Valley on our way back.'

I knew that once we rescued Palmer, we would leave behind maybe a quarter of a million dollars' worth of yacht, depending on its size. Over the years, I had watched half a dozen very expensive boats meet their watery graves.

'Works for me,' I said, watching him trace the trajectory on the map. As the one on the winch cable, I wanted to get the job over and done with quickly.

Ray, Brendan and I walked to the helicopter. Ray did his usual pre-flight inspection, making sure everything was where it should be. Still in my harness from the Skeleton Creek search, I jumped back into the rear cabin and checked my equipment for the second time that morning. If something was not needed it was left behind to lighten the load. Less weight meant more fuel, which would be spent while winching the yachtsman to safety – or searching for him if his yacht sank before we got there.

Ray soon had the engines screaming at full speed. He changed channels on one of the radios to check the latest weather report. The state was engulfed in a low-pressure system. Once he was ready, he requested permission from the control tower to take off.

'I've only flown in a pressure system this low once before,' Ray said in a quiet voice that I could hear through my headset. 'It was that yacht race five years ago, Cam.'

He didn't need to say anymore. I remembered the job well – the Big Bay yacht race around Port Phillip Bay, another yacht, another winch and sailor – only it didn't turn out so well. I shook my head to pack the memory away. I had a new job to concentrate on. Minutes later we were airborne and heading for the middle of Bass Strait. This job's urgency meant we got Air Traffic Control clearance for a quick departure out of Essendon Airport. There was some low cloud about from the storm cell sitting over Melbourne. Ray calculated a 75-minute flight to the yacht. That left us only thirty minutes to winch Palmer to safety before we had to head back to land and refuel. The timing would be tight.

The radio crackled to life. A voice from the Rescue Coordination Centre (RCC) relayed to us that they had been in contact with Palmer and had instructed him to wait on deck for us to arrive. They mentioned that they had also given him instructions to sink his yacht after I had landed on the deck.

'Confirm, he has to sink his yacht?' Brendan's voice was incredulous.

What the hell? I thought.

'Yes, confirmed. The yacht is in the main shipping channel,' the coordinator from the RCC explained. 'It can't stay there. It's gotta be scuttled.' He told us that once we had winched Palmer to safety we were to remain overhead and confirm that the yacht sank.

After this conversation with the RCC we discussed the rescue among ourselves over the intercom. As far as I was concerned, waiting around on deck while Palmer popped the yacht's sea valves was far too dangerous – the winch cable could get tangled in the mast and then I'd be in big trouble. But disconnecting myself from the winch cable and staying on the yacht came with its own set of dangers.

'Bugger that. I'm not waiting around for him to sink the yacht,' I said.

'Agreed,' said Ray. 'We don't have the fuel to wait around anyway.'

I suggested an alternative plan. 'How about he pulls the plug as soon as he sees the helicopter, then gets his arse back up on deck so we can winch him off and get the hell out of there?'

Brendan relayed our plan in slightly more professional language to the RCC, who agreed to pass on the new instructions to Palmer. With our plans in place we approached the hills along Victoria's southern coast. We flew low to stay underneath the cloud. At high altitudes, the ground is so far below that it seems like you're hardly moving. At lower altitudes, everything seems to move much faster. Low clouds on the hills near the coast blocked our way. Ray deftly banked to avoid them and sought an opening that he could sneak through.

We discussed our plan of attack over the intercom. This rescue would be a little more challenging because of Palmer's age. I'd never winched anybody that old before. How much could a 71-year-old participate in his own rescue? He might freeze or, worse, collapse. I would need a clear area on the yacht to be winched onto, probably the roof of the cabin. If he could climb up, Palmer would have to meet me there. Failing that, I would land in the water, get him to jump in and winch him up from there. We wasted precious minutes of fuel before Ray finally found his hole in the cloud. The coast was just on the other side of it. Before I knew it, we were over water. I needed to know what we were up against and looked out the window. The wind was whipping up some big waves, all of them covered in white caps and spray mist. *You've got to be kidding*, I thought. What sort of idiot would be out sailing in these conditions? I blew out a breath of deep frustration. *Every time someone decides to do something idiotic, someone like me ends up hanging from a winch cable.* I checked my mobile phone. It still had reception. I did something that I had never done before on a job – I typed a text to Susan: *Heading out into Bass Strait to winch someone off a yacht. Speak to you soon when it's all over.* I pressed send.

From the coast, we headed straight out to sea and soon lost sight of land. I checked my mobile phone one last time before the signal was lost. Susan hadn't replied.

Brendan kept his eye on the GPS and Ray flew onwards. While the Dauphin could handle the buffeting wind, it constantly dipped in the same way a light plane would in these conditions. Out this far, the water is usually a deep blue, but this time it was different. Beneath the surface, the sand had been whipped up by the storm and altered the sea's colour. It was murky green and ill tempered. From the air I could see wind veins – long streaks of white foam lace marking the direction and force of the wind. The closer we got, the more random and wild it looked. Bass Strait was a big washing machine and was certainly living up to its reputation. For the first time in years I felt my nerves starting to build. I quickly dismissed them.

To help focus, I readied myself for the winch. Just in case I ended up in the water, I emptied all my pockets: phone, watch, coins, wallet and, lastly, my lucky cigar. All left behind. I put on a survival suit over the top of my flight suit. It had a neoprene lining to keep the wearer's core temperature up and it was bright orange for high visibility. I put my harness back on and pulled down on the straps to tighten it, then repeated the procedure on my leg straps. The tight space at the back of the helicopter meant that putting on all my gear was like getting dressed in the back seat of a Morris Mini-Minor.

I connected my Y-piece to my harness and checked its quick-release mechanism. As its name suggests, the Y-piece is a Y-shaped short section of webbing that incorporates a large metal ring at one end to connect to the winch hook. It has a quick-release mechanism in the middle and two smaller metal hooks to attach it to the harness.

I checked the contents of my survival vest: mini flares, personal locator beacon and whistle – all tied to the vest with bright red lanyards.

Brendan disconnected himself from the intercom system, released his seatbelt and squeezed himself into the rear cabin. He set himself up next to the winch so he could operate it for me. He attached the nearest intercom lead to his helmet. 'Can you both hear me?' he said.

'Loud and clear,' I replied.

'Yes, Brendan,' said Ray.

I grabbed my rescue strop – a horse-collar-shaped harness that attached to the winch hook then looped around a person's body and tucked underneath their arms – and got it ready for the yachtsman. Even though we hadn't sighted the yacht, time was of the essence. I had to be ready to be winched out the door as soon as we located it. And since we had instructed Palmer to start sinking the yacht as soon as he spotted us, there was no time to waste. As far as fuel went, the clock was counting down.

I felt the nose of the helicopter lift and we began to slow down. Ray tried to descend but strong gusts of wind hit our rotor blades and forced us upwards. The blades started to make a slapping sound as Ray fought the wind and reduced power to get us closer to the water. We were directly over the yacht's last known position. We scanned the sea.

Ron's Endeavour was nowhere to be seen.

8

A CHILDHOOD DREAM

After seeing them at Melbourne Airport, I had to know more about these guys who flew in the police helicopter: who were these mythical beings? And, more importantly, how could I become one of them? No one back at the station seemed to know much about the Air Wing at all, but the consensus was that I'd have to wait until someone was carried out in a wooden box before I could get a job there. Suggestions I'd have a much better chance being promoted to Chief Commissioner did nothing to build my confidence.

Desperate for answers, I walked into the sergeant's office. John Booth, my supervising sergeant for the shift, was busy checking through the stack of paperwork left in the in-tray. Boothy had been around for a hundred years and I was certain that he would be able to tell me something about the Air Wing. I fired some questions his way.

'Boothy, do you know anyone at the Air Wing? Have you ever been out to their hangar? Have you been up in the police helicopter?'

His paperwork seemed far more important. I knew my relentless questioning would get under his skin and an answer would come eventually.

'What do the Air Wing actually do? Do they just fly helicopters?'

'For fuck's sake, Hardiman. Just ring 'em up and drive out there! They're just coppers!' Boothy always said what he was thinking, offensive or not. Why didn't I think of that myself? I made the call and grabbed the car keys.

•

I drove around Essendon Airport until I found the Air Wing's hangar. After ringing the doorbell at Hangar 104 I was greeted by a senior constable. He was dressed in his flight gear, wearing the signature blue leather jacket and an embroidered half-wing on his chest – the insignia of the police air observer.

He held the door open just enough to poke his head outside.

'Yes, mate?' he said.

'I was hoping someone here could tell me about the air observer role?'

'Ah, you want to be an air observer, do you?' he said.

'One day.'

'Come inside, then,' he said as he opened the door a little wider.

It was like meeting my favourite rock star and, after he introduced himself, in my excitement I couldn't even recall his name. He could have said his name was Charles Manson for all I know. We walked into the Air Wing's operations room, which I expected would be decked out like an aircraft control tower, complete with computer monitors and radios mounted into a giant wraparound desk. Instead, a single chair sat behind an office desk in the middle of a room, and a second desk had a few radios on it. The standard police firearms safe sat in the corner. He walked around the desk, sat down in the chair and, in one well-practised manoeuvre, pushed back from the table, crossed his legs mid-air and landed both feet on the table. He then reached over to the desk and picked up a television remote, pointed it to a television mounted high up in the corner and pressed mute.

I sat down on the only other chair in the room as he began to tell me about the role of the air observer.

'Well, for starters, similar helicopter operations to ours, like the Army and Navy, operate with two pilots. But we operate with one. We replace the second pilot with a trained air observer. So the air observer therefore has to assist the pilot with the management of the cockpit, navigation and radios. They are also in charge of the police side of the air operation – where the helicopter flies, what jobs it does and how it does them. The pilot is in charge of the flying side of the air operation – which means he keeps the thing in the air.'

The way he rattled on made me think that he had given the same speech to a hundred other coppers also wanting to become air observers.

'What type of person are they looking for?' I asked.

'Well, there are only twenty-two air observers on staff, most of them with more than ten years' General Duties experience behind them. When one of them finally leaves, their position is usually hotly contested by more than eighty applicants, most with ten years in the job and some of them with some sort of aviation experience. But it's probably best just to apply when a vacancy is advertised and not worry about everyone else. Needless to say, the applicant numbers are extremely high and vacancy numbers are low. Usually one.'

Although hearing his speech strengthened my resolve to get a job in the Air Wing, the figures he quoted eroded my confidence in securing one. With only seven years on the street and no aviation experience, I was in for one hell of a battle. A young copper like me could spend his whole career trying to get a job there and retire having never set foot in the place. But I had my whole career in front of me and there was no other place I wanted to be.

•

I started a regular schedule of waiting around the sergeant's office every other Thursday for the *Police Gazette* to arrive in the mail. The second it hit the sergeant's desk I'd snatch it away, rip it out of its plastic wrapper and flick straight to the section listing the vacant positions. None appeared for the Air Wing – until one Thursday when the unthinkable occurred. There wasn't just one air observer vacancy advertised at the Air Wing, but three. I could hardly contain my excitement. I read the advertisement a few times to make sure I wasn't seeing things. My excitement was short-lived, however, when I realised that with three vacancies, every man and his dog was going to apply. Application numbers would soar – the eighty originally mentioned were easily going to double. Each applicant would be thinking what I was: that this was their best chance of joining the Air Wing. The more I thought about the numbers, the more I realised my chances were poor. And then I remembered what the air observer had told me – it was probably best just to apply and not worry about everyone else. My application was in before the ink on my signature had the chance to dry.

Weeks later I received a letter informing me that I had to report to the Police Academy for an Air Wing physical assessment.

I nervously made my way down to the sports complex, not long before the other applicants showed up. Around twenty other coppers were selected for physical testing – I had secretly hoped there would only be three. We all got chatting, which for most of us was a good excuse to find out a little bit more about our competition.

Every applicant completed the standard physical strength and flexibility test with ease – push-ups, sit-ups and chin-ups. On top of that, we had to carry weights with our arms extended along a course to simulate carrying a person on a stretcher. Then it was off to the pool for a water assessment. I was confident with my physical strength and flexibility but was a little worried that my swimming would not meet the required standard, especially without a surfboard strapped to my leg. We started with a diver-drop into the water from a three-metre tower fully clothed. This was followed by a one-hundred-metre swim, then fifteen minutes treading water, finishing with a duck dive to retrieve a black rubber brick from the deep end.

One by one we entered the water. When it was my turn, I took a deep breath and executed a perfect scissor step from the dive platform and surfaced straight into the swim. I thought of nothing but making sure my swimming stroke looked at least half capable just in case the assessors were interested in technique as well as speed and distance. After the swim I went straight into treading water. For most of the time, I just lay back in a half-floating position waiting for the assessor to call me over to retrieve the rubber brick. I was out of the water before I knew it and pretty pleased with myself.

Then we were briefed on our final assessment – a single-breath, long-distance underwater swim that began after entering the pool and treading water a metre from the edge. Following a signal from the assessor we had to dive under the water and swim, fully submerged, as far as we could in one breath. We were not allowed to kick off from the side of the pool and there was no minimum distance we had to achieve, or so we were told. There was a mad scramble for the back of the line and I was lucky not to end up as first cab off the rank. I had a few in front of me and a chance to watch the exercise done a couple of times before my turn.

I entered the pool and began treading water and taking deep breaths to open up my lungs. I focused on holding my breath, not whether I could make the distance. On the assessor's command I took a final deep breath, lifted my chest out of the water, rolled forwards, dropped under the surface and started swimming. Flat out. No one said that our underwater swimming technique had to look pretty and mine – a cross between a sideways lunge and breaststroke – certainly wasn't. I held my breath until my chest ached and my brain was commanding me to breathe. When I couldn't resist any longer I broke the surface and gasped for air. I reckon I was underwater for no more the forty seconds. I looked back to where I had started and hoped that my efforts were enough. As I exited the pool the assessor recorded my distance – so much for no minimum requirement – and I was told to get dressed and return to my station.

I only had to wait four weeks to be told that I had passed the physical assessment and that I was shortlisted for an interview at the Air Wing's hangar. My confidence started to grow. All I had to do now was get through the interview.

On the morning of the interview I arrived at work with two police shirts – one to wear around the station and one just for the interview that I had ironed twice with a heavy coating of lemon-scented spray starch. My police cap, which only ever saw daylight for court, got a clean anyway. I scrubbed its white top with Jiffy kitchen cleaner and polished the black peak with a dishcloth that I'd borrowed from the station mess room. I closely inspected my uniform tunic, which had been hanging in my locker for a while since its last outing. Apart from a bit of dust that had gathered on the shoulders, it was something that any regimental sergeant major would be proud of – perfectly pressed with flat lapels and breast pocket corners snapped down. Its chrome buttons were glaringly clean and, most important of all, my name tag was centred exactly one centimetre above the right breast pocket, which I measured to be sure.

Not wanting to be late for my interview, I walked into the Air Wing hangar thirty minutes early. I parked myself on the blue vinyl two-seater couch in the office foyer while I waited for my turn. The foyer seemed to be the main thoroughfare between the aircraft hangar and the Air Wing's operations room and had a constant flow of traffic in and out. Everyone who walked past looked back at the couch, knowing that one of the applicants for the jobs would be sitting there nervously, waiting to be called. They all managed a smile as they walked past, probably more out of pity than politeness. Someone gave me directions to the mess room where I could get a drink of water – I must have looked like I needed one.

Walking into the mess room felt as conspicuous as walking into a wedding and slamming the church door during the 'I do'. It seemed like everyone in the hangar was taking their coffee break at the same time, and they all looked up at me. I refused to make eye contact and headed straight for the collection of glasses on the sink, hoping that a drink of cold water would settle my nerves. It didn't. For me, the air observer role was a lifetime in the making. I had a chance to turn a childhood dream into a reality. As for my police career, in my mind it was now the Air Wing or nothing.

•

Three panel members sat behind a long table against the back wall of the interview room. One of them was wearing metal police pilot's wings, another the air observer's half-wing. I stood in front of them and confidently threw a textbook salute, something I had not done since graduating from the Academy. Going by the looks of surprise on their faces, I don't think the panel had seen one for a few years either. Before sitting down, I removed my police cap and caught a brief glimpse of my cap badge mounted on the front of it. It was on upside down. For giggles an Air Wing staff member must have swapped it around while I was getting the drink of water. Under any other circumstances I would have had a good old belly laugh over it. But today, I shat my pants. I quickly sat down and placed my police cap on my lap with the badge away from the panel, praying that they hadn't noticed.

The most senior police member on the panel was the operations manager, Senior Sergeant Gary Lindsay. He introduced me to the Air Wing's chief pilot, Sergeant Ian Galt and the senior air observer, Sergeant Andrew Tait. Galt was a tower of a man. He was at least six-foot-five with hands the size of baseball gloves. I had no idea how his large frame could actually fit into the cramped cockpit of a helicopter, and with those hands it couldn't have been easy fiddling with all the helicopter's switches and dials. He had featured in a few articles in police magazines over the years – I knew he had transferred to the Air Wing as a senior constable, and rose to sergeant before becoming chief pilot. I figured he was the one I had to impress the most.

One by one they fired their questions at me. Gary Lindsay focused on police procedures, which I thought I had in the bag. Ian Galt was interested in getting to know me and my personality, and testing my ability to fit in with the unique dynamic of an Air Wing cockpit – a cockpit with both a pilot and air observer, each responsible for different but occasionally conflicting roles.

'Cameron, say you are the air observer in charge of the helicopter and searching for an armed offender in Fitzroy,' Galt said. 'You ask the pilot to descend lower so you can get a better look at the ground. The pilot does not want to descend the helicopter any lower. What do you do?'

'Sir, I would ask the pilot why,' I replied.

'The pilot tells you that he is not comfortable being any lower while there is an offender on the ground with a gun.'

'Sir, then I'd have a problem,' I said. 'If descending the helicopter lower was legal, I'd expect the pilot to do it.'

The conversation continued with Galt varying the scenario, adding legal height requirements, nearby construction cranes and a hospital. He even threw in a horse stud.

But the questions that really tested me came from Andrew Tait.

Tait handed me a standard bushwalking map of the Victoria High Country, covering the area around Mount Hotham and Falls Creek. He then fired off a list of map references for me to locate and asked me to describe the area within one kilometre of the reference grid. I also had to calculate rough compass headings for those locations and features. I was going okay for a while and was suitably proud of myself until he handed me a *Melway Street Directory*. Everything went downhill from there.

He bombarded me with questions that tested my ability to search for street names and features in the directory's index and search for map references at lightning speed. He didn't wait for me to provide him with a reference for the first street name before he gave me another one to find, then another. Before I knew it I had two or three names bouncing around inside my head, and I hadn't found any of them – Andrew was either timing my responses or seeing if I lost my temper and collapsed in a screaming heap. Then an instruction came that really caught me off guard.

'Cameron, your next reference is for Herring Island.'

Where the hell is Herring Island? I thought. I went straight to state maps and ran my finger along Victoria's coastline, from South Australia to New South Wales, searching for it. I knew the big islands – Phillip Island, French Island – and even some smaller ones, like Gabo Island. But I had never heard of Herring Island. I couldn't find it. I flicked over to the index of national parks, sporting grounds, schools and a whole host of other ground features. The index didn't have a list of islands, so I just flicked through a few more pages trying to buy myself a little time to provide a good reason why it was that I couldn't find Herring Island. It had to be a trick question.

'There is no Herring Island in Victoria, Sir,' I said with confidence.

'Isn't there?' he said. 'Okay, then your next reference is for Split Rock.'

I felt my stomach hit the floor. As I randomly flicked through the index for the second time, I thought, *How the hell am I going to find a bloody rock if I can't find an island?* Just in case I wasn't feeling enough pressure already, Tait explained in very clear terms why an air observer needs to be able to find and give map references quickly, no matter what map was in their hands – lives often depended on it. I knew exactly what he meant: my life was depending on me finding Split Rock.

'I don't believe Split Rock is listed in here, Sir.'

'Okay. That's all then, Cameron. We will let you know in a few weeks how you went today. Thank you.'

Fuck! I had just blown my best chance of getting my dream job.

•

A few weeks after my interview an envelope landed in my correspondence locker at the station. It had the blue Police badge printed in the corner and could only have been from the Air Wing. I had been trying not to think about the interview since I blew the last few questions, especially after discovering that both Herring Island and Split Rock were listed in the *Melway Street Directory* index under 'Places of interest'. I hadn't told anyone at the station how the interview had gone, hoping they would forget I'd even attended one.

I didn't have the courage to open the letter in front of my colleagues. I knew I had failed, I just didn't want to read it in print. I sat down on a desk next to my correspondence locker and stared at the letter. Once the room was empty, I opened it. I looked around to double-check no one was there, then I ran my fingernail along one edge of the envelope and pulled out the letter. I looked again to make sure no one could see me. I felt like I was about to read something that had 'top secret' stamped on it in big red letters. The first word I saw as I slowly unfolded the letter was one that I wasn't expecting: 'Congratulations'.

No more watching murderers walk around on bail. No more domestic violence merry-go-rounds. No more smacks in the mouth from idiots off their chops on drugs. I read the letter a second time, then a third. A huge smile began spreading across my face and tears welled in my eyes. I didn't care if anyone could see me now. I felt like running madly around the police station shaking the letter up high so everyone could see it. It was as if I had just found the last golden ticket in a Willy Wonka chocolate bar.

9

DAY ONE

It was late August 1992 when I walked across the hangar floor as a trainee air observer for the very first time. Two twin-engine Aérospatiale Dauphin helicopters sat along one wall, their tails pointing into the middle of the hangar, ready to be towed out onto the tarmac. Their doors were open, flight helmets hung from hooks above the seats with the crew members' names emblazoned across their backs in reflective letters. I wondered when I would run into the three guys I had spoken to at the armed robbery. I wondered if they would even remember me.

The Dauphin closest to the hangar doors was painted with red and white ambulance stripes and fitted with medical equipment. It was crewed by a police pilot and police air observer, with a Mobile Intensive Care Ambulance (MICA) paramedic as the third crew member. MICA paramedics undergo additional training over the standard paramedic, allowing them to perform intrusive interventions with patients, like administering drugs, intubations, chest tubes and myriad other advanced medical procedures.

The second helicopter, painted in police blue and white, was crewed by a police pilot and two police air observers and was equipped for Search and Rescue operations. A third Dauphin was parked in a service bay on the opposite side of the hangar with its engine cowls removed. Two engineers were standing on top of a brightly painted yellow platform wheeled up against the side of the helicopter, their hands buried deep inside the engine bay's braided metal pipe and wire intestines. In the far corner was a single-engine Squirrel helicopter. It was parked on a steel trolley because it had metal skids for landing gear and not wheels like its bigger brother, the Dauphin.

I had to contain my excitement. I didn't want anyone to see the new guy acting like a kid who had just been given the keys to the best toy shop in the country. Steve Collins and David Lord, the other two successful applicants, arrived shortly after me and I wondered if they were as excited as I was.

We had a two-year training program ahead of us that would end with an intensive course with the Air Ambulance. On completion, and after accumulating the minimum three hundred flight hours, we would be presented with the air observer's half-wing.

A large portion of the program was made up of navigation training, navigation being the main focus of an air observer's role. It consisted of both theory and practical day and night exercises conducted around the state and in the metropolitan area of Melbourne.

Gradually, the exercises increased in difficulty, with the targets getting smaller and harder to find. We went from navigating the helicopter to large wheat silos in the country or ovals and parks in the city, to finding a phone box, small laneway or the intersection of two dirt tracks. I relished the challenge.

There were a number of ancillary courses as well, including helicopter refuelling; obtaining a truck and dangerous goods licence, so we could drive the Air Wing's six-thousand-litre fuel truck; and the feared Helicopter Underwater Escape Training (HUET). That involved being strapped into a giant tin-can replica of a helicopter and dumped into a deep swimming pool. After the tin can was turned upside down, we had to release our seatbelts and get out. All of it was done blind. And as if that wasn't enough, random doors were locked.

No matter how long I could hold my breath for, it never seemed to be long enough. I really didn't like HUET training, not one little bit.

To get our flight hours up, we would be rostered on the police helicopter as an extra passenger in between training courses. We were known, by the experienced air observers, as 'self-loading cargo' – eighty kilograms of useless cargo taking up valuable weight that could be better used by eighty kilograms of fuel. That is, until we passed the winch crewman course, training to be what some call a 'rescue crewman' or a 'down-the-wire man'. Later we would train as winch operators, learning how to control the winch and send someone else down the wire, but our two-week winch crewman course came first.

After a few days of theory sessions and practising entry and exit techniques while the helicopter was parked in the hangar, my very first winch seemed like it would be as simple as they come. I sat in the helicopter's rear cabin as it flew around a large paddock, our training area for the day. Steve Collins was also doing his first winch and was sitting in the cabin as well. I put a rescue strop over my head, then underneath my arms. The helicopter slowed as it approached the middle of the paddock. A loud thumping noise started coming from the rotor blades. If you didn't know any better you'd think they were about to curl up and snap in half, but it was the pilot changing their pitch, giving the helicopter a little more lift as he slowed it down. It was the sound of a 'chopper'.

I sat in the rear cabin, nervously listening to every word the winch operator said to the pilot over the intercom. He gave the impression he was reading from a pro-forma set of instructions, but he was describing everything happening in the back of the cabin and outside the helicopter while giving the pilot directions in a clear monotone, and using so much jargon it sounded like he was speaking in a foreign language – one that I would eventually become fluent in.

The winch operator, who was one of our instructors, held the winch control pendant in his left hand (a pistol-grip-shaped handle with a small cone-shaped switch, like a witch's hat, and a second switch covered with a red safety guard). He pushed forwards on the witch's hat with his thumb and the winch motor came to life. I could hear the whine of the electric motor over the intercom. He reached out and grabbed the winch hook as it dropped from the winch mounted above his door. A little more pressure on the witch's hat and the winch responded in an instant, the cable unwound faster and the pitch of the whine increased. He pulled the winch hook inside the cabin and handed it to me. I heard my cue.

'Crewman has the hook,' the operator said over the intercom.

I threaded the hook through two metal rings at both ends of my rescue strop.

'Crewman is on the hook. Bringing the crewman to the door.'

The operator held the cable with his right hand and used the winch to pull me to the door. I shuffled along the cabin floor on my backside, the winch operator stopping me when my legs were hanging outside the helicopter. For a moment, I remembered the RAAF crewman sitting in the open doorway of the Iroquois helicopter all those years ago. I was just like him.

The sound of rushing air went through the intercom system as the wind and noise from outside hit my microphone. The winch operator casually leant over me and, with one hand, grabbed the intercom lead coming from my helmet and disconnected my helmet from the helicopter's intercom system. He didn't say a word. I had made my first mistake – I was supposed to disconnect myself earlier – but there was no time to apologise. With a tap on the shoulder I was lifted off the cabin floor and dragged out the door.

I was facing away from the helicopter with my full body weight on the cable, my legs dangling freely underneath me.

The wind rushing past the helicopter was hitting my body, trying to spin me around. The only thing stopping me was the operator holding on to a webbing handle sewn into the back of the rescue strop. It was as uncomfortable as hell with the nylon webbing riding up into my armpits. But nowhere near as uncomfortable as hanging forty feet from the ground on a six-millimetre-thick piece of steel cable, my life in the hands of a winch operator and pilot I hardly knew.

I was slowly lowered down below the helicopter body, then things started to speed up and I was heading for the ground in a hurry. I looked up at the underside of the helicopter. It was covered in removable panels all held in place by small spring retaining screws. Some panels looked like they didn't quite fit. What should have been a clean white fuselage was more a dirty white, discoloured by a thin film of black soot-like grime from burnt jet fuel and small brown stains from hydraulic leaks. Not the sort of things a new crewman really needed to see. But for me it could have been put together from vintage car scraps and I would have been just as thrilled to be hanging underneath it on a thin metal cable. As the helicopter pulled up to a hover in the centre of the paddock, my descent slowed. I touched the ground – one foot, then the other. My first winch was over in a matter of seconds, but the adrenaline lasted a lot longer.

I slipped out of the rescue strop and turned to look up at the helicopter hovering thirty feet above me. My feet were firmly planted on the ground but the downdraft coming from the blades was trying its hardest to knock me over. If the blast of air from the blades was enough to keep a three-tonne helicopter in the air, it was certainly enough to throw me off balance. The winch operator was still leaning out the doorway reeling off instructions to the pilot as he winched up the empty rescue strop. As soon as he had the strop in his hand the helicopter flew away, before returning to pick me up for winch number two.

Every winch from then on was done wearing a specially made winch harness that was far more comfortable to wear than the rescue strop. And we were not helped along by the winch operators – we would have to adhere to our own set of procedures, a sequence of actions and safety checks performed by the winch crewman that start when the winch operator opens the door of the helicopter and concludes when the door closes.

'The winch harness is perfectly balanced so you can turn yourself upside down if you need to,' said the instructor. 'Then if you're knocked unconscious for any reason, you will naturally rotate to the head-up position.'

Good to know, I thought.

Our winch procedures were broken down into single steps, each one executed in the correct order with perfect precision. I learned a series of hand signals that I could use to give the winch operator instructions while I was on the cable – move forwards, winch down, slow and stop. It was drummed into us that winching was only used as a last resort and conducted quickly, as helicopters are most vulnerable when hovering, especially in confined areas like among trees and up against cliff faces. But just in case things turned nasty during a winch, there was a pyrotechnic cable cutter installed in the winch housing and a set of manual bolt cutters in the cabin, right next to the doorway.

I was fascinated by the existence of the pyrotechnic cutter. In the event of an emergency during a winch, like an engine failure, the pilot and winch operator would each reach for a firing switch covered with a red safety guard. The winch operator's firing switch was on his winch control pendant and the pilot's was on one of the flight controls. After lifting the guard, the switch would be pushed forwards, activating a pyrotechnic charge that shot a chisel through the winch cable, sending it and the crewman to the ground, saving the helicopter and the rest of the crew. If the pyrotechnic charge didn't go off, the winch operator could use the manual bolt cutters to cut the cable. I was certain that the only reason both pilot and winch operator had a separate cable-cutter switch was that they could sleep better at night not knowing which one of them had been responsible for leaving their crewman behind.

The instructors reassured us that if the winch cable needed to be cut, the pilot and operator would first make sure that the crewman was as close to the ground as possible to increase his chance of survival. To date, the cable cutter has never been fired with a crewman on the cable. It has, however, gone off three times by mistake since the Air Wing started winch operations in 1979 – once because of interference from a strange radio transmission, another time because of a small amount of water that short-circuited the winch's electrical system. There was no explanation for the third.

To restore our confidence in the winch, the pilot and the winch operator's abilities to save us, we trained for an emergency that would call for the cable cutter to be used – a simulated engine failure while winching. First, we would be winched to the ground. The helicopter would then lose height rapidly and fly away as if one of its engines had failed and was therefore unable to hover. That was our cue to pull our quick release. It sounded easy enough.

Fellow new recruit Steve went first. The helicopter hovered over a large grassy area clear of trees and Steve was winched out. His feet were almost touching the ground when the helicopter dropped in height and started to fly away. Steve tried to reach his quick release but wasn't quick enough. As the helicopter reached full flight he was pulled off his feet, landing on the hard ground five metres away. He was dragged along the ground for thirty metres through half-buried granite rocks and kangaroo shit. Eventually he managed to pull his quick release and free himself. Steve staggered to his feet looking like he had just boxed with Mike Tyson for several rounds – and lost.

It was my turn next. Determined to learn from what happened to Steve, I had one hand on my quick release the second I was winched out of the helicopter. As my feet touched the ground I flipped open the cover on the quick release and pulled the ring. I separated from the winch hook well before the helicopter flew off.

•

In the second week of our winch crewman course, we moved to the water. Our procedures inside the helicopter were well practised and we now had to learn to use our equipment while it was submerged. The majority of our water winch training was done in Port Phillip Bay, where water temperatures fell as low as nine degrees Celsius – way too cold for swimming. The upside was that the bay was usually calm.

During my very first winch I was instructed to enter the water, check all my gear, give the winch operator the hand signal to winch me up, locate the slack cable under the surface of the water and then stay clear of it as it was winched in. The pilot hovered the helicopter thirty feet above the surface as the winch operator lowered me down. Entering the cold water was like walking into a freezing swimming pool a few inches at a time. My wetsuit did a lot to warm me up, but I first had to suffer through the cold slowly working its way up inside the neoprene, from my ankles to my neck.

Once in the water everything attached to my harness immediately sank. The quick release, the winch hook, and metres of slack cable winched out by the operator all disappeared. I had more than ten kilograms of weight trying to pull me down. Plus, what was previously calm water was now choppy thanks to the downdraft from the helicopter's blades, which also generated a fine mist of salt water that got in my eyes, making it almost impossible to see. Using one arm to tread water, I ran my free hand down the side of my body, finding the quick release connected to one of the two mounting clips on my harness. The quick release led me to its D ring, then to the winch hook, which was now dangling around my knees. As for the winch cable, that was swimming around my legs somewhere. I brought the winch hook to the surface, checked that all the connections were still together, then gave the operator a thumbs-up signal to winch me up. I held the winch hook away from my body as the cable slowly retracted. Then I waited for the winch cable to wrap around my legs or brush past my body. Only when I saw the cable rise up out of the water in front of me was I certain that I was in the clear. Seconds later the cable went tight and I was pulled out of the water.

For the rest of water training we picked up other members of the Air Wing recruited as pseudo survivors who were treading water or floating around in life rafts, and winched others in and out of stationary and moving boats. The last few water winches I had to complete before I passed the course were delayed while we waited for the helicopter to be serviced. Once that was done, there was a small window of opportunity between operational shifts to be self-loading cargo again and get my hours up for the last few winches, which were moved inland to Pykes Creek Reservoir near Ballarat.

Pykes Creek Reservoir was sheltered from wind on all four sides and would have been perfect if it wasn't so bloody cold. At the end of the day, I left Pykes Creek with a healthy dose of hypothermia and an authority signed by the chief pilot signalling my approval to operate as a winch crewman. I had written every winch into my flying log book with pride. I recorded training winches separately from the real ones, which I hoped would come soon.

10

SCOTIA

There wasn't a breath of wind in the air and Port Phillip Bay was dead calm. The captain of the *Scotia*, a beautifully restored wooden-hulled motor yacht, took advantage of the fine summer weather to sail from Queenscliff at the southern end of Port Phillip Bay to the St Kilda Marina for some much-needed repairs. His wife decided to accompany him.

The couple had just passed the halfway point on their journey when the *Scotia* started to take on water. The captain made a mayday call over the marine radio and it was picked up by the Water Police RCC. The Water Police immediately launched one of their boats but it was going to be some time before they were able to reach the yacht. The RCC came up with a solution: put a winch crewman on board until the Water Police launch arrived. If the boat sank before the launch arrived, the crewman would be ready to haul the captain and his wife out of the water.

That winch crewman was me. I was still in training to be an air observer, but I'd completed the winch crewman course a few months before and was now part of the helicopter crew. This would be my very first real winch and I secretly hoped that it would be so spectacular that my descendants would tell the story for years to come. I couldn't get my wetsuit on fast enough.

The *Scotia*, lovingly restored to its former glory, was now a lame duck, limping her way towards St Kilda Marina. By the time our helicopter hovered overhead I was sitting in the open doorway, my harness strapped up as tight as possible and connected to the winch hook. I was just itching for the winch operator to tap me on the shoulder and send me on my way. There were no nerves, just pure excitement. I leant out and looked below the helicopter. The water was crystal blue and as flat as a sheet of glass. If only it was a little rougher, if there were a few waves or even some wind and rain – something to make the winch that little bit more impressive.

My winch operator was Andrew Tait, the same Andrew Tait who had given me a hard time at my Air Wing interview. He tapped me on the shoulder, winched me out the doorway and down towards the *Scotia*. I landed on the cabin roof with a thud and disconnected myself from the winch hook, holding it out so the operator could see that I was off the hook so he could winch it out of my hand. I made my way along the side of the yacht to the cabin, where the captain and his wife were. The captain was standing at the helm, focusing all his efforts on steering. His wife was sitting behind him on a wooden bench seat with a large handbag by her side. They both looked remarkably relaxed considering they had just made a mayday call and were taking on water.

They welcomed me on board with a handshake. The captain made no mention of his motor yacht sinking or the mayday call. I stepped down into the main cabin and galley. The galley's cabinet doors were all open and swaying in motion with the yacht. Their contents floated around in waist-deep water. With that amount of water on board already there was no way the *Scotia* was going to make it to St Kilda, still fifteen minutes' sail away. I spotted two orange life jackets floating about on the far side of the cabin, close to the sleeping quarters. I waded over and grabbed them, then walked back outside and handed them to the couple.

'Put these on. I don't think your yacht's going to make it,' I said.

Both of them looked at me with absolute surprise – as if they didn't need to wear such things as life jackets and their *Scotia* was not going to sink. But they reluctantly did what I asked and put the life jackets on.

'Does this boat go any faster?' I asked the captain.

'This is about as fast as she goes,' he replied, tapping on the engine control lever, showing me that it was fully forwards.

We continued to limp towards the marina, waiting for the Water Police to turn up, the helicopter still circling above us until they needed to pick me up. When the Water Police finally arrived I made my way to the bow to catch the tow rope they threw to me, which I tied to the bollard on the *Scotia*'s bow. The police boat took up the slack in the rope and soon the *Scotia* gained a little more speed under tow, but not much. Certainly not enough to save it. I said my goodbyes to the captain and his wife, who were still convinced that their beloved *Scotia* was not going to sink, and let them know that the police boat would keep towing them and help if anything happened. I made my way back to the cabin roof and signalled for the helicopter crew to pick me up. The chopper lined up behind the yacht, slowly moving forwards and closing the gap between us. I saw the winch hook drop and then make its way down to me. When it was within my reach, I grabbed hold of it and fed it through the lifting ring on my harness. My job was done. I turned and looked back at the *Scotia* while I was being winched up to the helicopter. She was doomed. It took us six minutes to fly back to Essendon and in that time the *Scotia* had taken on so much water that she could no longer be towed. As her stern disappeared under the surface of Port Phillip Bay the Water Police cut the tow rope and she sank to the bottom of Melbourne's main shipping channel. The captain and his wife were plucked out of the water.

It was hardly the spectacular first winch that I had hoped for, but it was enough to cut the first notch in my belt.

11

MOUNT HOTHAM

For me, watching the evening news was a ritual. So was lying on the lumpy, uncomfortable couch with my dinner in a bowl resting on my chest while I ate it with a fork. I would keep an eye out for police stories like a hawk. What were the coppers doing today? Occasionally, I would see someone I knew standing at a crime scene or speaking solemnly to a reporter. I'd laugh as these normal blokes turned into stiff, formal police-speaking robots. They would turn our action-packed adventures into something more hygienic for public viewing. Criminals who were clearly guilty of committing a crime became 'persons of interest' on the nightly news. The husband dripping with his wife's blood and holding the murder weapon was now at the station 'assisting police with their inquiries'.

Unlike most viewers, for me the news would occasionally feature a story that I knew I would become involved in the following day. This was how I found out about the missing helicopter at Mount Hotham:

lying on the couch, eating yesterday's curry for dinner with a home-brewed coffee. According to the breaking-news story, a commercial helicopter had failed to arrive in Melbourne after leaving Mount Hotham, one of the popular Victorian snow resorts three hours' drive north-east of the city. The police Air Wing had sent a helicopter to join the search. It was 22 September 1993 and I was rostered on an office shift the next day, but that might change if the missing helicopter wasn't found before then. There was nothing quite like flying low over bleached-grey alpine gum trees dusted with white snow against the backdrop of a cornflower-blue sky. I had already spent five days at Hotham that winter, searching in vain for a missing bushwalker. The beautiful but harsh environment had swallowed the man whole.

There was a lighter side to the snowfields, which were a regular training destination during the winter months. When we weren't training we were playing – hard. At one ski field in particular we seemed to spend all of our off-duty time at the local watering hole, Hotel Pension Grimus, drinking from oversized beer steins and singing Austrian folk songs to a squeezebox played by the owner, Hans Grimus. We would end the night with a sobering snort of snuff. We were totally oblivious to the dangerous mix of alcohol and snow, and after one night out I found an observer wondering around the snow-covered streets in the early hours of the morning trying to find our accommodation. He was lucky he didn't die from hypothermia.

Snow trips also paid dividends. The ski patrol and resort staff knew how we operated, so if we had a job in the ski fields we always had fuel, communications that worked and a bed if we needed one. Jobs went like clockwork.

I packed my overnight bag.

•

The next day, I arrived at work right on time. Apart from one Dauphin, the hangar was deserted. The Air Ambulance was gone and so was the single-engine Squirrel – all had joined the search, no doubt. Bereft of their fleet, the engineers were office-bound, trying to look busy. Dermot Oakley, another air observer, was in the operations room leaning back on his recliner, feet up on the desk, deep in a phone conversation. As soon as he saw me, he said a quick goodbye to whomever he was talking to and hung up.

'Boss wants you and me up at Hotham. Chook is going to be our pilot. He's on his way in.'

Chook, known only to his mother as Rob McDonald, was an ex-Army officer and pilot. His ill-fitting flight suit and wild hair meant that he always looked like he'd just crawled out of a clothes dryer. 'Chook' came from the way he scratched around the fridge looking for people's leftovers. Conversely, Dermot Oakley probably should have been an officer in the Army. He certainly had the right haircut, and a love of fine military uniforms and accoutrements.

Chook arrived in all his crumpled glory and twenty minutes later we were heading for the alpine high country. The story as we knew it was that the missing helicopter with three people on board had taken off yesterday morning from Hotham. When it didn't arrive in Melbourne the

Search and Rescue authority in Canberra checked the flight radio traffic recordings and found an unidentified mayday call. All the recording said was 'Mayday! Mayday!', then nothing. Given that this mayday call came in not long after our missing helicopter took off from Hotham, and since all other aircraft were accounted for, it logically followed that the call belonged to it and that a crash would have occurred close to the take-off area.

In the hour-and-a-half flight to Hotham, we discussed the search and the chances of survival for the pilot and his passengers. The best-case scenario was that the pilot had managed to make an emergency landing in a clearing and he and his passengers were beneath the snow line, safe and well, waiting to be rescued. We didn't talk about the worst-case scenario. Whatever we found, our job would be purely observational. At that time, the police budget didn't stretch to owning more than two winches that were swapped between the two police helicopters and the Air Ambulance. Both winches were already at Hotham, so we were without one, which meant that if we spotted the downed helicopter we would have to leave the winching down of a winch crewman to another crew.

As soon as Mount Feathertop and the Razorback came into view, the vastness of the search area became obvious. I looked beyond the chiselled mountain range into the valleys below.

'Not a lot of places to land down there,' said Chook.

The area was blanketed in snow and random patches of cloud sat low in the valleys. The ground was steep and covered in a thick mat of gumtrees all dusted with snow.

The area was still as beautiful and as dangerous as I remembered. Incongruous to the landscape, buildings and cars soon appeared. On our Air Wing radio channel I called our fuel truck, which was waiting at Hotham car park. Air observer Grant Spurrell had driven it up late last night with its six-thousand-litre tank full to the brim. I told him that we were inbound for the car park and would appreciate a top-up before we started searching.

Chook flew a low pass right over the top of a car park in the centre of Hotham Village which had been made into a makeshift helipad. The signature whine of our Dauphin was enough to announce our arrival and clear the helipad of emergency workers. A couple of helicopters were parked there already. We landed off to one side near our fuel truck, where Grant was waiting with the hose out and the refuelling nozzle in hand.

We were then briefed by the search coordinator at the police station, next to the car park. The missing helicopter was a Bell Jet Ranger registered VH-FUX. The pilot, Andrew Anderson, had been hired to fly two Lion Nathan executives, Nick Schernickau and Tony Waddell, to Mount Hotham for a night's stay then a return trip. When they left Hotham the temperatures were at freezing and the mountain was surrounded by low cloud. It was hard to fathom why they didn't stay in Hotham another night until the weather cleared. My guess was that there was some underlying pressure to continue with the flight as planned.

The last reported sighting of the Jet Ranger came from a witness who watched it leave the helipad then fly into nearby Dargo Valley. The witness had taken photos of the helicopter until it disappeared under a patch of cloud. The search coordinator explained that the mayday call occurred approximately nine minutes into the flight, which meant the missing helicopter could be around eighteen miles away if it went down at the time of the call. That's if it flew straight and at full speed. The variables were many, but at least it gave the searchers a boundary.

Andy Anderson was well known within the helicopter industry, which explained the unprecedented number of helicopters involved in the search – a total of thirteen. That amount of aircraft in the search area was going to be a major problem. Some of the helicopters were privately owned and we didn't know whether the crews were experienced in searching. This also meant that while Dermot and I should have been only focusing on the ground and mapping our progress, our attention was diverted keeping an eye out for other helicopters straying into our patch.

We were given an unclear photocopy of a faxed topographic map with our search boundaries scribbled on top. It was of no use to us. I grabbed my red pen and quickly transferred the boundary lines of our search area onto a topographic map of Hotham that I had borrowed from our office. We were assigned the closest search area to the helipad – a five-mile arc stretching south from the top of Mount Hotham. It had been searched twice the day before, but we were a fresh set of eyes.

•

Trees grew against the steep slopes and competed for what little sun made its way to the south side of the mountain. The ground was covered with thick undergrowth and everything was covered with a layer of snow. The area was a patchwork of black and white with every shade of grey in between. The missing Jet Ranger was also white, with a fine black and yellow stripe. It would vanish into its surroundings if it was above the snow line.

I visualised the colour yellow – totally foreign in this landscape. I scanned the ground looking through the tree canopy, then would cautiously look up every few seconds for any stray search helicopters. The constant squinting did little to keep my eyes focused. We had been searching for almost two hours – it was time to take a break and feed our fuel tanks. I was sure that we all were starting to see imaginary objects on the ground, but everything got a second look. There were plenty of false alarms – a rock that glistened in the sunlight as its covering of snow started to melt, a piece of coloured rubbish or a flowering plant were enough to set off your alarm bells.

Just as we were about to head back to the car park to rest and refuel, I caught a glimpse of something on the ground partially hidden by a tree branch. It took a second or two to register. Was that something yellow? I wasn't really sure.

'Chook, I think I just saw something. Can you come back around to our right?'

'Yep.'

The helicopter rolled around. I had lost sight of whatever I saw behind trees but kept an eye on the area through the turn.

'Keep moving forwards, it's off to our right about ten metres.' I still couldn't see anything through the tree canopy, but we were getting closer. 'Five metres. Keep moving forwards. Four, three, two, one, standby.'

It *was* yellow I saw. The yellow stripe on the tail fin of the Jet Ranger.

'That's it,' said Chook.

To avoid disturbing anything on the ground, Chook moved downhill a little and the rest of the crash site slowly revealed itself. The tail boom of the helicopter showed itself first, then the cabin. The door was open, and someone was standing half out of the doorway. It looked as though they were looking up into the air while holding on to the door sill. This guy's alive? I had to take a second look.

He wasn't moving. We couldn't see anyone else, and didn't have time to explore further. We needed to get someone into the crash site, and quick. We notified the search coordinator and asked for a winch-equipped helicopter to put a crewman on the ground to check for survivors. We climbed higher and moved away from the site so we could pinpoint it on a map. The wreckage was less than two miles from the Hotham helipad. They hadn't made it very far.

Helimed One, a contract Air Ambulance from Latrobe Valley, east of Melbourne, answered our call and started heading our way. Helimed One's winch crewman was also a paramedic – Cam Robertson. If someone down there was alive, he was the man to help them. Seconds after Cam hit the ground we heard his radio transmission. Three people deceased.

The search for the Jet Ranger was over. It was now about recovering the dead. There was no need for the other search helicopters and our Air Ambulance to hang around Hotham anymore – we only needed one crew to recover the bodies. Dermot flew back to Essendon in one of our other helicopters while Chook and another observer, Dave Mills, stayed behind. Millsy was the office comedian and had a fantastic memory for stories about the hilarious times, full of little anecdotes played out with his uncanny impersonations. A shift with Millsy usually guaranteed a belly laugh or two, but not this time.

I also stayed on the mountain. A couple of extra days at the snow resort recovering the bodies was my reward for finding the helicopter. But before we could find them, two police Search and Rescue coppers had to be winched into the crash site to babysit it overnight. I didn't need to accompany Search and Rescue coppers on the winch cable, so I stayed at Hotham and waited for the coroner's assistant, Paul Evans, to arrive. I would have to winch him into the scene. While I waited, I took the opportunity to grab three body bags from the nearby medical centre and prepare our Paraguard stretcher – a portable, easily assembled stretcher, compact and light enough to carry on your back. By the time the helicopter returned, Paul Evans had turned up and was briefed on the winching procedure, which was pretty much to do as he was told, not grab hold of anything and keep his arms down.

As I winched in Paul and one Paraguard stretcher, I got my first close look at the crash site, which was steep and sat in the shadow of tall trees whose tops had been sheared off by spinning rotor blades, leaving behind jagged spikes of green wood. There was a deep trench gouged from the earth and a debris field of twisted aluminium, electrical wires and hydraulic pipes surrounding the wreck. The severed rotor blades nearby showed scars from their battle with the trees. The tail boom lay uphill, its two thin tail rotor blades still attached and largely undamaged – a sign that they were not spinning at full speed on impact. The Jet Ranger must have fallen out of the sky with little or no engine power.

As I got closer to the ground, I could see the body I saw from the air. It was Tony Waddell. I could tell from his thick black moustache. He was standing upright and half out of the cabin and looking up in the air, holding on to the door frame as though he was waiting for his rescuers to arrive. But he was dead now. His head was rolled back and his eyes and mouth were wide open – I'd seen the look before. He'd had no idea that he was almost impossible to find. Andy Anderson was lying on his back, only metres in front of the nose of the helicopter. He had his legs out straight and his arms beside him. And like Tony Waddell, he had no obvious signs of physical injuries. Nick Schernickau was inside the cabin. I caught only a quick glimpse of him when I was winched back into the helicopter. He was curled up on the cabin floor.

I returned to the helicopter and completed another winch to drop off the remaining Paraguard stretchers and three body bags. This time I took one of the Search and Rescue members who was ill and had to be evacuated out with me on my return trip. It was Bob Manks. Bob had been part of the police Search and Rescue squad for years and we had worked together on recent jobs – the search for the missing bushwalker one of them. He was hard as nails, so he must have been on his last legs if he was calling it a day. Once I got Bob into the helicopter he started hurling his guts out. Being the true gentleman he was, he used his police baseball cap as a makeshift bucket – and not the cabin floor. We flew back to the helipad and waited until the bodies were ready to be winched out.

•

Later that day, Millsy winched me into a tiny clearing in the trees not much bigger than a double bed. The first body was already waiting for me, cocoon-like, zipped up in its black shiny body bag and strapped into the Paraguard stretcher. I only had to take a step forwards, lean over and grab the stretcher's lifting ring and feed it onto the winch hook. Millsy left a coil of winch cable beside me so I could move around while he hovered above, waiting for my hand signal. The downdraft of the rotor blades parted the tree canopy. Small saplings and undergrowth whipped around. Dead branches broke off and flashed past, some striking my helmet visor.

I checked the strapping, securing the body to the stretcher, tucking in loose ends, tightening the carabiners on the ends of the four lifting straps. I set the tag line, a nylon line clipped to one corner of the stretcher, and gave the other end to one of the Search and Rescue members. He knew that he had to hold it tight as I was being winched up to prevent me from spinning out of control. Paraguard stretchers have a habit of acting like wind sails, catching the helicopter's downdraft and causing it to spin – usually slowly at first, but things can quickly get out of control. I was ready to go. I knelt down on one knee beside the stretcher and signalled Millsy to winch in the slack cable.

There was something about body bags that sent a cold shiver up the back of my neck. Their slick rubbery feel and zip running right up the centre from head to toe make them morbid-looking things, even when empty. I had no idea who I was picking up, but whoever it was, he was reasonably heavy. As Millsy winched in the slack cable, it began to tighten and lift me onto my feet. I dug the toe of my boots into the soft soil under the stretcher, fighting against the downdraft that was trying its best to knock me over. It was like trying to stand up in a cyclone, wind pushing me from every direction. The cable started to tighten again and I gave the lifting straps and winch hook one more check. Millsy winched in a little more cable. The stretcher left the ground first. I shuffled my feet as the weight of the stretcher centred itself underneath the helicopter. Then I was off the ground.

As I passed through the tree canopy, I reached out with both arms to fend off the incoming tree branches trying to shred my flight suit into rags. I got through unscathed. A few feet from the helicopter I grabbed the quick release on the tag line. At the very last moment I pulled the release and let the line fall to the ground, just as Millsy reached out to haul me and the stretcher inside the cabin. We returned to the crash site just before sunset and recovered the second body. The last one would have to wait until tomorrow.

•

Millsy and I weren't expecting the last of the three bodies to be ready until later in the morning, so we made our way to the nearest bar to debrief with two of the mountain's local coppers – Bruce Hall and Greg Brown. It wasn't by chance that we ended up debriefing with these two. They were both former air observers before transferring closer to the snowfields. And they loved a beer.

It was almost considered mandatory that visitors took part in a game or two of what the locals called 'Nails'. It was a simple game of skill where each player was given a four-inch nail lightly hammered into a playing board – a cross-cut piece of round log. One by one each player took a turn trying to hammer their nail into the log, one whack at a time. The challenge was that the hammer had a chisel end only a few millimetres wide. It was a difficult task when sober. If you missed your nail, you had to throw your drink down in one gulp. The last person whose nail was left standing bought all the other players a round of drinks.

It didn't take too many rounds before I was buzzing and seeing two nails in front of me, neither of which I could hit. Thank God I was still steady enough on my feet that I didn't need to hold on to the playing board – I could easily have lost a finger or two. I can't recall how many rounds we played but by the end of the night I was legless. Millsy must have been the same. He had a permanent grin from ear to ear and we hadn't paid for a single drink, which had nothing to do with our ability to play Nails. This was a Lion Nathan-owned bar and no one, staff or patron, would let us buy our own drinks. We had found their mates, Nick and Tony, and brought them home.

The four of us were the last to leave the bar. It was a beautiful night with clear dark skies covered in an array of stars. Everyone else on the mountain had deserted us, and so had the deathly cold wind, although I wouldn't have felt it anyway. The two snowmobiles that Greg and Bruce had ridden to the pub were still parked out front, unlocked with the keys still in them – it seemed that Hotham was full of honest people. We all looked at each other with eyebrows raised and cheeky smiles. We were like a bunch of rebellious teenagers on a mission to create havoc.

'Let's go for a ride! ... No, let's go for a race!'

With two experienced drivers up front, Millsy and I climbed on our mounts. The engines screamed as we waited for the start. The last thing I remember of that night was the race up to the Mount Hotham peak. Millsy was hunched over Greg, pretending to whip the hind quarter of the snowmobile like a Melbourne Cup jockey trying to get everything out of his thoroughbred. I lost my balance and fell off the back, hitting the snow and eventually coming to rest against a mound left by a plough. Bruce didn't even notice. The two snowmobiles continued up to the peak, totally oblivious that one jockey was missing. I might have lost the race, but boy did I sleep well.

•

The following morning, a little tired from last night's game of Nails, we winched the last body out of the crash site and delivered it to the temporary morgue on the mountain. Our job was over and it was time for us to pack up, fuel up and head for home.

The flight back to base was full of typical cockpit banter. Millsy and I recounted last night's mission to Chook. Of course, the final beer count was exaggerated, along with the game of Nails and the inaugural Mount Hotham Police Snowmobile Race. Chook was clearly disappointed that he was the responsible pilot and missed out on all the alpine shenanigans. There was no mention of the crash or the three bodies we recovered – that was all left behind us on the mountain.

12

BASS STRAIT

3 February 2005 – 1104 hours

We continued to scan the sea for *Ron's Endeavour*, spending valuable time and fuel. Ray flew in low, sweeping arcs, widening out from the spot the yacht should have been, following the assumption she was drifting with the current. Brendan and I looked out the side windows for anything that didn't fit among the swelling seas and the white-capped waves – a yacht or, worse, debris from a sunken wreck. There was nothing. Brendan tried to call the yacht again on the emergency marine radio channel. There was no answer. No sign either of a smoke flare. There was a bigger danger: if Palmer could see us, he would have followed our instructions and opened the valves, and would be standing on the deck of a rapidly sinking yacht. If he didn't have a life raft he might soon join the long list of lives that Bass Strait had claimed over the years.

We were scanning as sun broke through the clouds. Normally the appearance of the sun marks the end of a storm, but not this time. We were still surrounded by dark grey clouds. The wind buffeted the helicopter and the waves beneath were swollen and out of control. We were in the eye of the storm. Around ten valuable fuel minutes into the search, Ray said over the intercom, 'I'll go back to the original coordinates and we'll try again.' He pulled back on the control and the nose lifted. He then rolled the helicopter over to the right side and turned, rotor blades beating away. Gravitational force turned my flight helmet into a massive weight and for a moment I could hardly hold my head upright. Before Ray finished the turn, he spotted the yacht. 'Got him. He's three hundred metres in front of us, slightly right of the nose.'

Brendan craned to follow Ray's direction and spotted the yacht too.

'Seen,' Brendan said, immediately moving back to his station to prepare for the winch.

Ron's Endeavour was nowhere near where she was supposed to be. The wind and currents had pushed her far off course and it was pure luck that Ray spotted her. I leant closer to the window for a better look. The yacht was close, rolling and pitching from side to side on the waves. It looked like it was going to tip over. Another wave passed under it, rocking the yacht like a toy. It pitched over the crest before smashing back down. As we got closer, I saw steel cables strewn all over the deck. The aluminium mast had snapped in half and most of it was in the water, barely hanging on by its rigging and what was left of its sails.

Ray hovered in the best position for the winch. He checked the fuel. 'We don't have long,' he said, 'only about ten minutes. I'll sit right here. Ready to winch when you are.'

I could hear the urgency in Ray's voice. The yachtsman wasn't visible but that wouldn't stop me from going down. He was probably below deck pulling out the sea valves. Ray switched on the winch power and then set the circuit-breaker arming the emergency pyrotechnic cable cutter – I hoped they didn't have to use it, not out here.

13

VICTORIA – THE GARDEN STATE

They didn't call Victoria the Garden State just because of its well-maintained parks and gardens. In the early 1990s, cannabis growers were taking advantage of Victoria's reputation for having four seasons in one day – the perfect weather to grow marijuana. Some growers were making a sizeable profit from their crops, which were getting bigger and more elaborate as the growers turned greedy.

Each year around summertime, we would spend several days flying to far reaches of the state in the single-engine Squirrel helicopter looking for the elusive green weed grown in areas difficult to access by foot. There were a few characters at the Air Wing who seemed to find more than their fair share. One observer, Graeme Bradshaw, or 'Sniffy', was so named on account of his unique ability to smell the aroma of a single cannabis plant from one thousand feet. And one of our pilots, Jason Walburn, or 'Wally', had some sort of built-in cannabis radar that could zero in on the plant's particular shade of green.

Some growers employed all sorts of countermeasures to prevent their stash from being found by the law or stolen by a rival grower. We saw everything from military camouflage netting to electric fencing wires, even bear traps and fishing hooks suspended from trees. In those cases we would call in a winch-equipped helicopter and send in a crewman to pull out the plants.

In the summer of 1993, Wally and I had been searching the wheat belt around Horsham and Nhill for three days. We had a ground-support crew of local coppers from Nhill and Goroke plus Grant Spurrell, who followed us around in our fuel truck carrying thirteen thousand litres of jet fuel. Grant was the work prankster. He was the one most probably responsible if you ever found your clothing locker suspended high up on the engineer's crane, or the lining of your flight helmet smeared with black boot polish. You never could tell if the smile on his face was because he was plain happy, or if he had just masterminded a practical joke to end them all and you hadn't discovered it yet. I learned that Grant's favourite prank by far was turning badges upside down on the police caps of nervous applicants waiting to be interviewed for air observer positions.

We had some success over the three days of searching, but found only small crops. The plant count for the trip was nothing to get excited about. We were airborne early on our last day in the hope that we could check as many properties as possible before it was time to head home. It was a hot day, so we removed the helicopter's front doors and locked open the back sliding doors. There was a nice breeze coming through the cabin as we flew from property to property. It was like cruising country roads in a convertible. A stereo sound system would have made it perfect.

Being wheat country, the ground was covered in yellow fields as far as the eye could see, all bound by wire fences or well-worn tracks. Every now and then a small farmhouse sat in the middle of one of the fields, surrounded by lush green grass watered by a bore or rainwater tank. After checking so many, they all began to look the same. Each of them had the same lean-to, tin shed, rainwater tank and mandatory rusty old windmill.

As we flew over the small township of Netherby we turned and tracked west towards the South Australian border. An old farmhouse appeared on the horizon, surrounded by acres of wheat fields. It was no different to the others we had checked, except for a large fenced-off paddock area behind the house that was full of trees. From a distance, they looked just like pine trees.

We got a better look as we flew closer. Wally and I couldn't believe our eyes: they weren't pine trees – they were mature cannabis plants. There were thousands of them, all two metres tall with trunks as thick as fence posts and planted in rows like grapevines with black plastic irrigation pipes running to them from a large water tank. This wasn't the work of a local pot smoker growing a few plants for his own enjoyment.

I radioed our ground crews and told them to get up to Netherby as soon as they could. But the closest unit was more than forty minutes away – and we didn't have the fuel to wait that long. If there was someone in the house they would have heard us coming. So we got a little closer to have a good look around. It wasn't as if they would be able to flush all their cannabis down the toilet as the coppers stormed through the front door.

We flew right up to the side of the house and hovered only a few metres from the ground to see if anyone came outside, or at least looked at us through one of the windows. Dirt and bracken flew out from under us, peppering the length of the farmhouse. A section of corrugated iron covering a lean-to started slamming itself against its rafters, threatening to tear itself apart. If we couldn't see underneath something, we did our best to get the rotor wash to blow it over.

We were making a hell of a racket and if someone was in the house they would surely have shown themselves by now, thinking they were being invaded by the army. No one came out. The only sign of life on the property was a brand-new Toyota LandCruiser parked inside an open farm shed. A crop that size was not going to be left unattended – I was convinced that someone must have been in the house or hiding nearby.

Our fuel was getting low. We had just enough to fly out to meet Grant and the fuel truck, but not enough to hang around over the top of the house and wait for the fuel to come to us. Wally and I were left with no choice but to land the helicopter now. And if we were on the ground, we might as well search the house. We radioed our ground crews that we were landing and told them to hurry up.

I was armed with my police revolver. I was a copper first and an air observer second, so I usually carried a revolver and a set of handcuffs. Under normal circumstances our pilots would always stay with the helicopter, so Wally wasn't armed. He landed the helicopter in a grass paddock that ran alongside the property's driveway and shut down the engine. I told him to head around back and watch the rear door, while I crept up to the front door. It was open. I stopped and listened for any sounds coming from inside the house. All was quiet.

I drew my revolver from its holster, then crept through the front door and down the hallway, my revolver leading the way. I was treading carefully, trying not to make a noise on the old wooden floorboards. I checked each room that ran off the hall until I reached the kitchen. Dirty dishes were stacked in the sink and the rubbish bin was overflowing. I walked out the open back door, lowered my revolver and met up with Wally. Someone had left in a hurry. We both walked over to shed to where we saw the LandCruiser parked prior to landing. It was gone. *Shit!* We had only been on the ground for fifteen minutes, but that was enough for whoever was driving the LandCruiser to get a head start on us.

Airborne within two minutes, we used our remaining fuel to quickly search the area for the LandCruiser. We climbed straight up to two thousand feet to get a better view. To the north of the property was the Little Desert – hundreds of square kilometres of low arid plants and sandy tracks. If the LandCruiser made it to the desert we would be able to see it from this height. If not, we would certainly see the trail of dust it would have left behind as it tore up the track. We checked all the minor roads that weaved through farming properties. The only cars we saw were the marked police cars speeding towards the farmhouse. The LandCruiser had vanished. Although we had the cannabis, we had lost the chance to catch the grower.

There were several thousand mature female plants growing on the property, all of which had to be pulled from the ground by hand. There was also another thousand mature male plants that had already been harvested. A semitrailer was used to cart them to the local rubbish dump, where they were burnt. They would have made for one hell of a bonfire if you were standing downwind.

I later found out that the crop was being looked after by an Italian man who had hidden inside while Wally and I buzzed the farmhouse. As we were landing, he had snuck out the back door and made his way to the LandCruiser, then driven across the farm while we were searching through the house. He had laid low for a few hours at a nearby property – which was why we couldn't spot him. Two days later he was on a plane out of the country, but he was eventually tracked down to a small town somewhere in Europe with 175 thousand dollars in his pocket – his modest payment for babysitting the crop.

Wally and I thought that our seven-tonne marijuana haul was pretty special. But a couple of months later another crew stumbled on a cannabis crop in the state's east hidden in thick bushland – Sniffy Bradshaw found it, of course. Once it was spotted, Sniffy was dropped off in a nearby clearing and had to walk in. The helicopter crew stayed overhead, giving him directions over police radio. Just as he was about to break through the scrub, he tripped over a log and fell into the small clearing where the plants were growing. He stood up and brushed himself off, and when he looked around he found that he was surrounded by plants that he had only ever seen in photographs – opium poppies.

Each one of their seed pods had been scored for harvesting. The idea that opium was only grown overseas was blown out of the water the second Sniffy fell over that log.

Despite Sniffy and his crew's record find, our crop was much bigger and featured as a cartoon in the *Herald Sun* drawn by the late, acclaimed Jeff Hook.

•

Large cannabis crops weren't just found on isolated country properties. Every now and then the distinctive shape or colour of the cannabis plant would catch the corner of my eye as we flew over the suburbs of Melbourne.

Large crops often led to bigger and better things, and this certainly happened one afternoon while on a job in the Air Ambulance with Wally, a few years after the Netherby crop. From Essendon we tracked towards the country town of Warragul, a thirty-minute flight south-east of Melbourne, where we were to pick up a hospital patient and bring them back to The Alfred Hospital. The route to Warragul had us flying directly over the rural suburb of Devon Meadows, on the outskirts of Melbourne. Wally and I were both sitting back in our seats. The autopilot was on and we were deep in meaningless conversation to pass the flight time.

Devon Meadows is full of small farming plots growing everything from vegetables to flowers. I looked out the window and caught sight of a small patch of cannabis green. I leant closer to the window and looked behind us as we flew onwards, but it was out of sight. I was almost certain that I had seen a crop of cannabis plants growing out the back of an old weatherboard farmhouse but, travelling at two hundred kilometres per hour, I wasn't absolutely sure.

We picked up our patient and flew them to The Alfred Hospital. I didn't get the opportunity for a second look at the farmhouse or to work out where exactly it was in Devon Meadows, but I reckoned I had it narrowed down to within a few square kilometres. After refuelling at Essendon, I arranged for a plain clothes police unit and a couple of detectives to head out to Devon Meadows while we returned in the Air Ambulance and searched for the farmhouse. As we started to slow down over Devon Meadows, the farmhouse showed itself again. Growing on a small plot cut deep into a mass of wild blackberry bushes were thirty mature cannabis plants.

From the air, I directed the coppers to the property and they were more than happy to knock on the door. Not to miss out on the chance to do some police work on the ground for a change, Wally and I landed in the vacant land opposite the property to give them a hand. Unfortunately, the farmhouse was abandoned and appeared to have been so for some time.

We gathered around the seven-foot-high blackberry bushes trying to work out a way of getting to the crop without falling victim to the blackberry barrier of razor-sharp thorns – the reason why the grower had planted them there in the first place. There were no irrigation pipes leading into the blackberry patch so there had to be an access point for someone to water the plants. We scoured the outside and eventually found a small tunnel cut into the blackberries. Wally and I decided to leave the crawling to one of the other coppers – a very small one.

I was pretty happy with my find and I made sure Wally knew it. It wasn't often I got the upper hand when working with him and I enjoyed rubbing it in. But Wally couldn't help himself. He started searching around the property with his neck stretched high like a hunting dog. He spotted a large opaque plastic-covered greenhouse on an adjoining property, more than a hundred metres away. There was something casting a shadow from within and through a small plastic section no bigger than an A3 sheet of paper that had come loose at one end of the greenhouse, Wally's cannabis radar zoomed straight inside. Ping!

'I reckon there's more in those greenhouses,' he said.

'Bullshit, Wally, how the hell can you tell that from here?' I replied.

Wally mentioned his flimsy suspicions to the local detectives who decided to walk over to the greenhouse and check it out. Wally waited. He was keen to see if his cannabis radar was still in top form, whereas I was hoping to rub things in a little more. Minutes later, I saw one of the detectives emerge from the greenhouse and stick a single thumb up in the air. It turned out that the greenhouse was full of mature cannabis plants with an estimated street value of around half-a-million dollars. The rest of the shift with Wally was unbearable.

14

SAN REMO

In the days of healthy state government budgets, we would patrol in the helicopter for a few hours, picking up whatever jobs came over the police radio. But when the purse strings were tightened we had to stay on the ground and wait for the jobs to come to us. With helicopter running costs at 3600 dollars an hour we understood the restrictions. But we didn't like 'em.

Unfortunately, things were tight in April of 1994, and with no flight hours for anything else but jobs, my training came to an abrupt halt. After checking the helicopter and rescue equipment one quiet day, I snuck into the ambulance office for some covert TV viewing and a sneaky nap on the comfortable vinyl couch, if no one else had beaten me to it. But this time I wasn't the only one of our crew who was looking to hide. I opened the office door, generating a frenzy of activity inside. Fearing that it was the boss walking in, feet were quickly removed from the coffee table and everyone in the room sat up straight like students expecting their headmaster. Someone grabbed the nearest magazine and pretended to read it, upside down, while another pressed every button on the remote control to try to stop the video – an adult video that would not have been approved by the boss – and send the screen black. There were huge sighs of relief when they saw it was me at the door.

In these lean flying times, there was a bit of bored-teenager behaviour exhibited by a few of these grown men. Someone's car once ended up hoisted to the top of the hangar crane that was reserved for lifting out helicopter engines. If things were really quiet you might find the passenger's side of your car decorated with pages from a porn magazine, only to realise it after receiving disapproving looks at traffic lights or pulling into the driveway at home.

There was barely standing room in the office with the Air Ambulance crew and the rest of my crew all crammed in there, but soon the Air Ambulance crew left on a job and I took a seat beside our pilot, Andy Baker, and our air observer and winch operator, Damian Waugh.

Bakes was a bit of a larrikin, even when he was flying. The first time I met him he climbed out of a helicopter after landing and looked down at his feet. 'Don't know why I can't fly straight today,' he deadpanned. I followed his gaze and saw that his shoes were on the wrong feet. Despite Bakes's inability to distinguish right from left, he still managed to fly a helicopter. Damian was the complete opposite. He knew left from right, and which foot went into which boot – as long as those boots were handmade and highly polished.

We all sat there hoping to get a job soon. Any job would have been better than watching the movie that was showing. The operations controller called us over the intercom.

'Can you guys get airborne to back up the Air Ambulance going to a rescue.'

We couldn't get to our feet quick enough, switching the video player off as I left the room empty. Minutes later we were airborne too and on our way to San Remo, a coastal town ninety minutes' drive south of Melbourne. A teenage fisherman had been pulled from the sea after his boat had been washed onto rocks by waves. The Air Ambulance was heading there and our job was to look for his three fishing companions, who were still missing. On the way there we received word over the police radio that the three missing fishermen had been found. All of them had drowned. A police boat that was nearby had already recovered one of the bodies and was attempting to get the other two. Damian decided to keep heading to San Remo just in case they couldn't get to the other two bodies by boat.

As we approached San Remo I could see that the offshore wind was causing a swell, which rolled in towards land before crashing onto rocks in sprays of white. We got low enough to see the police boat sitting outside the swell as the two remaining bodies were pushed into the rocky gutter cut into the base of the cliff. There was no way the police boat could get in close enough to retrieve the dead fishermen. Their bodies were stuck in the gutter and wouldn't last long under the constant pounding of waves against the sharp rocks. We headed towards the top of the cliff, where the Air Ambulance had landed. Their crew was already treating the teenage survivor. Two uniformed coppers had walked down the only access to the platform, a set of old, weather-beaten timber stairs. They were standing at the base of the cliff keeping their distance from the waves as they rolled into gutters and over the platform. The bodies of the two fishermen were just visible, floating in the white water. Bakes turned the helicopter in a wide arc, then descended into the landing area and put the helicopter on the ground next to the Air Ambulance. The injured teenager was the grandson of one of the drowned men, and a bunch of relatives had already made their way to the landing site. They crowded around him as he was loaded into the Air Ambulance. One was alive. Three were dead. In equal measures there was elation that the teenager had survived and devastation that his grandfather and friend were being smashed against jagged rocks at the bottom of the cliff.

I prepared myself for the expectations that always arrived when we did – people seemed to think that the helicopter crew could fix everything. I kept my distance; relatives were the domain of the General Duties coppers.

Damian turned to Bakes. 'They want us to get the bodies out. What do you reckon?'

'There's a bit of a tailwind, so it might be a little rough,' Bakes shrugged. He was fine either way.

'I'm in. It's up to you, Cam,' Damian said.

'I'll give it a crack,' I said nonchalantly.

The final decision to winch out the bodies was left to me. There was an unwritten rule when it came to winching – if one crew member didn't feel comfortable with it, it didn't happen, no questions asked. And in this case there was no one here to be saved. I was back in the helicopter and my wetsuit before Bakes had started the engine. I would like to think that the family being there didn't influence my decision, but even if I had serious reservations, how could I refuse to try with them there? I admit that ego did play a small part as well.

I sat in the open door of the helicopter attached to the winch cable as we climbed into the sky. I looked back and saw the Air Ambulance helicopter's blades start to turn. The teenager would be receiving treatment at The Alfred Hospital in less than forty minutes. I watched the family stare in hope as the Air Ambulance flew over to the rocks.

Suddenly, like a buzzard around carrion, the Channel Seven news helicopter appeared out of nowhere. The voice of their pilot came over our radio.

'Polair 30, this is Hotel Sierra Victor. Are you going to try and winch these two out?' There was a note of incredulity in his voice.

'Yes, mate,' said Bakes, as if he flew near cliffs and retrieved bodies every day.

'Mind if we tag along and get some shots?'

'Be my guest,' Bakes replied.

Bakes flew the helicopter into position. It wasn't the perfect hover and I could see him working the controls, trying to keep us steady in the tailwind. Waves were pushing huge volumes of water into the gutters where the bodies were. From our proximity I could see they were floating face down, with arms outstretched. They were stuck in the surge of water that was flooding the gutter, then emptying.

Damian tapped me on the shoulder. I checked the winch hook and harness. It was time to step outside. I was caught in the downdraft and began to spin as I was winched below the helicopter steps. I could feel Damian controlling the winch through the cable, stopping and starting as Bakes flew in towards the centre of the gutter. Suddenly, I was in the water, my entry exactly timed to land close to one of the bodies. I reached out and grabbed a handful of the drowned fisherman's clothing and held on tight. Then I wrapped my legs around him, clinging to him and bracing myself as the water flowed out of the gutter, trying to drag me with it.

I threw the rescue strop over the fisherman's head and fed his arms through it, one after the other, until the strop was around his torso and wedged under his armpits. I then held him tight again as the next surge of water filled the gutter, forcing me into the jagged rocks. I turned around and with my feet pushed myself off the rocks. I was ready and gave Damian the hand signal to winch me up – a thumbs up. I kept hold of the fisherman and held down his arms to stop him falling out of the rescue strop. Then waited for Damian to haul me out of the gutter.

In the water, the body was just a swirling, heaving mass. Out of the water and on the way up to the helicopter it became the teenage boy's grandfather. He was facing me, his head rolled back and his mouth wide open. His skin was a waxy grey and his tongue had swollen up to almost fill his mouth. The water had turned his eyes glossy like melting ice cubes. Clear of the water, I could see immediately why he had drowned: he was wearing rubber fishing waders. The minute he hit the water, the waders would have filled and dragged him under. Out of the water the weight of the his waders was enough to snap the shoulder straps and send them tumbling inside out. The water rained out of them. Held on only by the tight-fitting boots, the empty waders swung in the breeze as we were both winched up to the helicopter.

Damian winched me high enough to reach the step and hold on. Bakes swung the helicopter away from the cliff and up to the rock platform. He hovered over it as Damian winched me down to the ground. As soon as I touched down I released the body onto the ground and slid the rescue strop off him. I gave Damian the thumbs up again and he lifted me off the ground, ready to winch out the second body.

The second fisherman was easier to winch out as the swell had calmed. Plus, I'd had some practice. Within ten minutes both bodies had been left on the rock ledge, ready to be retrieved by the General Duties coppers and returned to their grieving families as we flew off and left them all behind.

●

Before we knew it, just as we were about to head home for the day, we got another call. In Sorrento, a few miles further along the coast from San Remo, a young man and his dog were stuck on a small ledge on the side of a cliff at the back beach. He'd got caught out by the rising tide and had climbed onto the ledge to escape the incoming waves. After a quick flight to Sorrento we arrived overhead, spotting the young man and his dog waiting for us.

Damian winched me down to the cliff's edge. I got myself a firm footing on the ground, then leant backwards over the edge, letting the winch cable take my body weight. When I was ready I gave Damian a hand signal to winch out – one finger pointing to the ground scribing small circles. The faster the circles, the faster Damian would winch out the cable. I walked down the side of the cliff, forcing my feet hard against the rocks, as if abseiling. When I reached the young man and his dog I gave Damian the signal to stop winching out by tapping the top of my helmet.

There was just enough room on the ledge for me to plant the balls of my feet, and the winch cable was still tight enough so I wouldn't fall if I lost my footing, I'd just swing out over the water and have to try again.

'Hey, mate, I'm going to slip this harness on you, then pick up your dog, okay?' I said.

The young man nodded, clearly lost for words.

I fitted the soaking wet rescue strop around him, just like I did with the two dead fishermen. Luckily, he had no inkling who had been in the strop before him. I then picked up his extremely large Rottweiler and wedged the dog in between us. I gave Damian the thumbs up. Seconds later the helicopter moved away from the cliff. I followed, stepping off the ledge and swinging out over the water, taking the young man and his Rottweiler with me. It was a short winch. The three of us remained on the outside of the helicopter, dangling on the winch cable. The young man was terrified, but the Rottweiler, with its long tongue flapping in the breeze, seemed more than happy to look around and enjoy the scenery.

I held on to the helicopter's step to keep us from spinning around while Bakes hovered over to the top of the cliff. Damian then winched us down to the ground and I sent the man and his dog over to a waiting copper.

•

The flight back to Essendon Airport was straight up the middle of Port Phillip Bay. I sat on the floor in the back cabin and looked up at Bakes and Damian who were busy in the cockpit. The distant Melbourne skyline was neatly centred in the middle of the windscreen. Bayside suburbs were slowly rolling past the window on my right. I looked back at my day – winching two dead bodies out of the sea, then a guy and his dog off the side of a cliff. Despite the fact that two people had died that day, I had at least helped one person. It was at that very moment that I realised that this was the job that I was put on this earth to do. I was right where I belonged.

This photo was taken only minutes after graduating from the Victoria Police Academy on 12 July 1985. I had just turned nineteen and was about to start a policing career that would span more than thirty years. (Author's collection)

Shaking hands with Chief Commissioner Sinclair Imrie 'Mick' Miller at my graduation. Little did I know that within a few years I would transfer to the Victoria Police Air Wing. The Air Wing was the brainchild of Chief Commissioner Miller and was established in 1975 with two fixed-wing aircraft. He then bought the first of three police helicopters in 1979 – the French-built Aérospatiale SA365C Dauphin. (Author's collection)

Winch training in Port Phillip Bay, transferring people in and out of a six-person life raft. The orange suits worn by the winch crewman and his survivor were Mustang survival suits, meant to increase the wearer's survival time in freezing water. (Author's collection)

Almost the perfect transfer. The winch crewman can be seen pointing a finger up and scribing circles, the hand signal for the winch operator to 'winch up'. (Author's collection)

Winch operator practice in Port Phillip Bay. We would throw a brightly painted wooden cross into the water, then try to catch it using a grappling hook attached to the winch. The cross was named Great Expectations, after a yacht that went missing in 1990. (Dermot Oakley)

Winching the second of two deceased fishermen from the rocks at San Remo in Victoria's Gippsland region. (Coroners Court of Victoria)

Thousands of mature cannabis plants growing among eucalyptus trees on a remote property near the town of Netherby, in the western districts of Victoria. From a distance the cannabis plants looked like small pine trees. (Author's collection)

This is how those cannabis plants ended up. The guy in the blue singlet must have had a cracking time. (Author's collection)

The Bell Jet Ranger VH-FUX minutes after taking off from Mount Hotham. Three people died in the crash: Andrew Anderson (the pilot), Nick Schernickau and Tony Waddell. (Coroners Court of Victoria)

The wreckage of Robert Baulch's truck after he collided with the back of a car travelling without lights at night on the Western Highway near Bacchus Marsh. Robert died before he could be cut free from his truck. (Coroners Court of Victoria)

After receiving our Royal Humane Society of Australia medals for rescuing Ron Palmer from his stricken yacht, *Ron's Endeavour*. Left to right: Me, Ray Pitts and Brendan Francis. (Jessica O'Donnell/*Herald Sun*)

Susan and me following my graduation from the Australian Federal Police College in Barton, Canberra. Not long after, I boarded a plane for the Solomon Islands. (Author's collection)

Makeshift repairs to the shattered windscreen of a Toyota HiLux after a night of rioting in Honiara, Solomon Islands, in 2006. With no spare windscreens in the whole of Honiara, chicken wire was the next best thing. (Author's collection)

Patrolling along Chung Wah Road in Chinatown, Honiara, the morning after riots. Very few buildings in Chinatown were left standing. (Author's collection)

Ghost Point Track near Marysville after the 2009 Black Saturday bushfires went through. James Gormley and Julie Wallace-Mitchell's car can be seen on the track (middle right) with a fallen tree in front of it, blocking its path. (Leigh Hunter)

The 271 kilograms of cocaine that were smuggled into Australia inside wooden crates containing ride-on mowers. We substituted the cocaine with icing sugar and I delivered the crates to the importer, who was later arrested. He is now serving nineteen years in jail.
(Michael Clayton Jones/*The Age*)

15

BAPTISM OF FIRE

Our Air Ambulance was the only one of our helicopters that operated around the clock, so its crew spent a week working night shifts on standby, which really meant they were in bed asleep.

I was only a few weeks off training with the Air Ambulance – the last course I had to complete before I would be fully qualified as an air observer and would be issued with my half-wing. Until then, I had to spend my week of night shifts in the operations room monitoring the police radio and telephones. The closest I got to the helicopter during the week was to tow it out for the crew while they dragged themselves out of bed for a job.

It was well past 11 p.m. and the last member of the afternoon shift had gone home. I had closed the hangar doors and turned all the lights out – a mammoth task due to the number of lights and switches dotted around the hangar. It was almost time to put my feet up and waste a few hours watching television when Air Ambulance observer Millsy wandered into the operations room. He was suffering from night-shift hunger pains, the only known cure for which was takeaway from Mamma's Pizza in Essendon. Delivered, of course.

I announced the arrival of the pizzas over the hangar intercom. Even before I hung up, the ambulance office door on the other side of the hangar swung open and the crew poured out like disturbed ants. They hadn't even finished their first slice of pizza when the first ambulance call of the night came in. There had been a car accident on a country road near Bendigo.

I jumped on the tractor and towed their helicopter out to the tarmac while they grabbed another slice. By the time they took off, their pizzas were in the oven staying warm for their return. I didn't hear much from them over the radio as most of their communications were with the Air Ambulance controller, a paramedic who worked in another operations room in the main Air Ambulance office on the other side of the airport. So I sat back in my chair with my pizza box on my lap and enjoyed every slice.

Finally, I got a call over the radio from Millsy saying that they were airborne from The Alfred Hospital and would be back at the hangar in five minutes – the job had taken them nearly two hours. Just in case I had fallen asleep in my chair, the pilot decided to execute the tightest turn the helicopter could handle right over the top of the hangar on arrival – more commonly referred to as a 'beat-up'. The noise created by the slapping blades was loud enough to shake the corrugated iron sheets covering the hangar roof. If anyone was standing in the hangar at the time they would have been rained on by nuts and bolts loosened by the vibrations, or worse, a decade or two's worth of pigeon shit that had been deposited on the rafters.

With the helicopter refuelled and back in the hangar, we all met in the mess room. Millsy went straight over and grabbed the pizza boxes, threw them on the mess room table and then filled me in on the job they had just attended.

'Two cars had a head-on along the highway just outside of Colac,' he said. 'One of the drivers was trapped. One guy was barely conscious, pinned down by the dashboard and steering wheel. Everyone looked at this bloke and thought he wasn't going to survive cutting him out. Then this doctor turns up out of nowhere and says we need to amputate this bloke's leg.'

Millsy stopped. He had a look of discomfort on his face. Not because he was experiencing the job for the second time, but because his pizza had spent so long warming in the oven that it tasted like the recycled cardboard box that it was delivered in. He kept chewing, slowly, as if he was trying to eat an over-boiled Brussels sprout. After forcing a swallow and taking a swig of Coke, he got back to his story.

'The doctor cut right through this bloke's leg muscles, then his tendons. Then, he grabs a saw.'

I reached for another slice of pizza while I hung off every word.

'It only took a few seconds to cut through the bone. When the doctor was done, he puts this bloke's leg into a plastic bag and hands it to me!'

I would be rostered on my first Air Ambulance shift in a few weeks. *I might end up getting a job just like this one*, I thought. Despite the fact that someone had been seriously injured and had lost a leg, I still couldn't bloody wait. It never occurred to me at the time that being able to eat pizza while discussing the roadside leg amputation of a crash victim in all its gory detail without so much as a second thought was not normal behaviour. But it was certainly normal for us.

•

In May 1994 the other two trainees, Steve Collins and David Lord, and I underwent the intensive three-day course with the Air Ambulance. Out at ambulance headquarters in Doncaster, in the eastern suburbs of Melbourne, we covered all the equipment and procedures so that we'd be able to assist the MICA paramedics on any job that was thrown at us. We were trained to identify and draw up drugs in a syringe, assemble intravenous lines (IV), set up equipment for intubations and fit monitoring equipment to patients. Afterwards, we spent a week working in a road ambulance alongside MICA paramedics, followed by a supervisory period in the Air Ambulance helicopter, until both a qualified air observer and MICA paramedic believed we were ready to work unsupervised.

Finally, after nearly two years of training, I became a fully qualified air observer. I had my brand-new half-wing sewn onto the right breast of my flight suit – it had been handed to me in the mess room after a very short speech by one of our sergeants during the morning coffee break.

All I wanted to do now was put my skills into practice.

•

My first job with the Air Ambulance came on an unusually hot autumn day as I was storing a few water bottles in the helicopter. The location was only a six-minute flight away from our hangar. By the time we arrived at the Dunlop Tyre factory in Campbellfield, a road crew was treating a worker whose arm was jammed inside a piece of heavy machinery. His injuries were far too severe to risk transporting him to hospital by road.

Phil Hogan was my paramedic. He had been with the Air Ambulance helicopter since it started back in the mid-1980s. He was one of the most patient and thorough people I knew – everything you wanted in a paramedic. If the toy manufacturer Lego used a real person to model its Lego man on, it was Phil – they were spitting images of each other. Just as we got airborne, Phil passed me a bag of Hartmann's solution and an IV kit, and asked me to get it ready. Hartmann's (or Ringer's lactate) solution is used to replace fluid and also build up blood volume. At first I thought it was a test, but because we would be landing at the job in no time at all Phil wanted everything ready to go.

I gave the pilot, Tony Griggs, the final directions to the factory and then started putting the IV line together. It reminded me of one of my favourite television shows from when I was a kid, *Emergency*. I was addicted to it. The two firemen, Jonny Gage and Roy DeSoto, seemed to give all their patients IV Hartmann's, whether they needed it or not.

I had practised putting IV lines together in the office using kits that had passed their use-by dates, but there was never any urgency when I was sitting on the vinyl couch. Now I tore open the plastic bag and pulled out all the pieces from inside. I pushed the sharp spike at the end of the line through the rubber bung on the fluid bag. I then primed the line and drip chamber before closing off the valve and proudly handing it back to Phil.

All went quiet in the cockpit. Phil coughed into the intercom, 'Ah mmm … Cam.'

'Yes, Phil?'

'Ah, it looks like we may need a little more practice here,' Phil said in his usual quiet, polite voice.

My IV line was a complete failure. I had pierced the fluid bag with the spike and there was more air in the IV line than there was fluid. The drip chamber, which should have been half full, was bursting with fluid. I would have liked to have blamed the cramped cockpit but had to accept it was just a stuff-up, and I apologised to Phil for my pathetic attempt. Jonny Gage and Roy DeSoto never stuffed up an IV line.

'Here's another one. Perhaps we don't rush it this time.'

I turned around and took a fresh kit from Phil. 'Thanks, Phil.' My second attempt was much better, and I handed it back to Phil just as we started our descent into the factory. There was a long grass strip near the factory's front gate and the driveway between the front of the factory and its security fence. The road ambulance crew were on the driveway waiting for us with the patient, who was already lying on their stretcher ready for us to load him up. We pulled up into a low hover in the centre of the grass strip and the helicopter crept forwards, landing as close as possible to the ground crew and patient without blowing them over. Phil and I didn't wait – we gathered our gear and went straight to the patient, leaving the pilot to shut the helicopter down. Our patient didn't look that bad from a distance. He was sitting upright and deep in conversation with the road crew. I even saw him laugh.

'We may not be taking this guy, Cam. I'll check him out first,' Phil said.

The road ambulance paramedics gave Phil a briefing on the patient's injuries and how he got them. He was working on a machine that wound steel reinforcing wire onto hot rubber truck tyres when a wire caught his arm and dragged it into the machine. The wire sliced through his wrist right down to bone before running along his arm, removing muscle and flesh up to his bicep. Then the machine stopped, leaving his arm wedged up to his shoulder.

One layer at a time, Phil removed the four inches of gauze and padding around the worker's arm. He peeled the final layer back gently with the worker sucking on a Penthrane stick like it was an alcoholic pop – which explained why I saw him laugh. As the wound dressing lifted I couldn't help myself and took a look. What was underneath certainly didn't look like someone's arm. A lump of meat and tendon was hanging on to a white humerus, the bone in the upper arm. It looked just like the offerings in the local butcher shop's window. Glossy blobs of custard-yellow fat were stuck to skin and muscle. I was surprised how very little blood there was – I assumed that the main artery running down his arm was untouched.

'Cam, we will be flying this man to The Alfred Hospital,' Phil said.

I wasn't surprised.

Phil handed me our Propaq monitor – a portable machine that continually monitors and records a patient's vital signs – to hook up to the worker.

The blood pressure cuff and pulse oximeter went on without much trouble, but I drew an embarrassing blank when it came to hooking up the three colour-coded electrocardiograph (ECG) leads to our patient. I had managed to place the sticky dots on his bare shoulders and left hip ready to clip the leads on. But I couldn't remember which sticky dot the colour-coded leads connected to. I had stuffed up for the second time on this job and was looking at another apology. Luckily for me, Phil had noticed the dumbfounded expression I had on my face. Without missing a beat, he subtly reached over and grabbed one of the ECG leads and clipped it onto the sticky dot on the patient's hip. With the first lead on, I managed to work out the other two.

Phil took hold of the worker's uninjured arm, searching the inside of his elbow for a vein to insert an intravenous needle into. I was prepared this time. No more stuff-ups. I handed him an arm strap and had a roll of clear tape and a valve flushed with saline ready. All I needed from Phil was the size of the IV needle he wanted to use. He asked the patient to clench his fist a few times to see if the vein would show itself. I couldn't see anything and I suspected Phil couldn't either. A few rubs and taps on his arm did nothing to reveal a vein for Phil to drive the needle into. Even so, Phil held his hand out, ready for the needle.

'Fourteen-gauge please, Cam.'

I had no idea where he was going to put it. Obviously Phil could see more than I could. I held out a fourteen-gauge needle by its protective sleeve, sharp end towards me. Phil removed the needle and gently placed it against the worker's skin and lined it up with the vein.

'There will be a little sting in your arm,' Phil said.

There was no way the worker was going to feel the sting by the way he was sucking on his Penthrane stick.

'Okay, we're ready to go.'

The needle was in. Phil was not only a paramedic, he was a magician.

With the patient loaded, we got airborne and headed for The Alfred Hospital. My first ambulance job was a success, as far as the patient went – we got him to hospital alive. I am not sure if his arm was ever saved but it would not surprise me if it was eventually amputated. As far as my efforts went, though, the job was a total failure. I resigned myself to the fact that when I got back to the hangar I would spend the rest of my shift in the ambulance office going over the equipment, putting it all together and pulling it apart again, until it was burnt into my memory.

But I didn't get the chance. We received another eight calls that day and only returned to base when we were desperate for fuel.

My last job came in just as we were starting the helicopter up at The Alfred Hospital helipad to head home. Tony had been replaced earlier in the day when his shift had finished. There had been a car accident on the West Gate Freeway, less than two kilometres away, and the injured driver was already out of his car and ready to transport to hospital. We landed on the freeway. The new pilot, Tim Morgan, reduced the engines to idle. It was far quicker to load the patient 'hot' (with the engines running) than it was to do a two-minute engine shutdown and another start-up.

I jumped out of the helicopter with our paramedic to get the patient. I felt the heat coming off the roadway and could see the blurred heat haze surrounding the helicopter's exhaust outlets. We pulled the stretcher and patient out of the road ambulance and wheeled him over to the helicopter to load. The intense heat coming from the exhaust was like a furnace. I angled the back of my head towards the exhaust to create a little more protection with my helmet. I felt sure that the paint on my helmet was blistering and it wasn't enough to protect my shoulders – my skin was burning underneath my flight suit.

Once the patient was loaded I quickly closed all the doors and got myself away from the exhaust, then gave the pilot a thumbs-up signal that we were ready to get airborne. He ran the engines up to full speed while I climbed in the back of the helicopter with the patient and paramedic. It was only a two-minute flight back to The Alfred Hospital.

While the paramedic drew up a cocktail of drugs into syringes I began setting up an IV line and the Propaq monitor and connected them to the patient. I had had plenty of practice since the job at the Dunlop factory that morning and it was all done by the time we touched down on the hospital helipad. The whole job took less than fifteen minutes. My first shift on the Air Ambulance was a baptism of fire, but by the shift's end I knew it all back to front.

16

BASS STRAIT

3 February 2005 – 1120 hours

Brendan popped the door open and the wind and the roar
from outside rushed in. These sounds and those of the turbine
engines and crashing waves were muffled under my helmet.
Brendan reached outside and grabbed the winch hook. He
pushed his thumb forwards on the winch controller in his
other hand, pulled the winch hook on board and handed
it to me.

With his eyes fixed on the yacht, Ray manipulated the
helicopter's flight controls. Small but frequent movements
maintained our position behind the yacht.

'Crewman has the hook,' Brendan announced over the
intercom.

I snapped the ring of my harness into the winch hook
then the rescue strop, watching as the hook's gate clicked
shut each time. I was as ready as I was ever going to be.
Looking outside and seeing how rough it was, I just wanted
to get this job over and done with.

'Crewman off coms,' I said as I disconnected my helmet from the intercom, no longer able to hear Brendan and Ray. All I could hear now was the roar of the helicopter and the rush of wind. Any communication from this point would be done through hand signals. Brendan used the power of the winch to drag me to the doorway, stopping me once I reached the opening. I now had the perfect view of the yacht. *Ron's Endeavour* was being thrown around in the waves like an inflatable toy. There was still no sign of the yachtsman.

Fear was starting to take hold and this surprised me. My heart began pounding like it was going to burst out the front of my chest and my gut was churning just like the water below me. Sweat dripped from underneath my helmet and ran down my cheeks. I had to get a grip. I slowed my breathing. *Breathe in. Breathe out.* I had to stay calm and concentrate on the yachtsman and nothing else.

I could see him now. He was wearing a yellow one-piece survival suit and standing in the companionway, both hands locked firmly onto a handrail. He was waiting for me. The rescue looked good – there was a small clear area right in front of him. I leant over to Brendan, my hand sheltering my mouth from the wind. 'Try to land me right in front of the yachtsman first.'

Brendan nodded, tapped me on the shoulder to let me know he was ready. I let the winch cable pull me out the door, suspending me outside the helicopter, sixty feet above the water, nothing below me but ocean. I held on to a handle on the doorframe. When I was ready, I gave Brendan a confident nod, then let go.

As I was winched below the helicopter the wind caught my body and I started a slow spin. I tried an old trick of putting one hand out to catch the wind and counteract the spinning. It usually worked, but not today. The wind wasn't playing nicely. I felt every variation of the winch. It unwound smoothly, then it stopped with a slight bounce, then it started again. I continued the descent, gradually getting closer to the yacht. Brendan and Ray were obviously trying to time my landing with the swell of the sea and the fall of the yacht. The perfect landing would have me drop when the boat dropped. An ill-timed landing would have me drop as the yacht rose over a wave and then we'd both crash into each other. Given the unpredictability of both the sea and the wind buffeting the helicopter, either landing was as likely as the other.

As I got closer the yacht climbed a wave, closing the gap between us. Just as I was about to connect, it rolled over the crest and vanished beneath me. Two more attempts failed. On the third I touched the deck with both feet, then slammed down hard as Brendan quickly winched out spare cable so I wouldn't be pulled from the yacht. Extra cable whizzed past my head, piling up in a coil beside me. I was on board. It was the perfect winch.

Palmer was right in front of me, still hanging on tight. I wasted no time. I took the rescue strop and lifted it above his head. He yelled something to me that I couldn't hear over the noise. Unbelievably, he pushed the strop away, turned and disappeared into the cabin.

Fuck! What the hell was he doing? I'd missed my only chance to get him off the yacht quickly. Whatever it was he went back to get, it wasn't worth it. I turned around and looked up. Driven by the wind and waves, the helicopter and yacht were now moving apart and the helicopter was taking the coil of winch cable at my feet along with it. I could see Brendan leaning outside the door, with one hand on the cable, madly giving commands to Ray, trying to position the helicopter back above the yacht.

A huge wave approached from the opposite direction. It was a monster. Spray blew off the white foam that marked its crest. It had to be at least seven metres high. That's almost a two-storey house. As it got closer, the yacht rose and I could see what was coming – I was going to get catapulted overboard. I desperately grabbed at the winch cable. If it was wrapped around anything, I was a goner. I followed the winch cable and saw it was wrapped around a pole that held the wind generator. Fucking hell!

The gap between the helicopter and the yacht was still growing. I looked down at my feet. The coil of winch cable was almost gone. Any second now there would be no slack left and I'd be dragged into that wind generator. The yacht felt like it was about to tip over the wave. With all the strength I could muster, I flicked the cable as hard as I could in one giant whipping motion. Relief. It flipped over the top of the wind generator and was clear of the pole.

Brendan was letting the winch cable out as fast as he could – but it just wasn't fast enough. I stepped towards the direction of the helicopter and braced myself. Suddenly, the cable went tight. Snap!

17

MOUNT MACEDON

It was a typical late-night country accident – on an unlit single-lane carriageway two cars had collided head-on. With no lighting on the ground, I was in the Air Ambulance heading into a massive area of black at the base of Mount Macedon, north of Melbourne. The flashing beacons on the emergency vehicles at the scene appeared first as tiny flickers of red and blue lights. As we flew closer I could make out the accident scene. Two cars were sitting in the middle of the road. Both their fronts were caved in, one more so than the other. A firefighter was standing next to the oil and petrol stain on the roadway with his hand on the firehose's trigger, ready to cover the wreck in a mist of water if the petrol ignited.

Two paramedics were already in the back of their ambulance treating one patient who had just been cut from his car, the one with its roof peeled back like an empty soup can. The local copper was there leaning over the bonnet of his police car busily writing in his notebook, probably jotting down the car and driver details, or sketching the scene, just in case the accident turned into a coroner's inquest. There were State Emergency Service volunteers everywhere dressed in their bright orange overalls, easily outnumbering all the other uniforms on the ground.

According to my map there was a sports oval only a kilometre or so from the accident scene. With the road paramedics already looking after the patient, we chose to land on the oval instead of on the side of the road. Although we landed on unlit country roads all the time we couldn't justify the risk of striking a powerline over the roadway when there was a perfectly good oval so close by. Wires and helicopter blades don't mix. If a powerline caught in the rotor blades, the helicopter would spin out of control and most probably wipe out every emergency vehicle and person at the scene, like a massive tornado of twisted metal and jet fuel.

We were all hyper-vigilant about powerlines. Only a couple of weeks earlier, pilot Bryan Aherne and I had approached an accident scene on a country highway. The tall trees that bordered the narrow stretch of road made for a tricky landing. It was in the middle of the night and raining so heavily that Bryan had to crawl the helicopter sideways while looking through his open storm window – a small window flap on the side of the windscreen. As best as he could, Bryan swept the area with the Nitesun – a thirty-million candle-power spotlight attached to the outside of the helicopter, controlled by a witch's-hat button on the flight controls. It looked clear of powerlines. Just to be sure I radioed the coppers on the ground to double-check. It wasn't until after we landed and got out that we both saw the single powerline spanning the roadway directly behind the helicopter's tail – we had missed it by a matter of feet. We were bloody lucky. Even though I had known it already, that job reinforced the need to always assume there were powerlines, everywhere.

Our paramedic, Nigel Newby, contacted the road ambulance by radio and asked if they could drive the patient up to the oval. The road paramedics answered straightaway – they would come to meet us. I figured we would have our patient at The Alfred Hospital within forty minutes and I'd be back in a warm bed not long after that. Mike Tavcar, 'Trolley', was the pilot. He was another ex-Army pilot and, oddly enough, also held a degree in genetics. I had no idea how these two fields managed to merge, but I could picture Trolley wearing a white lab coat and performing some weird experiments more than I could picture him wearing an Army uniform.

Trolley circled around the oval and lit up the ground with the Nitesun. He searched the ground for obstacles. There had to at least be the standard country oval windbreak of large pine trees along one side or a single powerline to the clubhouse.

When we were both happy that it was all clear we turned towards the oval and began a slow descent into its centre, which was marked by a recently mown cricket pitch. Trolley pulled up into a hover ten feet above the ground. Seconds later our downdraft caught up with us and there was an instant storm of grass clippings swirling around us. Trolley hovered over to the fence gate, the grass clippings following close behind.

Just as our blades stopped turning, the road ambulance headlights lit up the oval – the crew hadn't wasted any time. I jumped out of the helicopter and waved the road ambulance over. They drove towards us and began reversing towards the helicopter. The ambulance's rear cabin was all lit up, with one paramedic sitting in the chair monitoring the patient. He wasn't exactly busy so I assumed the patient was doing okay. I much preferred to see this when an ambulance pulled up with a patient, rather than two paramedics frantically trying to keep the patient alive.

I walked beside the ambulance watching that it didn't back into our rotor blades and knocked on the side window for them to stop when they were close enough to unload the patient.

Nigel didn't want to load the patient into the helicopter until he was sedated and intubated – that is, fed oxygen through a tube leading directly down into his lungs – so he jumped in the back of the road ambulance and went to work. I stood at the ambulance's open rear door with our equipment case in front of me, ready to hand Nigel whatever he needed. When we were treating someone in a road ambulance we made sure we used as much of their gear as we could get our hands on first, rather than ours. Some may call that stealing, I called it good equipment management.

I could see that the patient had a head injury that was haemorrhaging, all packed heavily with layers of thick gauze pads, each one layered on top of the other once his blood had soaked through to the surface. His blood-soaked shirt had been cut straight down the centre with trauma shears and hung in shreds beside the stretcher. Nigel quickly got an IV line into the patient's arm and started to load him full of fluid to replace all the blood he had lost, then got straight onto sedating and intubating him.

When Nigel was ready we loaded the patient onto the helicopter and prepared to get airborne. He probably still wasn't stable enough to fly, but he certainly wouldn't have survived unless he got to a hospital soon. Trolley turned the batteries on then moved the fuel control levers to the start position, his thumb resting on the ignitor button, just waiting for the go-ahead from Nigel to start the first engine. As I was walking around the front of the helicopter I heard Nigel call my name.

'Cam, in the back. Quick!'

The patient's heart had stopped and his oxygen level had dropped to zero. Nigel started chest compressions. I opened our drug case while he rattled off the long list of drugs he needed. I started loading up the syringes. When the first of the syringes was ready we swapped roles. I leant over the patient, placed one hand over the other and continued the compressions. Nigel then injected the drugs into his IV line. The patient's chest was soft like a down pillow and I could feel broken ribs underneath my hands, clicking together with every compression.

Doing cardiopulmonary resuscitation for real is never like using the clean and sterile training mannequins at the local first aid school. It is always hurried, performed under immense pressure, usually in less-than-ideal conditions. On top of that, the patient likely has ghastly injuries. My latex gloves were slipping on his chest from my sweat pooling inside them and the patient's blood on the outside.

Nigel and I kept swapping, alternating between chest compressions and drawing up and injecting drugs, all the time adding another layer of gauze to the patient's haemorrhaging head injury. After a drug was administered we continued chest compressions long enough to give it a chance to work. And then we stopped so that Nigel could check to see if the patient's heart was beating on its own, or if his chest was rising and falling. Nothing. We began another round.

Eventually we had gone through every resuscitation protocol – drug cocktail, chest compressions, checking oxygen levels and responses – several times over, more than what was required. There were no signs that his brain or body were functioning on their own.

He had died. And he was no longer our patient. The reality was that transporting a dead body was not a good reason to tie up an Air Ambulance that could be needed to save a living patient, so we left the driver with the road ambulance crew. They would take care of him.

We were back at our hangar thirty minutes later. It was a quick job after all but quick for all the wrong reasons. The next hour or so was spent in the hangar, the paramedic replenishing all the drugs and equipment we had used on the driver, while Trolley and I cleaned out the back of the helicopter. It looked like the floor of a wartime triage tent. A pool of dark congealed blood sat in the stretcher's drip tray. In record time, we had the helicopter cleaned and re-stocked, ready for the night-shift crew relieving us at 11 p.m.

I never gave the accident a second thought. Like the others I had attended before it, I put it behind me the second I walked out the hangar doors. Even if I had needed to process the night's events, there wasn't any time – I was rostered back onto the Air Ambulance in eight hours. I went home to bed.

18

MINOTAUR

I was hoping for a quiet afternoon shift in the operations room. Most of the office staff would be knocking off soon and there would only be the Air Ambulance crew and me left in the hangar. I wanted to use the quiet time to clear up some outstanding paperwork, then kick back in the operations room chair, throw my feet up onto the table and watch some evening television. But my hopes were dashed when I walked into the operations room and it was packed with pilots and observers all talking about a winch rescue that the Air Ambulance had just done. Anything that generated that much talk must have been big.

There was discussion about whether the crew should have done a winch in the first place and who might have stuffed something up. That was the general theme of most post-rescue discussions. From what I could gather, something had gone wrong during this winch. On the Air Ambulance, paramedics were the dedicated winch crewmen and the police air observer was the winch operator. During this winch, the paramedic on the end of the winch had been injured.

I left the crowd and walked into the mess room in search of the cleanest and least-used coffee cup. Guy Griffiths, who was the observer on the Air Ambulance helicopter, was in there making himself a tea. Guy's face was pasty white – he looked like he had just had all the blood sucked from his veins.

'You okay, Griff?' I asked.

'I thought I'd killed Rakka,' he mumbled. He turned around and continued to make his tea. Griff was never much for conversation. He was a gravedigger before he joined the Police Force, so I suppose he wasn't well practised at office chitchat, and he certainly wasn't interested in any more questions from me.

Back in the operations room, everything had gone quiet and the crowd was now focused on the television as the afternoon news report came on. The newsreader opened with the headline story: 'Three fishermen were winched to safety today in a dramatic sea rescue.' The well-scripted news piece couldn't adequately describe what really happened during the rescue, but the video footage taken by their news helicopter did.

Three fishermen were on board the fishing trawler *Minotaur* when it became stranded in Bass Strait, south of the township of Wonthaggi. The trawler had taken on water and its electrical system had short-circuited, knocking out their marine radio. The crew called for help using a satellite phone. With their GPS also out of action they couldn't give the rescuers their exact location, but they believed they were around ten to fifteen miles from the coast.

Bryan Aherne was the Air Ambulance pilot, and a damn fine pilot at that. He had a habit of lowering his grip on the flight controls just before he was going to execute a manoeuvre that would have been a show stopper at the RAAF flying displays I saw as a kid. Bryan and Griff, along with paramedic Mark Lamb – known as Rakka, short for rack of lamb – had been searching a fifteen-square-mile area off the coast at Wonthaggi for nearly two hours and hadn't had any luck locating the *Minotaur*.

Two media helicopters had also joined the search. Even though their main priority was to collect footage, they could always be counted on for contributing to the search effort. Letting them film the rescue was the least we could do for helping to find whoever was missing. Some of our pilots also flew the news helicopters while they were on leave, so the chances were high that the pilots were actually some of ours.

Low on fuel, the Air Ambulance crew decided to head back to land and top up their tanks, before returning and expanding the search area. Just as the crew were pumping the last few litres of fuel into their tanks, the pilot from one of the media helicopters called them on the radio. He had located the *Minotaur* anchored twenty miles off the coast. The Air Ambulance was airborne within minutes and flew straight for the *Minotaur*.

As far as fishing trawlers go, the *Minotaur* was a small one – around ten metres long. It had the typically large foredeck and a small wheelhouse towards the stern. Its main mast had broken away and it, along with all the rigging, was strewn across the deck. As the twenty-foot waves rolled through, the trawler climbed up the wall of water then, just as it was about to tip over the top of the wave, the anchor rope snapped tight, dragging the bow of the trawler down into the trough of the waves.

Against the forty-knot headwind, Bryan used flotsam and sea foam as a reference point to keep the helicopter in position over the trawler's bow, while Griff winched Rakka onto the foredeck. Rakka had just called one of the fishermen over, so he could put him in the rescue strop, when the *Minotaur* rolled over the top of another wave. The winch cable suddenly snapped tight and pulled Rakka off his feet and into a pile of rigging lying on the deck. He was then lifted off the deck and thrown over the handrail into the sea.

Bryan felt the forces on Rakka through the helicopter's flight controls. Griff reacted instantly, feeding more cable out to create some slack and prevent Rakka from being pulled out of the water when the next wave rolled through. But he couldn't get the cable out quick enough. It snapped tight again and Rakka was hauled out of the water. Now the boat's anchor rope was running over the top of Rakka's quick release. He was caught. Tension quickly built up between the anchor rope and winch cable. The anchor rope finally gave way and Rakka was flicked away.

Every second of the rescue played out on national television. I felt the pit of my stomach sink as Rakka was released from the anchor rope. For a split second he was limp and lifeless. He was winched back up to the helicopter, injured and clearly shaken. By the looks on the faces of everyone else in the operations room watching the television, I was not the only one horrified by what had happened.

The crew decided against any further attempts to winch Rakka back onto the trawler and opted to winch the fishermen out of their life raft instead. Bryan contacted one of the news helicopters and asked their pilot to relay some instructions to the fishermen using their helicopter's satellite telephone – to tell the fishermen to deploy their life raft into the water, tie it to their vessel and jump into it. They'd be winched up from the raft. The media chopper relayed the message. Unfortunately, our helicopters weren't equipped with any type of telephone, especially expensive satellite ones.

Bryan then hovered over the *Minotaur* for another forty minutes with the needles on the engine gauges pecking at the red line, while Griff and Rakka winched all three fishermen to safety from their inflatable and heavily padded life raft, which was far more forgiving than the trawler and its anchor rope had been.

Watching what happened to Rakka made me realise – for the very first time – that while you're on the winch cable, you're utterly helpless. Your life is in the hands of the pilot and winch operator. Perhaps that's why at my Air Wing interview, Ian Galt was more interested in knowing about me, the person, and not whether I could find Herring Island or Split Rock in the *Melway Street Directory*.

The TV footage also hammered home that no matter how much we tried to look after each other, Mother Nature was far more powerful and commanded absolute respect. But I knew, too, that if a winch job came in at that very moment that was just as dangerous, there would still be a fight between the winch crewmen over who would get to do it. I for one would have thrown my hat in the ring – an oversupply of egos and a collective addiction to adrenaline meant there was never a shortage of volunteers.

19

BACCHUS MARSH

As the crow flies, the town of Bacchus Marsh is an eighteen-minute flight from Essendon Airport and lies in a valley surrounded by hills. At night, the hills around the town are invisible among the black unlit countryside. In the spring of 1996 we were called to attend a car accident on the Western Highway at the base of one of those hills. My pilot, Wally, made sure we were flying high enough to avoid them.

The flashing red and blue lights of emergency vehicles were hidden by the hill until we were pretty much on top of the accident scene. A car and semitrailer had collided on a stretch of the highway just west of the township. The semi was upside down, with its prime mover hanging off the road in a grass drainage ditch along the side of the highway and its refrigerated trailer still attached. The car was in front of the semi with its rear end caved in.

'Looks like the truck's rear-ended the car,' Wally said.

'There's one deceased and one trapped inside the truck,' said Phil, our paramedic for the shift.

Before landing, we circled the scene. Wally turned on the Nitesun. He moved the beam of light along the highway and into the unlit paddocks beside it to check for powerlines. The local police had blocked off the whole section of highway. Wally landed the helicopter on the highway as close to the scene as he could. Phil and I climbed out with our two cases of equipment and headed straight to the truck. We walked past one of the two road ambulances at the scene. A young guy was sitting in the back of it being treated. He looked like he was in his early twenties, long sun-bleached hair, a real surfy type. He was the driver of the car involved in the accident and looked relatively fine to me. His passenger didn't fare so well, though, having been thrown through the windscreen. His body was lying in the grass drainage ditch not far from the truck.

The other road ambulance crew were already with the truck driver and they quickly briefed Phil. The truck driver was trapped inside the wreckage. He couldn't be cut out because of the risk of serious injury from the truck collapsing if cutting it weakened the wreckage. There was very little access to the truck driver – a narrow space in the mangled sleeper cabin behind the driver's seat. One of his legs was partially sticking out of the space where the driver's door used to be.

'We can only get IV access to his leg. He can speak through the space behind the cabin,' said one of the paramedics.

'The ditch is partially filled with water and there's diesel leaking from the fuel tank,' said another paramedic. 'CFA have detected leaking battery acid and are trying to disconnect the batteries.'

The grass around the cabin had been flattened by the constant flow of emergency workers coming to reassure the driver that a heavy haulage tow truck was on its way; it was the only tow truck capable of pulling the huge semitrailer upright.

Phil didn't waste a minute. I watched as he crawled inside the sleeper cabin. From inside, Phil could see the driver's head.

'My name's Phil and I'm a paramedic,' I heard Phil say.

'Robert Baulch.' The upside-down truck driver sounded clear. 'Can you just get me out of here?'

That would be my first question too if I was in his position.

'We're doing the best we can,' said Phil. 'How are you feeling?'

'I can't feel my legs,' said Robert. 'They're pinned.'

The fact that he was hanging upside down could have explained the lack of feeling in Robert's legs, but it could also have meant that he had suffered a spinal injury. Phil wriggled back out of the wreck and asked me to prepare some drugs for pain and nausea.

While I got the syringes loaded Phil had a quick conference with the other emergency services about the best way to get Robert out. Once the drugs were drawn up, I crawled into the cabin to keep Robert occupied and awake.

'We're in a bit of a bind here, Robert,' I said.

'Yeah, tell me about it,' he said.

'There's a heavy haulage tow truck coming,' I said to keep the conversation going. 'Should be here soon. It will lift your truck and we can get you out.'

I crawled out of the truck and Phil climbed in behind me, injecting the drugs directly into Robert's arm. For the next twenty minutes Phil and I took turns in keeping Robert company. As much as he could, he talked back to us. Phil had managed to get a pulse oximeter from our Propaq monitor onto Robert's finger to measure the amount of oxygen in his blood, concerned that his oxygen levels were not high enough to keep him alive for long.

In the tiny dark corner of the cabin, alone with Robert, everything seemed to stand still. We were in our own little bubble while outside discussions about the heavy haulage tow truck and logistics carried on. The truck seemed to be taking forever and both Phil and I pressed the coppers at the scene to check for an arrival time. But all they could give us was, 'It's on its way'.

I don't know how long Phil and I had been talking to Robert when he stopped answering. Phil grabbed Robert's arm and gave it a shake to try to rouse him. There was no response.

'Quiet!' Phil yelled. The talk outside stopped. Robert's monitor was beeping, warning us that his oxygen levels were dropping rapidly. *What bloody happened?* I thought.

There was no longer any concern about injuring Robert further, now that he was unresponsive and his oxygen levels were dropping. Phil called over the firefighters who had all the hydraulic cutting equipment and told them to cut Robert out now. But they never got the chance. While the crews were getting the cutting equipment ready, Phil forced his arm into the cabin through a small gap beside Robert's seat, allowing him to feel his neck for a pulse. There wasn't one. Robert was dead.

We watched the Propaq monitor as Robert's oxygen levels slowly dropped to zero.

There was nothing more we could do.

We packed up our equipment and headed back to the helicopter, updating the coppers as we walked past. The accident was now a double fatality.

Forty minutes later the helicopter had been refuelled and restocked, and was parked back in its bay inside our hangar. I joined Phil and Wally on the vinyl couch in the Air Ambulance office for some late-night television. We didn't talk about the accident and the two people who had just died. Instead, we debated who was going to walk across the hangar to the mess room and make some coffee. We had to be ready for our next job and the caffeine would help.

•

Months later, Phil came to see me in the office. He had something he wanted to show me.

'Do you remember that truck accident at Bacchus Marsh?' he said.

'How could I forget?' I said, surprised he actually asked.

'While the driver was trapped, he managed to ring triple-O on his mobile phone.'

'Is there a recording?' I asked.

Phil pulled a compact disc from his pocket and both of us sat there and listened to the call, which was incredibly clear. Every creak and shuffle was as clear as if it was happening right next to us. We tried to match the sounds we heard on the recording to what we remembered was happening at the scene. There was Phil squeezing in and introducing himself. There was Robert telling us that he couldn't feel his legs. There was me chatting away to him, trying to take his mind off things. Every word we said. It was all there.

We both listened with rapt attention.

There was a faint gurgling sound. Then silence. It was the sound of Robert drowning in his own vomit. The sound of Robert dying.

Phil then told me that he was called to the coroner's inquest and filled me in on the rest of the story. It turned out that the bleached-hair surfer guy we had seen on the night was driving his car while he was off his head on drugs. His headlights didn't work, so he drove with his head out the window, following the fog lines painted on the side of the road. Robert drove up behind him. By the time the car appeared in Robert's windscreen it was too late.

20

BASS STRAIT

3 February 2005 – 1122 hours

Everything went black. The roar of the helicopter and the sea was gone, replaced by the sound of rushing water. I remember feeling the winch cable snap tight when I was on the yacht, but nothing more. And then I was underwater and disorientated. All the air in my lungs had been knocked out of me, like I had just been hit by a truck. Every fibre of my being urged me to take a breath, but I couldn't. My chest screamed in pain as my lungs demanded to be filled. I was terrified. Terrified that my next breath would fill my lungs with sea water and I'd drown.

21

CAIRNS BAY

Cape Schanck on the Mornington Peninsula had always been a popular spot for paragliders. One summer an experienced glider pilot named Peter Bird launched himself off the edge of a cliff overlooking the Flinders Blowhole and was searching the coast for the thermals that would keep him up in the air. But a gust of wind caught him by surprise. He lost control of his paraglider and hit the cliff wall. The glider's canopy collapsed and Peter fell onto the rocks below in a small inlet at Cairns Bay. He was injured and stuck in the cove surrounded by a wall of rock. There was no way out. And with the tide rising, he'd soon be underwater.

By the time we arrived over the cove the sun was sitting low above the horizon, casting a dark shadow over it. Thirty-metre-high black granite cliffs surrounded it on three sides. Ground crews couldn't get to Peter without climbing gear, which they didn't have, and there was no room for us to land. We could see Peter below us, sitting on a rock ledge, close to the base of the granite wall. Waves were lapping around him and he was supporting his leg, which was obviously injured.

Trolley was my pilot. He suggested flying into the cove and hovering a few feet above the water so our paramedic, Shane Foster – Fozzie – and I could jump out, grab Peter and load him back into the helicopter. The rescue would be all over in a few minutes. Fozzie had worked on the Air Ambulance helicopter for a few years and was an experienced paramedic. Nothing seemed to faze him, and Trolley's plan certainly didn't.

We flew out to sea then turned around and crept slowly into the cove. We watched the tips of the spinning rotor blades as they passed alongside the granite wall. Initially there was a three-to-four-metre space between the cliff wall and our rotor blades, but as we moved forwards the cliff wall closed in and the gap got smaller. If Trolley had sneezed, our rotor blades would have hit the granite, disintegrating into a million pieces. The wind was coming from offshore, which was behind us and made hovering unstable. Trolley was battling with the flight controls trying to keep the helicopter steady as we entered the cove only a few feet above the water. Fozzie and I moved over to the doorway and got ready to jump.

As Trolley slowed to a hover, sea water sprayed up from underneath us, covering the helicopter's windows in a light mist that made it difficult to see. Trolley reached over with one hand and opened his storm window so he could see the tips of the rotor blades spinning only metres from the granite.

Suddenly I saw a flash of colour in the corner of my eye. It was the paraglider's canopy. The downdraft from our rotor blades was generating its own little whirlwind inside the cove, which caught the canopy, lifting it off the rocks. It started to spiral up into the air like a mini twister. It kept climbing until it was only seconds from being sucked into our rotor blades.

'Clear! Move back!' I yelled.

Trolley instinctively lifted the nose of the helicopter and increased power. We climbed up and out of the cove, backward – we had to find another way of getting Peter out. We came up with an alternative plan. Trolley spotted a small rocky ledge near the cove's entrance. He reckoned that he could hover the helicopter close enough to the ledge that Fozzie and I could throw the gear onto it, then jump out and climb down to Peter. While Fozzie got Peter ready, I would secure the canopy then make my way back to the ledge. I would then call Trolley on the portable radio to come back and pick me up. It was the only plan that we could think of – Fozzie and I agreed to it.

Trolley flew over to the ledge then turned the helicopter around and moved it sideways until the ledge was only few metres from the cabin door. The wind was coming from our right now, forcing the helicopter towards the ledge. Trolley held it there, his hands and feet working the flight controls, fighting the wind. He looked like he was trying to balance on top of a giant exercise ball. Fozzie started to throw our gear out the door. When the last piece of equipment landed on the ledge, Fozzie sat in the doorway and watched the movement of the helicopter over the ledge. When it was close enough, he jumped.

Then it was my turn. I grabbed a portable radio and moved to the doorway. And when I got the opportunity, I jumped.

As my feet touched the ledge a gust of wind hit the helicopter; it rocked from side to side and the spinning rotor blades dropped to head height. Luckily Fozzie and I saw them coming and ducked. Trolley rolled the helicopter to the right and dived away from the cliff. It was a manoeuvre reminiscent of the old Spitfire pilots peeling away from formation to battle the enemy – typical Trolley.

We waded out into the waves and were waist high in water when we got to the glider pilot. Waves were still lapping around him and it was only a matter of time before he and the ledge he was sitting on would be underwater. After a quick introduction, Fozzie took a look at Peter's injured leg. It was a mess. He had a compound fracture of his femur – the large bone in his upper leg was broken, its jagged end poking through his thigh. It had to be immobilised so the bone couldn't do any more damage to his leg tissue or, worse, sever his femoral artery. But before Fozzie did that, Peter was going to need some pain relief.

Fozzie rattled off what he needed out of the drug kit, and I got it ready – a green Penthrane stick and two syringes, one of morphine, for pain, and the other of Maxolon, to counter the nausea caused by being loaded full of morphine. With no time to set up an IV line, Fozzie flicked the safety caps off the syringes and jammed the needles straight into Peter's leg. I stuck the inhaler in his mouth and told him to suck like mad – at least until the morphine kicked in. Peter relaxed. The relief from the morphine was quick.

Trolley had since flown back and landed on top of the cliff. He stayed there on the ground with the engines running and blades turning, watching our every move and waiting for my call. I set up the portable stretcher and laid it out on the rocks beside Peter, then we gently moved him onto it. Fozzie strapped his legs to the stretcher, stopping them from moving about.

A copper and paramedic suddenly appeared out of the surf, both soaking wet, their uniforms hanging off them like heavy rags. They had huge grins on their faces and were obviously proud that they had reached Peter. I wasn't.

'Where the hell did you guys come from?' I said.

'We dumped our gear in the next cove over and swam around the point,' one answered.

'How are you going to get back?' I asked.

'You can fly us out, can't ya?'

Although two extra sets of hands were welcome, we hadn't planned to rescue three people from the cove. And we hadn't burnt off much fuel flying down there, so we had the extra weight still on board, meaning we couldn't add the additional weight of the copper and paramedic. If we did, we wouldn't get off the ground. Our only option was to drop off Peter at the waiting road ambulance, then fly back into the cove. Hopefully by then a little more fuel would have burnt off, and we could winch the two out.

'We'll have to get this guy out and come back and get you both,' I told them.

With Peter strapped to the stretcher, I asked the copper and paramedic to help move him to the centre of the cove and away from the granite wall. It would give the helicopter a little more breathing space around the rotor blades.

We were ready. I called Trolley on the radio but he didn't answer. I started waving my arms above my head to get his attention. He saw me and lifted the helicopter off the ground. I turned to the copper and asked him to gather up the paraglider canopy and place some extra-large rocks on top of it.

Trolley flew towards me, low across the water, pulling the helicopter nose up to slow down and turning the tail around to fly sideways, closing in on the ledge. Trolley executed the manoeuvres with all the confidence of a pilot flying in a well-rehearsed air display. I watched as he fought with the wind, pushing the helicopter towards the ledge. For a split second it came close enough for me to jump. I launched myself into the cabin and used a length of webbing attached to a hard point on the floor to haul myself on board, while Trolley rolled the helicopter away from the edge. We then flew cautiously back into the cove. Fozzie was standing over the stretcher with his arm held up waiting for the winch hook. Waves were lapping around him.

We flew forwards, inches at a time. Trolley monitored the rotor blades as they spun past the granite wall on his side of the helicopter, while I watched them on my side. The wind was still blowing into the cove from behind us and Trolley was working hard to keep the helicopter steady, moving its nose slowly over Fozzie. Salt water sprayed up into the cabin from the waves. I could taste the sea on my lips.

I started to lower the winch hook down below the helicopter as Trolley slowed to a hover. Fozzie was right underneath me. He reached up and grabbed the winch hook, then attached it to the stretcher's lifting rings, then to his harness. His right arm shot out and he gave a thumbs up. Fozzie was ready. I winched in the cable lifting Fozzie and Peter out of the water. Trolley moved the helicopter backwards and climbed a little higher away from the granite rocks as I brought Fozzie and Peter up to my doorway and hauled them both on board. The road ambulance was waiting for us back at the blowhole. Trolley kept the rotors spinning as Fozzie and I unloaded Peter, then we jumped back into the cabin and prepared to winch out our drenched colleagues.

We got airborne and flew into the cove for a third time. The tide was rising, forcing the copper and paramedic to move further into the cove. Again, we watched the tips of our rotor blades as they slowly passed alongside the granite wall, Trolley pulling the helicopter up to a hover once we were over the top of our colleagues. One at a time we winched them up and into the cabin. Trolley had *just* enough power; luckily we had burnt off enough fuel. When they were both safely on board I resisted the urge to give them a serve for swimming into the cove and putting more people than just themselves in danger.

As usual, not much was said during the trip back to Essendon. I suppose we were all coming down from our highs. I know I was. It had been a few months since my last rescue and having adrenaline pump through my veins again was as intoxicating as I remembered. I loved every second of it.

22

MY LITTLE SECRET

How hard could it be? It was just a transport job – fly from Essendon to the country town of Horsham in the far west of the state, land at an oval where a road ambulance would be waiting with our patient, then fly the patient back to The Royal Melbourne Hospital. But the winter weather had really settled in. There was a thick layer of cloud moving slowly over our hangar that couldn't have been any higher than a thousand feet, and we were being bombarded by some of the heaviest rain I had ever seen. Everyone told me that these were the kinds of jobs where you really earned your pay. The main ambulance helicopter was being serviced so we were in the spare Dauphin. All the rear passenger seats had been removed and the ambulance equipment transferred over. At least when my pilot Killer and I arrived at work, the transfer had already been done – there was nothing worse than swapping helicopters mid-shift under the pressure of a waiting job.

I would like to say that Killer got his nickname after an heroic performance in which he saved a young schoolgirl from being attacked by a hoard of outlaw bikers, but it was just derived from his surname Kellerman. The air observer working in our operations room decked himself out in rain gear and towed us out to the fuel bowser to top up our two main fuel tanks and then our auxiliary tank, while Killer and I sat in the cockpit and prepared for the flight. We formulated a plan to fly direct to Horsham Airport, then turn towards the township, flying the last few miles at low level. Our paramedic sat quietly in his seat against the back wall.

The Dauphin had nothing in its arsenal of flight instruments for flying in bad weather that set it above any other small aircraft. Apart from a simple autopilot system, it had a pressure altimeter (ALT), which indicates the helicopter's height above the ground; an automatic direction finder (ADF), which receives signals from ground-based transmitters and displays their direction using a needle on a compass rose; an air speed indicator (ASI); a horizontal situation indicator (HSI), which is a fancy magnetic compass with receivers that pick up navigation beacons; and then the instrument that I reckon is the most important of all: the artificial horizon (AH). The AH tells you where you are in reference to the horizon, like during a turn or when the helicopter is upside down.

All these instruments were for flying in bad weather – but only from airport to airport or radio beacon to radio beacon. They were useless when trying to find an intersection on an isolated country road or a hiking trail in the mountains. For this we went back to basics – we drew a pencil line on a paper map and used a ruler and protractor to work out the track and distance. Then we would use an EB6 navigation computer to work out how long the trip would take given the helicopter's air speed and adjustments for any wind.

The word 'computer' might suggest that the EB6 was a fine piece of electronic gadgetry, but it was actually just a metal slide rule that enabled us to perform basic time and distance calculations. On the back was a clear plastic disc surround by a compass rose that you could mark the wind speed and direction on, then use it calculate the effect on the helicopter's heading and speed. The first time I ever saw a navigation computer like the EB6 it was being used by the navigator on a Lancaster bomber in the classic 1955 movie *The Dam Busters*. And it hadn't changed since.

There was a tap on my storm window. I could barely see the operations guy through the rain. He was doing his best to keep himself dry, pulling his rain hood over the front of his face. I opened the storm window just enough to hear what he wanted but not enough to flood the cockpit with the incoming rain.

'How much fuel do you want in the auxiliary tank?'

'Fill it up, thanks.'

I switched the wiper blades on and watched them struggle across the windscreen, leaving streaks across it with small clean patches between them. The wiper blades on the Dauphin must have been old stock from the Citroën car factory that were sold off to Aérospatiale to put in their helicopters. Luckily we only needed to see through the windscreen for take-off and landing. Nothing too important.

There was a tap on Killer's side window – the tanks had been filled. Killer gave our soaking wet refueller a thumbs up. The drenched man then jumped on the tow tractor and sped off towards the shelter of the hangar. In the time it took to fill our tanks, rain had made its way through a tiny gap in the heating vents in the cabin roof and a small puddle of water had started to form on the floor between our seats. Luckily the water hadn't hit anything vital.

It was on flights like these that I wished I was the one working in the operations room, leaning back in my chair, warming myself in front of a heater.

Killer started the engines. He lifted the helicopter off the ground and hovered over to the runway. He lined up for take-off, just like a plane would, only we hovered ten feet above the ground waiting for Air Traffic Control to approve our flight to Horsham and grant permission to take off.

I reached up to the top of the dashboard and turned on our global positioning system (GPS). It was a basic GPS and only contained the locations of hospitals and some country airfields. I scrolled through the list of airports looking for Horsham, then wrote down the track, distance, and our estimated flight time on my kneeboard – a small folder strapped to my right thigh that held my navigation equipment, paper maps and a notepad.

Ninety minutes in shit weather. It was going to be a long trip.

We lined up over the broken white line that ran down the centre of the runway. A dome of yellow light sat over the top of the city in the distance, all the lights of Melbourne reflecting off the bottom of the thick layer of cloud. We received our clearance to take off and were instructed by Air Traffic Control to track for Ballarat. They would tell us when to turn and head for Horsham Airport. Killer pushed the nose of the helicopter forwards and we began to accelerate, skimming only metres above the runway. The broken centre lines disappeared underneath my feet. At sixty knots, he pulled the nose up and we climbed, entering a thick layer of cloud shortly after. Killer was already on the clocks – flying using the instruments – and probably didn't even notice.

We turned right and established ourselves on the track to Ballarat while we continued to climb to our assigned altitude of 5500 feet – high enough to keep us above all the hills along the way. Flying the Dauphin in cloud was like speeding along a gravel road in a old Volkswagen Beetle at two hundred kilometres per hour with a bedsheet draped over the windscreen. White cloud vapour rushed past and raindrops peppered the windscreen like tiny bullets. Flashes of white light from our anti-collision strobes bounced around the cockpit and we were being thrown around in our seats in turbulence. It was going to be like this for most of the trip.

Killer's eyes were glued to the instruments and so were mine. We were constantly monitoring all the navigation and flight instruments, making sure we were on track and everything was functioning as it should. Our paramedic was busy in the back of the cabin sorting through his gear, probably as a means of keeping his mind off the turbulence.

He hadn't said a word since we jumped into the helicopter. When we reached 5500 feet, Killer switched the autopilot on, made some small adjustments to correct our heading and altitude, then leant back in his seat almost relaxed, his hands close to the flight controls just in case. I don't think any of us trusted the autopilot.

I could see the blurred disc of the rotor blades cutting through the cloud – it was like a spinning plate balanced on a stick high over a circus performer's head. Helicopter blades are incredibly flexible and absorb a lot of the shock from turbulence. Even so, we were still getting pounded inside the cockpit like a Volkswagen Beetle hitting pothole after pothole. White cloud vapour continued to rush past us and the sound of the tiny droplets of rain hitting the windscreen got louder. The puddle of water created by the rain leaking through the ceiling was getting bigger by the minute and things were starting to rattle inside the cockpit. Without warning the helicopter entered a steep dive to the right – our autopilot had failed. My body lifted off the seat. I imagined that this was what going over Niagara Falls in a barrel would be like. Killer casually took hold of the controls and brought the helicopter back level. We had lost five hundred feet in a matter of seconds. Killer seemed unfazed by the whole thing and blamed it all on the helicopter's 'gremlins'. I reckon his heart never even skipped a beat – unlike mine, which was beating fast enough for the two of us.

Expecting the autopilot to fail again, I reached for what I called my secret hand hold. The seats in our helicopters were made of thin moulded fibreglass that formed a rolled lip around the front edge of the seat. It provided the perfect handle to hold on to. The best part about it was that I could reach it from between my legs and no one else in the helicopter could see me do it. It had been my little secret for years, having discovered it on my very first flight in bad weather almost ten years earlier. That time too, the autopilot put the helicopter into a nose dive. In a moment of sheer panic I reached out for anything I could grab hold of. Ever since, that rolled lip around the edge of the seat provided me with a small amount of comfort during turbulence.

By now Killer and I were somewhere near the small township of Myrniong east of Ballarat when the gremlins continued to wreak havoc. We lost all power to our main navigation instruments. It's not much of an issue if you are flying in blue skies and can just look out the windscreen to get your bearings, but we hadn't seen the ground since we departed Essendon Airport.

'What the fuck?' Killer took the words right out of my mouth.

He instinctively grabbed for the flight controls and levelled us out using our standby AH, while I held on to the seat a little tighter. The standby AH was one of the few cockpit instruments that was still working, probably because it ran off a separate power circuit to all the other instruments. Killer reached for the circuit-breakers for the autopilot and navigation instruments and reset them. It did nothing to fix the problem.

He calmly radioed Air Traffic Control and told them that we were in cloud and had lost most of our navigation instruments. Air Traffic Control answered us straightaway, giving us instructions to maintain our current heading and altitude while they came up with a plan to get us out of the bad weather. Quickly, I hoped.

We had a standby compass mounted high just above the centre of the windscreen, and it was still working. It was a small ball with compass markings on it floating around in a sphere filled with clear oil. The sort of thing you would find in a kid's two-dollar lucky dip. It wasn't the easiest thing to read and had a ten- or twenty-degree compass error just from bobbing around with the movement of the helicopter. Knowing how low-tech these helicopters were, it was probably a ping-pong ball in its previous life – and it bounced around like one. Between the standby AH and the ping-pong ball, we had enough to continue to Horsham. It was going to be just as difficult to turn around and head back to base as it was to carry on. The crappy weather was still over both Melbourne and Essendon airports, so all aircraft were landing on instruments – the ones we didn't have.

Air Traffic Control's plan was that we change our heading slightly to track direct for the Nhill airport a few miles further out from Horsham. A front of clear weather below our altitude was moving through Victoria and was expected to reach Nhill any minute. If the weather gods were nice to us we might be able to descend out of the cloud without hitting any hills, then turn around and scud run it to Horsham. Scud running was a term used to describe flying close to the ground to avoid low cloud – named after low, patchy cloud formations, not the Russian missile.

I took out my paper map and quickly drew a pencil line from Essendon Airport to Ballarat. We had been flying for exactly fifteen minutes since leaving Essendon. I drew a cross to mark our current position based on our speed and flight time. We were over the western edge of Ballarat. I then drew a pencil line from the cross to our new destination, Nhill. Our new track would have us flying directly over the Pyrenees Ranges. That meant more turbulence was on its way. Exactly what we didn't need. Killer turned onto our new track and the turbulence increased the second we hit the ranges. All we could do was ride it out, constantly checking our two working instruments. Killer caught a rare glimpse of the ground through a passing gap in the cloud beneath us. He swore that he saw a group of house lights on the ground, which, according to him, was not far below us. So the town or houses he saw must have been in the hills.

'What's that town down there?' Killer asked.

I looked at my map. There were plenty of small towns nestled among the hills to choose from. But the only one that was anywhere near my pencil line was the tiny township of Amphitheatre. So I gave Killer my expert opinion.

'It's Amphitheatre, I think.'

Killer took a quick look at his map. For the length of time we had been flying we should have already passed Amphitheatre. It meant that we had a massive headwind. I reached into my nav bag and pulled out my EB6 flight computer and wiped the dust from it. I used it to recalculate our ground speed based on the time it took to fly from Essendon to Amphitheatre then used that speed to work out the remaining flight time to Nhill.

Killer grabbed his flight computer too. His looked a little more impressive than mine. For a start, mine was so large and heavy it would kill someone if I ever dropped it from the helicopter. His was made of lightweight plastic and was small enough for him to keep in the breast pocket of his flight suit – he must have bought his own. In between checking our instruments, we both quickly turned a few bezels on our computers and came up with the same answer. We were down to eighty knots ground speed. The headwind was hitting us at forty knots – more than seventy kilometres per hour. We had been flying in cloud at temperatures just above freezing and the inside of the cabin was starting to turn into an ice chest. I was starting to feel it despite being dressed in a multitude of layers, including a wool scarf, gloves and my leather flying jacket. Killer was working up a sweat at the controls and probably didn't notice how cold it was.

Although we had no intention of flying any higher, where the air temperature would be below zero, there was no guarantee that the temperature outside would not drop below zero, causing the moisture on the helicopter to turn into ice. Unfortunately, the Dauphin lacked the de-icing stripes that lined the leading edge of the rotor blades of some more advanced helicopters. Icing was something we needed to avoid, since without the de-icing stripes, the aerodynamic shape of the blades would change and they would no longer produce lift. This trip had already turned into a flight from hell and we didn't need icing to add to our list of problems. So Killer and I reverted to our standard method of ice detection – we both shone a small handheld torch along the outside edge of our windscreen looking for ice crystals. Killer checked the outside air temperature gauge down near his right knee, giving it a gentle tap to make sure it wasn't stuck. It wasn't below zero yet, but it was pretty damn close. The strong westerly wind was hitting the side of the Pyrenees Ranges and being thrown straight up at us.

We didn't have long to go before we would be clear of the ranges and things would calm down a little. But it seemed that Mother Nature was having one last crack at us before letting us go. The turbulence was getting worse, the rattles in the cockpit were getting louder, and my fingers were starting to cramp from holding on to the seat.

Killer was working hard keeping us level and on track, while I continued to monitor instruments and check our progress on my map, hoping that the second we burst free of the cloud I could identify some features on the ground and mark our exact position.

'We should be clear of the ranges in ten miles, Killer.' It was as much a comment to Killer as it was to reassure myself that we would soon be able to descend out of this awfully shitty weather and into some clear, smooth air. I could then let go of my secret handle.

Air Traffic Control called and confirmed we were about to clear the ranges. As we left the Pyrenees behind us, we could both feel the turbulence subside. Holes in the cloud started appearing in front of us and patches of dark ground passed underneath. Gradually the cloud thinned out and then it vanished altogether. Everything went calm. The sky turned into a large star-filled dome. Clusters of lights from country towns appeared in front of us, joined by trails of car lights like tiny red and white glowing ants.

I can't describe the feeling of immense relief that came over me at that very moment. We had made it through the weather unscathed and I could finally let go of the seat. Killer and I had earned every cent of our pay that day and were lucky we only had to fly in the shit weather and not land in it.

The electrical failure could only have been caused by the water leaking through the overhead heating vents. But despite the best efforts of our engineers to fix the problem, water leaked through the same tiny gap in that Dauphin every time I flew in it in shit weather.

23

GAME FACE

Not long after the flight to Horsham, I was called to a job that none of us ever wanted to get. I had been with the Air Wing for seven years and, so far, had managed to avoid getting one like this: a toddler had been run over by a car in the family driveway. We jumped up from the vinyl couch and stormed out the door, leaving magazines strewn over the floor, the television on and half-full coffee mugs abandoned. We were airborne in minutes.

It was chaos on the ground. Two paramedics were already working on the toddler on the driveway. The ground around them was littered with discarded plastic IV bags and empty syringe packets. The house was at the end of a small suburban court, but the court wasn't big enough for us to land on. I spotted a playground nearby and got straight on the police radio asking for one of the ground units to come and pick us up. I saw a copper run straight to his highway patrol car and take off in the direction of the playground – he knew the urgency.

I climbed out of the cockpit and grabbed the equipment we needed, then ran for the patrol car. I ducked my head as I passed underneath the spinning blades, our paramedic close behind me. We jumped into the patrol car and the driver accelerated away before we had even closed the doors. There was no time for the usual introductions with our driver, instead he gave us a quick run-down of what had happened at the house. Seconds later I was stepping out of the car and walking up the driveway.

Two road paramedics were kneeling over the toddler. He wasn't moving. They told us that the injured child's mum was backing the car out from the carport to wash it in the driveway and didn't see that her two-year-old son was playing behind it. There was a lady standing near the front door of the house crying uncontrollably. I assumed she was the mum. A young uniformed policewoman was standing beside her with one hand on her shoulder, trying to comfort her. I'm sure the young copper was struggling to find the right words. I was glad it wasn't me. In my General Duties days, I had been reasonably well practised at generating conversation with distressed people, but I couldn't have done it now.

The sound of a helicopter landing created some interest and a crowd of people had started to gather on the footpath and street out front. We were conspicuous in our flight suits and I felt eyes on us as we walked up the driveway. The crowd no doubt expected us to perform miracles.

Our paramedic got straight to work, with the road paramedics now assisting him. There seemed to be a great deal of respect within the Ambulance service for our helicopter paramedics. I suppose it was because they too had worked as road paramedics for several years and were trained as MICA paramedics as well.

I laid the equipment cases in front of me, opened the lids and started getting the equipment ready. I grabbed the laryngoscope – a foldout blade attached to a handle. The paramedic would need it to clear the toddler's airway and help insert an intubation tube into his lungs. I removed the adult-size blade that was always fitted to it and replaced it with the infant blade, which was not much bigger than my little finger. I removed the pulse oximeter, with its paediatric-sized sensor fitted to a cartoon-covered bandaid, then the kids' Laerdal mask and bag – a flexible mask that can fit over a toddler's mouth and nose – and the tennis-ball-sized bag to pump air into his tiny lungs.

It wasn't long before our equipment cases looked empty, and with the toddler showing no signs of improvement our paramedic was starting to run out of options. He asked me for the intraosseous needle. There was always one in our equipment case, but this was the first time I had ever been asked to get one ready. It's a hypodermic needle with a round, palm-sized grip on the end, much like a hand engraver's tool. It's used mainly for kids and is inserted directly into the leg then screwed through the bone and into the marrow. Drugs are then fed through the needle. It's barbaric but can be lifesaving.

Our paramedic swabbed the insertion site, halfway along the child's lower leg, then took the needle from its packet and with gentle pressure forced it into his leg with a slow twisting motion. The toddler didn't flinch. The paramedics worked on him for nearly thirty minutes, managing to intubate him and get fluids and drugs into his system through the intraosseous needle. The Propaq monitor was connected to sensor tabs on his skin. The toddler's little body was functioning – barely.

With the help of paramedics manually squeezing oxygen-enriched air into his lungs with the Laerdal mask, the child was getting the oxygen he needed and was eventually stabilised enough to be moved. One paramedic picked him up and laid him on the ambulance stretcher – he looked tiny on the adult-size bed. I pushed the stretcher down the driveway with our paramedic following alongside, watching the equipment and squeezing the Laerdal bag. Mum followed, still sobbing and being supported by the policewoman.

We made our way through the crowd in front of the house, which had grown since we first arrived. It was time to put my game face on. The face that showed just the right amount of empathy even though I felt nothing at all. At some point in my career I had become totally emotionally immune to trauma. Perhaps it was a defence mechanism, a means of survival. I had worn the same game face when I told a lady that her husband had just committed suicide in the back of his green Toyota, and a father that his daughter had just been murdered, masking the fact that I was numb to it all. My game face was just as important as the uniform I was wearing, so I had to get it right. I didn't want to give someone false hope from the slightest of grins – or rob them of it with a scant frown. There was no need to ask the crowd to move. Everyone took a step back, a path opening between them and the waiting ambulance.

A police car turned up to the park while we were loading the stretcher into the cabin. The toddler's mum was sitting in the front passenger seat. On jobs that involved kids this young we would usually take one of the parents in the helicopter with us, but there were other children still at home so Mum would have to make her way to the hospital a little later. I walked over and helped her out of the police car, then took her over to the helicopter. She walked slowly with her head bowed. Her whole body was trembling. While our paramedic was inside the cabin getting her son ready for the flight, she was given a chance to say a few words of comfort to him before we took off. She leant over, whispered into his ear and gave him a gentle kiss on the forehead.

As I walked her back to the police car, I asked if she was able to find someone who could drive her to the hospital. I didn't think she was in any state to drive. What do you say to a mother who has just run over her young son who may not survive? I would have liked to say that everything was going to be fine and her son would be okay, but there were no guarantees.

'We'll take care of him,' I said, still wearing my game face.

I walked back to the helicopter as the engines started and the blades began to turn.

There were tubes and wires hanging everywhere from the toddler's tiny body. His chest was rising and falling, as it was supposed to, and his heart was beating like it should. He was weak, but at least he was alive. The staff at The Royal Children's Hospital had been told that we were coming and had made their way to the helipad in the park behind the hospital. They were waiting for us as we landed.

As the engines started to shut down, I stepped out of the cockpit and walked around to the other side of the helicopter, gripping the handle on the patient's door, ready to open it. The nursing staff were already standing at the edge of the helipad, waiting for my signal to approach. I waved the staff over as the rotor blades slowed to a stop.

From the helipad, we wheeled the stretcher through the back door of the hospital and onto the first floor where the Intensive Care Unit (ICU) was. The corridor that led to the ICU was lined with seamless blue linoleum flooring and stainless-steel strips to protect the walls from being damaged by passing stretchers. Framed mementos adorned the corridor – pictures and poems from the families of patients past, some as a thanks for the lifesaving treatment provided by the incredible team of doctors and nurses, others celebrating a child's short life.

We passed through a set of secure doors and into the ICU. It was full of humidicribs in darkened rooms. Parents of sick children were sitting beside each crib, reaching in through the access ports to hold their child's hand or stroke their hair. Some of the lucky parents had smiles on their faces – hopefully our patient's mother would soon have a smile on her face too.

The ICU staff gathered around our toddler and got straight to work while listening to the paramedic's handover, which detailed the child's injuries and the list of drugs he had been given. Then we pushed our empty stretcher out of the ICU. Our job was done.

Any time I returned from jobs that involved kids there would be at least one air observer who would warn me that it would be much harder to handle if you had children yourself. Unsurprisingly, it always seemed to be a guys with kids who told me that.

I was never sure how to take this advice, or if it was advice at all. But I wondered, if someone who had kids found jobs like this difficult to handle, why would they want to work here? When I eventually went on to have children of my own, my view on this didn't change. Somehow, at the start of each shift, I was still able to flick an imaginary switch in my head, severing the link between work and my emotions and home life. As far as I was concerned, emotions would only get in the way, preventing me from doing my job well. Maybe that's why it never crossed my mind to find out if the toddler survived or not.

24

BASS STRAIT

3 February 2005 – 1123 hours

Everything was black. I couldn't breathe. Then I broke the surface. I had just long enough for a quick gasp of precious air and a glimpse of the yacht as another wave rolled over the top of me. I kept fighting, trying to force my way up towards air. It seemed impossible. I was being dragged deeper and deeper by a massive weight.

There must have been thirty feet of slack cable now underwater, thirty feet of slack cable dragging me under. If I was going to have any chance, all of that cable would have to be winched in before I could get to the surface.

The waves were relentless, attacking me from all angles, like lions toying with their prey before a kill. I broke through to the surface just as a wave rolled over me. Another valuable window to take a breath.

And then, in a split second, I was out of the water and in the air, swinging uncontrollably like a massive pendulum.

I rose rapidly as the helicopter climbed to pull me out. I felt the jolt of the lift through every bone and muscle in my body from what was now the second strain on the cable. It couldn't handle too many more.

I looked up. I could see Brendan working hard, using his body weight to push against the swinging cable to try to slow the pendulum down. It had little effect, but he and Ray didn't miss a beat. I started moving back towards the yacht. They were using the swing of the pendulum to try to land me on deck again. Timing my landing with the swing of the cable and the pitching and rolling of the yacht had to be perfect. If it wasn't, I would be smashed into the hull.

I looked for Ron Palmer, the yachtsman. He still wasn't on deck. He needed to be there when I landed. If not, I would be thrown off the yacht again and we wouldn't have the fuel for another attempt. I started to think about what I would do if the helicopter had to head back to land and refuel. Maybe I could swim over to the yacht, then deploy its life raft? Palmer and I could stay in that while the helicopter refuelled and *Ron's Endeavour* sank. We certainly couldn't leave him out there alone.

As I swung over the yacht, I stretched my foot out to see if I could stop the pendulum and land. Palmer suddenly appeared and tried to reach out to grab hold of me. We both missed, and I overshot the yacht. As I swung back I could feel myself being winched up and then lowered again. Brendan was going to have another crack. We missed again. Our only chance now was to winch Palmer out of the water. I hoped he was prepared to jump overboard.

I landed in the water right next to the yacht. I was able to keep my head above water, at least for now. The hull was close and provided me with some protection from the waves that now seemed to be coming from the opposite side. The yacht climbed up the side of a wave – as it rolled through, I followed. The stern lifted out of the water as it tipped over the crest, showing its clean blue-painted underside. I quickly reached out and placed my hand on the hull and pushed myself away from it as it came crashing down. Jets of water shot out in all directions as the yacht smacked into the trough of the wave. That was close.

I signalled Palmer to tell him to jump into the water. He remained still, not moving from the cabin doorway. A look of bewilderment on his face. Maybe he just didn't understand my hand signals.

'Get in the water!' I yelled.

Bewilderment changed to fear. He hesitated. If he didn't get into the water, I might never get hold of him.

'Get in the bloody water!' I screamed.

He started moving towards the outer railing, then stepped over it. He then stopped.

'Hurry up!'

The yacht climbed up another wave. He crouched down, still holding on to the rail. He was taking his time. Time that we didn't have.

The yacht rolled over the crest – I followed. I reached out and touched the hull again. The yacht pitched over the top of the wave and then crashed back down. The yachtsman lost his hold and fell into the water. I swam over and grabbed hold of him. We quickly drifted to the back of the yacht and immediately lost any protection from the waves. They hit us hard, pushing us both underwater. I struggled to find the rescue strop in the chaos. I needed to get both of us out of the water. We were getting pounded.

As a wave pushed me under, I closed my eyes and searched around for my quick release. I found it, then reached for the winch hook attached to the other end. Its weight had made it sink down near my knees. I broke the surface and took a quick breath – then I was underwater again. I felt my way along the winch hook to the rescue strop. I broke the surface and took another breath. I held the strop in one hand, grabbed the yachtsman with the other, then lassoed the strop over his head. He was of no assistance – he had no idea how to help and I had no time to explain it to him. I grabbed hold of his arms and fed them through the strop.

I held out one arm and gave Brendan a thumbs up to haul us both out of the water, knowing it would take him a few seconds to winch in the slack cable. In that time, I could tighten the rescue strop's chest strap. Suddenly another wave hit; its power was incredible. I lost my grip on Palmer. He was attached to me and I could not even see him or touch him. I was being thrown around underwater. I felt a third jerk on the cable and suddenly we were both climbing above the waves. Christ! This time with two bodies on the hook. How many more of these shocks could this bloody cable take?

Something was out of place. The yachtsman and I were face to face and he was holding on to the winch cable. He should be hanging below me. Fuck, the rescue strop was down below his waist. I never got the chance to tighten the chest strap before the wave hit. I panicked. He couldn't be winched like that. Within seconds we were thirty feet above the water looking down at the predatory, man-eating waves circling beneath us.

Without warning, the yachtsman lost his grip and fell backwards.

He was a goner.

25

WEST GATE BRIDGE

Suicides off Melbourne's West Gate Bridge were as common as the mud that lay on the banks below it. They were almost a weekly occurrence but rarely reported in the press for fear of encouraging copycats. At fifty-eight metres above water, the bridge had a perfect success rate. As far as I knew there had only been one person who had survived the jump – for a few minutes, at least.

Years ago, Grant Spurrell and another air observer, Barry Barclay, had found a man face down in the water after he had jumped. They were about to call in a police launch to retrieve the body when he rolled over and started moving. Barry jumped out of the helicopter and dropped almost eighty feet into the water. But the man died in Barry's arms only minutes later.

Tonight, we were heading there to search for a jumper, more commonly referred to as a body. A driver crossing the bridge had reported seeing a young woman climb over the handrail and jump. As we left Essendon Airport I could spot the lights from the bridge's two massive supports that form triangles pointing skywards.

As we got closer my pilot, Mark Kempton, slowed the helicopter and descended below the bridge. He hovered the helicopter over the water and kept it steady using the bridge's western pylon as a hover reference. Alan Cross was our paramedic. He was a man of more than one nickname. Crossy (for obvious reasons) and Aggro. I wasn't sure if the latter nickname referred to his uncanny resemblance to the children's puppet or his fierce temper. Perhaps it was both.

Crossy sat near the stretcher while I used the Nitesun to search the dark water. From his position in the pilot's seat, Mark was the first to spot something.

'I've got her down here,' he announced through the intercom. 'Ah, and she's ... waving.'

It took a couple of seconds to process what I was being told – that the woman had survived the fall.

'I'll move over and put her on your side, Cam.'

I opened my door and held it out at arm's length to get a good view of the water below as Mark moved the helicopter sideways.

'You should be able to see her coming under you now, Cam.'

There she was, only her head visible in the water. She was alive, all right. But God knew how long she would stay that way. I got straight onto the police radio to find out how long it would take to get a police boat to her. The radio then went silent while the operator contacted the Water Police. Every second of waiting felt like an eternity. Mark didn't want to wait for the answer and was keen to winch her out of the water now. I agreed, so I asked Crossy to get ready to do a winch. I was about to call the radio operator to tell him what we were doing when he came back to me with an answer – thirty minutes.

She wouldn't last that long. If the fall hadn't killed her, then surely her injuries would prevent her from keeping her head above water for much longer.

'Air four-nine-five. We will be off the air while we put our crewman in the water,' I announced over the police radio.

I quickly undid my seat harness and squeezed myself into the rear cabin while Mark held the helicopter in a hover.

Crossy already had his winch harness on and handed one to me. I threw it on loosely and secured myself to the nearest anchor point. I couldn't recall if Crossy had the foresight to put a wetsuit on before we left the hangar – he certainly didn't have any time to do it now. I went through our winching procedures quickly, confirming every move with Mark. When Crossy was ready, I slid back the side door, pulled the winch hook on board and handed it to him. I then leant out the door and took a quick look below – the woman's head was still above the water, but only just.

I winched Crossy out the door and sent him on his way.

The pitch-black water made it difficult to gauge how far Crossy was from the surface, especially when it was as flat as glass. I slowed the speed of the winch a little, just in case it was closer than it looked. She was still above water, so we had time. I kept an eye on Crossy and the woman while frequently scanning around the helicopter, making sure that the rotor blades were clear of the bridge's pylons and that we hadn't descended without noticing – easy to do when winching at night. I also checked above the rotor disc – being under a bridge was a first for me. But then again, so was a night-time winch.

As I looked up through the spinning rotors I saw two uniformed coppers leaning over the bridge's handrail shining their heavy metal torches down at us. I remembered from my General Duties days that those torches didn't have wrist straps and weighed a tonne. If one was dropped onto our rotor blades it would all be over.

Crossy was twenty feet above the water and right over the top of the woman when I saw her head vanish underwater. She didn't come back up. I pushed the winch up to full speed and the whine of its motor screamed through my headset. Crossy hit the surface of the water, travelling at the winch's maximum speed of 175 feet per minute, accompanied by a massive splash of white water. He disappeared, and I waited. Only a few seconds passed before he resurfaced. I didn't know how he did it, but he had dragged the woman to the surface with him. She wasn't moving and was a dead weight. I watched Crossy throw the rescue strop over her head and feed each of her arms through it.

I didn't wait for a thumbs-up signal and started winching in the slack cable straightaway. The winch cable ran through my hand as it wound onto the drum above my head. I felt it snap tight and the helicopter rocked a little as it took their weight.

I gave Mark the all clear to climb up ten feet – just enough to pull Crossy and his passenger out of the water. I pushed the winch to full speed again, slowing only as they approached the door. I then reached out and grabbed a webbing handle on the back of the strop, and when I got a confident nod from Crossy I pulled them both into the cabin.

'Clear to rotate, Mark.'

We could see The Alfred Hospital trauma centre from the bridge. Mark pushed the nose of the helicopter forwards, picking up speed quickly. He turned and headed straight for the hospital helipad.

Crossy pushed the woman into the back corner of the cabin. Her body was limp and her skin pale, almost ghost-like, and I couldn't see her chest rising and falling. I figured she was dead. Crossy grabbed a Laerdal mask and bag, placed it over her mouth and nose and squeezed air into her lungs.

It was a two-minute flight to The Alfred Hospital's trauma centre, so we radioed ahead to warn them we were coming in with a critical patient. The second our wheels touched the helipad, Mark gave the waiting trauma team the okay to approach under the spinning blades. Crossy crawled out of the helicopter and dragged his patient along the floor with him, both of them still harnessed up and attached to the winch cable. Water poured out of the cabin and onto the concrete helipad.

He and the woman disappeared into the trauma centre surrounded by a team of medical staff, Crossy still squeezing air into her lungs. He hadn't missed a beat.

After the helicopter was shut down, Mark and I finally got a chance to take a breath.

'Well, that was different,' I said.

'Sure was,' Mark replied with a slow nod.

•

A few days later, Crossy was at The Alfred Hospital and had a chance to check on his patient. She was conscious and talking, even though she had massive internal injuries and had broken almost every bone in her body south of her hips. She confessed to Crossy that she wanted to commit suicide after having a fight with her boyfriend. It was only after her feet had left the bridge railing that she realised she didn't want to die.

26

GUNGA DIN

Weighed down with a hull full of scallops from a successful night of fishing, the trawler *Gunga Din* was struggling to make it back to port before daybreak. Diesel engines laboured below deck as they pushed the trawler up and over the fifteen-metre-high Bass Strait swell.

The crew had joined Captain Ken Schwarzenberg in the warmth of the wheelhouse for the home leg, holding on tight to any solid object within reach and chatting about the celebratory beers they'd share later at their local pub. They didn't notice the rogue wave approaching. It hit the fourteen-metre trawler, rolling it so hard onto its side that it almost tipped over. Sea water swamped the rear deck and flowed into the open hull. Unable to handle the extra weight, the stern started to sink. The captain drove the engine throttles forwards in an attempt to drag the stern out of the water, but the engines choked to a stop. He had enough time to make one mayday call over the radio before the *Gunga Din* started to sink.

With no time to deploy their life raft, the crew jumped into the freezing water as the *Gunga Din* headed for the bottom of Bass Strait. The fishermen struggled to stay afloat, weighed down by the heavy layers of their warm clothing. Miraculously, one of the *Gunga Din*'s life rings had come loose from its mount and shot to the surface, appearing within arm's reach of one of the crew. The men huddled together holding on to the life ring that was barely capable of keeping the four of them afloat.

It was just after two in the morning, and the freezing men were stuck in the middle of Bass Strait, alone and in complete darkness.

•

That night I snuck into the pitch black of the crew rest room, careful not to wake up my pilot, Wally, and our paramedic, Neil. They had gone to bed hours ago. I always waited until I could barely keep my eyes open before jumping into bed – usually around the time American infomercials came on the TV.

It was always a battle to fall asleep at work, especially after spending hours on high alert expecting to be called to a job at any minute. The crew rest room was rigged for sleep, with the thermostat set to warm and the windows covered by old grey hospital blankets that made better window coverings than bed linen because they felt like steel wool.

Since the Air Ambulance helicopter was the only helicopter that operated twenty-four hours a day, if D24 called the Air Wing and requested a helicopter to attend a police job, it was up to the Air Ambulance's observer to decide if the job was urgent enough for them to attend. For that reason, the air observer's bed was strategically placed next to the doorway of the crew rest room, so the rest of the crew were not woken up when the observer working the operations room entered to run a job past him.

The steel-frame bed squeaked as it took my weight. There was no avoiding it. The beds were hand-me-downs from some hospital – made of solid steel tubing welded to four trolley wheels, with thick wire-spring netting as the base. I pulled the blankets up around my shoulders, closed my eyes and hoped for a good night's rest. Although the wind outside was gathering intensity and doing its best to stop me from sleeping. The hangar roof creaked and the large metal doors moaned with each gust of wind.

I was almost asleep when I heard the faint ring of the D24 phone. The operations guy was right onto it. I knew the drill: if there was a job, it would take him about two minutes to hear the request then walk from the operations room to the rest room. Unless he turned it down. And on a cold and windy night like tonight I hoped that he had. Nonetheless, anxious energy began to build. Right on cue, the door squeaked open and light broke into the room.

'Cam, there's a job,' he whispered. 'A mayday call from a fishing trawler taking on water in Bass Strait.'

I opened my eyes. I couldn't turn this job down. In the dark, I reached for my flight suit and called to the pilot and paramedic. 'We've got a job, guys.'

As we all got up and dressed in our flight suits, the operations guy filled us in on the details. The RCC had received a mayday call from the fishing trawler *Gunga Din* saying that they were ten miles south off Cape Schanck and taking on water rapidly. When they tried to call the *Gunga Din* back, there was no answer.

The operations guy left us so he could jump onto the tractor and started to tow the Air Ambulance out of the hangar and onto the tarmac while Wally, Neil and I climbed on board. We were airborne minutes later and heading for Cape Schanck. I sorted through my mess of a navigation bag looking for a map that covered that area. I marked a spot ten miles due south off the cape, then drew a quick pencil line to it from Essendon Airport. The city lights below vanished the minute we flew over the bowl of the bay. Nineteen minutes later the lights of San Remo appeared, and in no time at all we were over Bass Strait. Flying at two miles per minute, we would be over the search site in five minutes.

Over the radio, the RCC told us that a container ship in Bass Strait had heard the mayday call and had diverted to the area. As we got closer I could see the huge container ship anchored in the dark water. Crew were dotted around its perimeter, shining torches into the water. Wally turned on the Nitesun and illuminated the container ship. Waves were pounding the sides and it was rolling in the swell.

I called the container ship on the radio. The quality of the communication was scratchy but I could make out what the captain was saying, even with his strong foreign accent. One of his crew had reported hearing voices coming from the ship's starboard side. I asked the captain how long it had been since then. I didn't like the reply – at least ten minutes.

It had now been forty minutes since the mayday call. Wally pulled the helicopter around to the ship's starboard side and adjusted the Nitesun, scanning the surface of the water from left to right, covering as much area as he could.

'There's no debris in the water,' I said over my intercom. I'd never seen a fishing trawler deck not covered in a collection of buoys, plastic fish boxes and endless coils of rope – if the *Gunga Din* had gone down here, there would be debris floating on the surface. Like me, Neil looked out the windows and scanned the water below.

I wasn't confident in finding the trawler crew at all, alive or otherwise. 'We're looking for heads bobbing in the water. No chance,' I said, shaking my head. Bass Strait was just too unforgiving.

After half an hour of searching we had covered an area up to half a mile away from the container ship and failed to spot anything. We were using fuel at a faster rate while we hovered and our nearest refuelling point at Sorrento was a ten-minute flight away. Wally calculated that we had enough fuel for another forty minutes of searching.

As the observer, it was my call as to whether we continued. I decided to give the search another twenty minutes. We also had to consider refuelling so we could respond to other medical emergencies. I started our twenty-minute countdown. The time went fast and I could tell Wally was getting tired when he rolled the helicopter forwards, then flew a slow orbit above the container ship before pulling into a hover at the same spot. Just as it was time to call it off and head for home, Wally jolted the helicopter.

'I think I've got something!' he said.

'Bullshit,' I said in disbelief.

Wally rolled the helicopter over to the right to get a better view of something in the water. At the same time, he moved the Nitesun, keeping his eye fixed on the water.

I kept my eyes on the radar altimeter (RADALT), making sure we didn't get too close to the water.

'Shit! It's them. Four of 'em.' Wally was dead serious.

I leant over to Wally's side of the cockpit so I could see out of his window. Sure enough, there they were, four of the luckiest guys on the planet bobbing up and down in rough seas while clinging on to a half-submerged life ring. Miles from land. It got busy in the cockpit. Banter was replaced by strategising – how were we going to get these guys out of the water?

It had only been a few months since our bosses had reluctantly approved winching at night. Our chief pilot, Ian Galt, and two observers, Neil Davey and Steve Collins, did the Air Wing's very first night winch to save the life of a teenager stranded on the roof of a car during some floods. They had no training and no lighting to do a winch at night. So they declared a 'mercy flight', which allowed them to throw the rule book out the window in order to save a life. The powers that be wanted to crucify the chief pilot for doing the winch, but the declaration of a mercy flight was his get-out-of-jail-free card. We started night winching soon after, but not over water. It was still forbidden because it was far too dangerous.

Wally moved the helicopter to position the four fishermen directly in the Nitesun's beam. I immediately got on the marine radio and notified the RCC. There were only a handful of options for rescuing the four fishermen and we had to find the best one in a hurry, by process of elimination. It was far too dangerous for the container ship to try to pull alongside the men in these conditions – it could run right over the top of them. The only other option was for us to stay overhead for as long as our fuel would allow and hope that a smaller marine vessel close by could get here on time. If we found ourselves running on fumes, I could drop a marine marker flare out of my storm window.

I broadcasted on the marine radio requesting any vessel in the area capable of picking up the stranded fishermen. A fishing trawler, *Pinta 3*, answered my call. The captain's voice boomed over the radio. He sounded excited. I understood enough of what he said buried in wind noise and static. The *Pinta 3* was twenty minutes away. We had just enough fuel to wait that long. Right on time, the trawler pulled into the Nitesun's beam. A crewman leant overboard, reaching for one of the survivors. As soon as the rescue was underway, we turned and headed for fuel. We made it to Sorrento with only a few minutes to spare. As Wally shut down the engines, we heard over the marine radio that all four fishermen had been pulled to safety.

As we headed back to Essendon, it struck me that four lives could have been held in the balance for the sake of a minute's worth of fuel, or by the chance turn of the Nitesun's beam. Four dads or husbands or fathers were saved that night because I decided to go to the job, even though I hadn't been convinced they would still be there to be rescued in the first place.

So much boiled down to sheer luck.

•

The story of the crew's miraculous survival appeared in the newspaper the next day, and after reading the article I realised that the fishermen were far luckier than I first thought – one of them in particular. As they clung to the one life ring, their Captain Ken Schwarzenberg kept his crew – Paul Hopkins and brothers Dean and Bill Thow – focused by telling them that he was confident that his mayday call had been picked up and a rescue helicopter was on its way. But after twenty minutes floating in the cold water Dean, the youngest of the crew, started to freeze. Thinking he was endangering the rest of them, he told his brother that he was going to let go of the life ring – he was ready to die so that his brother and friends could live. The captain convinced Dean to hold on for a little longer. He did, and we turned up.

27

PORT PHILLIP BAY

It was Boxing Day 2000 and the Big Bay Race around Port Phillip Bay was well underway. Sailing conditions were perfect. No one could have possibly forecast the dangerous and unpredictable weather phenomenon that was about to hit the field – a microburst. Instead of a storm's usual sideward flow, in a microburst air flows straight down, hits the surface of the earth, then punches violently outward. Microbursts have been known to bring down passenger jets.

The *Spirit of Downunder*, skippered by Laurie Ford, was leading the race when the microburst hit. All hell broke loose on deck. The spinnaker partially collapsed while it was being lowered. It refilled with air, lifting its handler off the deck and throwing him metres through the air before he crashed into the mainsail. In a steep lean, the yacht's boom and mainsail were dragged in the water. Lindsay Dack, a 43-year-old crew member, was thrown overboard. One of the crew activated the man-overboard alarm and a mayday call blared over the marine radio. Laurie jumped overboard to help his mate.

Horizon Spirit heard the distress call and spotted the two sailors in the water in front of them. They were both hauled on board. By that time, Lindsay had stopped breathing.

•

The phone rang in Hangar 104's operations room. It was the RCC. Two people were in the water off Carrum, one of them feared drowned.

The job could've been given to either the police helicopter or Air Ambulance. The preference was the Air Ambulance, as having a paramedic as the winch crewman gave the people involved a better chance of survival. But on this day the Air Ambulance was stuck at The Alfred Hospital dropping off a patient, so the police helicopter got it.

Ray started the helicopter while Dave Lord, the other air observer, and I strapped ourselves in. Dave Lord, or Lordy, was one of the air observers who started at the Air Wing the same day as me.

The weather was deteriorating rapidly as the wind increased. The main storm front was moving over Geelong to our west. As we flew over the West Gate Bridge, I grabbed my wetsuit and started suiting up. Dave had acted as the winch crewman last time we worked together, so this time it was my turn. We would be overhead in under fifteen minutes. Squeezing myself into a wetsuit in the confined area of the cabin where you couldn't even stand up was not exactly fine choreography. I was wrestling with thick black neoprene and building up a serious sweat. When I was finished I was steaming hot – hitting the cold sea water would be a welcome relief.

The yacht was easy to spot. The Big Bay Race hadn't been called off and the yachts that were still racing were under sail, leaning against the wind with long streaks of white water trailing behind them. But *Horizon Spirit* was stationary, its sails were down and it was pitching and rolling with the waves.

The waves weren't huge, so they were nothing to worry about. What did worry us was the pitching and rolling of the yacht, which turned the mast into a dangerous obstacle as it whipped from side to side. It would be far too dangerous to attempt to winch me onto the deck – the winch cable could get tangled up in the mast or its rigging or, worse still, the mast could hit me. Winching me into the water was the only solution. I could then swim over to the yacht.

Lordy winched me out and placed me only a few metres behind the yacht. As soon as I hit the water I released myself from the winch hook and swam straight over to the back of the yacht. It had the typical chiselled transom of a racing yacht – impossible to climb unassisted. Two of the crew threw me a rope line. I grabbed hold and they pulled me in and helped me on board.

Lindsay was lying on the deck near the bow, face up, with his arms by his sides. I walked over to him, shedding my equipment as I went and dropping it onto the deck – helmet, gloves. I didn't need them anymore and they would just get in my way. His face was drained of all colour, that unmistakeable shade of blueish grey, and his eyes were wide open, shining like melting ice. I felt the carotid artery in his neck. There was no pulse. I repositioned my fingers. Nothing. I watched his chest hoping to detect some movement. Nothing. I could feel the eyes of the crew burning holes through me, all of them watching and expecting me to do something. Anything. I had to try, even though all the signs pointed to it being too late.

There were remains of vomit around his mouth and chin. After washing it away with some sea water that had flooded the deck, I tilted his forehead back. I asked one of the crew members to kneel beside me to start chest compressions and count to five, out loud. He positioned himself. *One ... two ... three ...* They were good compressions. I could tell by the sound of air being expelled from Lindsay's lungs. I clamped his nose closed with my hand and with his jaw held open, I leant in.

... Four ... five ... I pressed my mouth against Lindsay's, covering it completely. I gave him two full breaths, then lifted my head and wiped the taste of sea water from my mouth. I continued.

Everyone on the yacht watched on. They were all hoping for a response from Lindsay, but I knew there was a big difference between blowing air into someone's lungs and them coming back to life. After several cycles of breathing and compression, I checked Lindsay's neck for a pulse. There was nothing. We continued. *One ... two ... three ...* Then I heard a helicopter approach – it was the Air Ambulance that had flown straight over from The Alfred Hospital. It positioned itself in a hover just off the back of the yacht. I turned up the volume on my portable radio and waited for them to call me. When they did, I quickly answered before getting straight back to CPR.

They had returned with one of our paramedics and were preparing to winch him and his equipment onto the yacht to help. I looked back at the helicopter. The paramedic was in the doorway and already connected to the winch hook. His equipment was tied together with some webbing and sitting next to him. He was all ready to go. But the yacht's mast was in between the deck and the helicopter, swaying erratically from side to side. There was no consistent direction or timing to its movement – it went in whatever direction the waves commanded.

The risk of the mast hitting the paramedic was far too great and his equipment would be useless if it went into the water. Even if winching were an option, Lindsay was not responding. I called off the paramedic and stopped CPR. Lindsay was dead. We motored towards Sandringham Marina where the local coppers would be waiting. I called the helicopter and told Ray to land somewhere nearby.

I sat with my back to the weather, which had quickly become worse. Waves were now crashing over the side of the yacht, sea water pouring into the cabin from behind me. I could feel cold water running down my back. The thin summer wetsuit did nothing to prevent me from freezing.

Lindsay's body was lying in water that had pooled on the deck and was rolling from side to side with the movement of the yacht. There was nothing to cover him with. This was no way to treat the dead. All I could do was slide my feet forwards and wedge them under his back to keep him still.

As he lay there in front of me I couldn't help but think that I should have tried to get the paramedic on board the yacht. Maybe he could have brought Lindsay back. Or perhaps I should have continued CPR for a little longer.

As we pulled into the shelter of the Sandringham Marina I noticed the crowd gathering. Police, yachties and onlookers, who never failed to show themselves in times like these. As the yacht pulled alongside the pier I didn't wait. I stepped off as the local uniformed senior constable stepped on. I made my way through the crowd packed onto the tiny landing. I didn't stop for a chat or the usual debriefing – I would call the senior constable later.

Ray and Lordy were sitting in the helicopter waiting at a nearby oval. As I approached I held my arm out to my side, scribbling a circle in the air with my pointer finger – the hand signal for Ray to start the helicopter. The engines clicked over and the blades started to turn.

I jumped in the back, secured myself to the cabin floor and put on my flight helmet.

'No good, Cam?' Lordy asked over the intercom.

'Nah. But I gave it crack,' I replied.

28

BASS STRAIT

3 February 2005 – 1125 hours

I tried to grab hold of Palmer as he fell backwards but missed. I felt a punch behind my shoulder – it was his foot. I reached down and took hold of one of his legs. *Don't let go*, I thought to myself, *Whatever you do, don't let go.*

His arms were flailing about trying desperately to grab on to something. He managed to reach the rescue strop underneath his knees and pull on it hard, lifting his head up. His eyes were wide open, staring at me, silently begging for me to do something. Then he lost his grip and was upside down again. I was holding on as tight as I could.

The pain was intense. A sharp burning sensation coming from deep within my shoulder, as if a large needle was being driven into the joint. I started to panic. Palmer was getting heavier and I couldn't hold on for too much longer. We were still high above the water and I was going to lose my grip on him at any second.

Brendan must've been able to see what was happening. I needed to get back in the water, and fast. I looked up towards the helicopter hoping that Brendan could see the desperation on my face. The pain in my shoulder was torture and any minute now my arm was going to explode out of its socket.

'Mate, I've got you!' I yelled to Palmer. Not even sure if he could hear me over the roar of the wind and waves.

I felt movement in the cable. We were heading towards the water again. Brendan saw we were in trouble. Before we hit, I took a deep breath, cramming as much air into my lungs as they could handle. We went straight under.

The next thing I remember was feeling intense pain and the winch cable grating across my ribs as Palmer and I were lifted from the water – the cable had wrapped around my body and when the wire was winched in I was lifted out of the water by my shoulder. The weight of two men on the cable forced my arm and shoulder joint to flex in a way they were never meant to.

This time Palmer was hanging upright, his head centred against my chest like it was supposed to be. While I was in the water, I must have pulled the rescue strop out from underneath Palmer's legs, thrown it over his head and then fed each of his arms through it. I must have tightened the chest strap and given Brendan the thumbs-up signal, extending one arm up and out. But I can't remember doing any of it.

The winch up to the helicopter seemed to take forever.

I placed my hands on the yachtsman's shoulders. A belated attempt to reassure him. I could feel the acceleration as Brendan pushed the winch to its limits. Finally, it would only be a matter of seconds and I could reach up and touch the helicopter. I turned and took one last look at the yacht. Soon it would be resting on the bottom of Bass Strait along with the countless other wrecks that had fought the strait and lost.

We slowed down before reaching the doorway and I placed my hand on the skin of the helicopter. We were safe.

•

There was an uneasy quiet in the helicopter as we flew over the coast, leaving Bass Strait behind us. I sat against the back wall of the cabin. I was on my way down from a massive high. It was intoxicating, as if I'd just got away with the crime of the century and was home free.

Palmer sat motionless on the cabin floor in front of me, a puddle of sea water forming around his feet. He was staring out the window, where there was nothing to see but ocean.

Brendan broke the silence. 'I'm Brendan, this is our pilot, Ray, and that's Cameron in the back.'

'Ahh. Ron Palmer,' he said in an English accent, his voice barely loud enough to activate his microphone. 'I should say thank you for the lift, gents.'

'Pleased to meet you, Ron. Although I wish it could be in better circumstances,' I said.

'Yes, yes indeed.'

'Ron, we just have to make a quick stop for fuel then we'll head for our hangar at Essendon Airport,' Brendan said.

'Thank you.'

Maybe it wasn't the best time for idle chitchat. What do you actually say to someone who has just seen his prized possession sink to the bottom of Bass Strait? But I had one question I had to ask him.

'Ron, when I landed on the deck, why did you turn around and go inside the cabin?' I said.

'I was told by your Coast Guard to open my sea valves once the helicopter crewman had landed on the deck,' he answered.

I was aghast. Our message for him to pull the plug as soon as he saw us approach had never been delivered.

•

The airport at Latrobe Valley was quiet as always, typical for a regional airfield. It was the home base of one of our counterparts, Helimed One, a Bell 412 Air Ambulance helicopter that serviced the eastern part of Victoria. I used to think that we attended a lot of gruesome car accidents, but we had nothing on these guys. East Gippsland was notorious for high-speed head-on collisions along its many sections of straight highway.

Ray hovered over to the Helimed One hangar and landed right out front. As soon as the wheels touched the ground he hit the timer on the helicopter's clock and waited the two minutes for the engines to run at idle before shutting them down.

I slid back the cabin door and sat there, my feet hanging out over the tarmac. I stretched out my right arm and rotated it around my shoulder, trying to get some movement back. It had seized up like some rusty old engine part. I could feel pain along my ribs just under my left arm. It felt as though I'd had a layer of skin removed.

The engines let out a hiss as Ray pulled back on the fuel control levers, starving them of fuel and shutting them down. The rotor blades slowed. At the right speed, Ray reached up to the controls above his head and pushed the rotor brake's lever forwards. The rotor blades ground to a halt.

I stepped out first. Warm water heated up by my body drained out of my survival suit and onto the tarmac. I was back on land.

The Helimed One accommodation rooms were dark and unkempt. Perhaps we had just disturbed them engrossed in a movie. Most likely, we had just woken them up. Palmer and I accepted the offer of a hot shower from their crewman, Billy Smits. Billy had been a crewman on Helimed One for years. He was part of the furniture, a company stalwart.

Steam was soon billowing out of the shower cubicle as I dialled up the hot water. It felt like torture with a thousand needles as the hot water hit my icy-cold feet and hands. I gritted my teeth and groaned, hoping my extremities would thaw quickly. I felt a sting as the water hit my ribs and legs. I looked down – both were covered in deep red grazes. They could only have come from one thing: the winch cable.

I crossed my arms against the wall tiles, leant forwards and rested my head against them. Then closed my eyes. The steaming hot water hit my shoulders and ran down my back, slowly washing away the salt-water residue stuck to my skin. I noticed my body trembling. I tried to turn the hot water up, but it was as hot as it could be. Eventually the intense heat turned my back and legs cherry red – but it also slowed down the trembling as my body went numb.

I stayed in the shower a little longer. I began to think about the few seconds that I was stuck underwater, terrified that I was going to drown. But I didn't, I survived. And Ron Palmer was rescued.

Then why, after having been on such a high, did I now feel like a failure?

•

I was halfway through a cup of instant coffee when Palmer finished his shower. Billy was kind enough to lend him some dry clothes, underwear included. They weren't most men's taste in underwear but under the circumstances Palmer was not in any position to refuse the offer. Palmer looked more of this earth now. I offered him a mug of coffee and he took it with both hands. I could see the delight on his face as he closed his eyes, smelt the aroma and took his first sip. When we got back to our hangar at Essendon, Australian Customs were waiting to process him for landing in Australia. Soon after, he was in a cab and on his way to his sister's place for a long overdue visit, while Ray, Brendan and I were summoned to the operation manager's office for a debrief on the rescue. The debrief was a quick one. Each of us recounted the rescue from start to finish. It was interesting to hear what Ray and Brendan had seen from above. Brendan was expecting to find me floating in the water without legs after I was thrown from the yacht and out of sight. Ray felt the jerk in the controls of the helicopter and knew something had happened. He asked Brendan if I was okay. But Brendan had lost sight of me and couldn't answer. As for Palmer falling backwards and me holding on to his legs, Brendan hadn't noticed from his position directly above us. He winched us both back into the water because he figured something must have been wrong.

The debrief ended with a few questions from the operations manager. How did the equipment hold up? Was there any training we could do to better prepare? We didn't hold back and gave him the answers that he probably didn't want to hear, although he was scribbling a few notes in his diary. I only had one question of my own. 'Why weren't our instructions delivered for the yachtsman to open his sea valves when he saw the helicopter and be back on deck waiting when I landed?'

The operations manager dropped his chin and stared at the carpet. It was a dead giveaway that he was feeling a little uncomfortable. 'The Rescue Coordination Centre's phone has a block on making international calls so they couldn't call him and pass on your message.'

There was silence. I didn't know what to say.

•

When I got home, I told Susan about the rescue – the heavily edited version, anyway. I didn't want to worry her with all the gory details.

Palmer spent the rest of the day doing phone interviews with the media. I heard one of the interviews on ABC Radio. It started off okay but, like the Bass Strait weather, it turned nasty quickly. Palmer was accused of being careless entering Bass Strait in a storm and placing himself and his rescuers in great danger. It ended after the interviewer suggested that Australian taxpayers should not bear the financial burden of his rescue, and he should pay for it himself.

I felt sorry for Palmer. The poor bloke had been smashed by waves all night, strung upside down and nearly drowned beneath our helicopter, and then watched on as everything he owned sank to the bottom of Bass Strait. Now he'd be thinking that the Australian Government was going to hunt him down and extract payment. Welcome to Australia, Ron. I suspected he wouldn't agree to any more interviews from then on and would probably try to escape back to his home in Canada as soon as he could pay for his airfare.

•

I had the following day off and woke up with pain and cramping in my right shoulder. I wasn't sure if it was from holding on to Ron's leg or from the winch cable when we were both hauled out of the water.

But the pain in my shoulder was overpowered by thoughts of the rescue. It was like a motion picture was playing in my head on an endless loop. In an attempt to divert my racing mind, I decided to head to the local cafe for coffee, but there was no escape. The morning's newspapers were scattered all over a bench inside the cafe and I could see the bold headlines: 'Record storm leaves chaos trail', 'Worst storm in 150 years' and 'Spirit of Tasmania pounded by wild seas'.

I thought that if I couldn't get the rescue out of my mind, I might as well read what other people thought of it. I gathered a copy of each paper and sat and read through them all. It seemed as though it was some storm we were in yesterday. The search for the teenager swept off the bridge into Skeleton Creek and the rescue of Ron Palmer were hidden among far bigger news stories like the wave damage to the Spirit of Tasmania ferry and the widespread flooding around Melbourne.

With the endless motion-picture loop still playing, I eventually realised that there were some pieces missing. I had no recollection of being thrown off the yacht and hitting the water, or of re-fitting the rescue strop on Palmer, no matter how hard I thought about it. I had no idea why I had blanked out during those moments. I contacted a close friend, Joe Gazis, who was also a police psychologist. Joe was one person who was always prepared to tell you exactly how it was – he called a spade a spade. I asked Joe about my memory loss. He told me that the mind has the unique ability to block out things that it believes may be damaging, even though the body continues to function normally. I didn't think it was a big deal – I remembered everything else and that was more than enough to keep my mind busy. But it did explain my memory loss during the Russell Street bombing nearly twenty years earlier.

I struggled to fall asleep that night – the motion picture was playing again. Eventually I did, but only a few hours before I had to be back at work.

Later that morning I stood in front of my locker and put my flight suit on. I folded my gloves the same way I always did and, after slipping my talisman into my leg pocket, I walked out into the hangar and tossed my flight gear into the helicopter, then headed to the mess room to sort through the coffee mugs. It was business as usual, and I found the perfect way to stop the endless replays – work.

•

A few months passed, and I found that my interest in flying had faded. I'm not sure if it was the rescue of Ron Palmer that caused the change. But now, if I was given the choice between flying around the city at night for a few hours, or staying back at the hangar by myself, I'd take the hangar – and I did. I found myself spending more and more time at work hiding away from people and helicopters.

Part of me still believed that I was made for the job, but I knew I couldn't keep hiding. I decided my only option was to leave the Air Wing and Victoria Police. But where do old air observers go to die? It wasn't like dream jobs were thick on the ground. I toyed with the idea of going back out to a station and starting again where I left off – chasing a promotion to sergeant or applying to become a detective. But that would be like turning my career clock back thirteen years. Was there a job for a 38-year-old copper like me who had been away from General Duties policing for more than a decade? I had some important career decisions to make, and only I could make them.

Steve Collins, the other air observer who started at the Air Wing the same day as Dave Lord and I, suggested that I apply for the Australian Federal Police (AFP). He had joined them a few years earlier and had just returned from six months in the Solomon Islands. And he was about to head to Cyprus for twelve months. They were looking for experienced coppers to be deployed on overseas peacekeeping missions.

Peacekeeping! Now that sounded like fun. I applied.

29

MY LAST JOB

It was my last flying shift at the Air Wing, almost thirteen years to the day since I had first walked through the hangar doors. I had accepted a job offer from the AFP and after a few weeks training in Canberra I would be sent to the Solomon Islands as part of an Australian assistance mission to the country.

I was just about to clean out my clothing locker when that familiar amplified ring echoed through the hangar. We had a job – probably my last job in a helicopter. A car had been stolen in Carlton. Normally this wouldn't warrant getting the helicopter airborne, but the car had a baby asleep in a capsule on the back seat.

The suburb of Carlton was abuzz with people heading out for a meal in Lygon Street, the popular Italian restaurant district. The streets were littered with parked cars, but we were only interested in one – a red Subaru station wagon. I was hoping that the car thief would notice his passenger, then panic and dump the car close by. If not, the car could be a couple of suburbs away in the time that it took for us to fly out to Carlton.

We flew the helicopter in slow parallel tracks over the suburb, searching the streets and picking out cars in every shade of red. We checked each one with a slow left-hand orbit. I started to think that the car thief hadn't noticed his tiny passenger and we needed to widen our search area to include the surrounding suburbs. I was just about to call our office and ask for them to send the Air Ambulance out to help search when I spotted a red station wagon parked alongside a row of cars. It looked like it had been parked in a hurry – its nose was pulled into the kerb and its back end was poking out onto the road. It had a similar shape to a Subaru wagon but I wasn't certain and a slow orbit couldn't confirm it. I requested the nearest ground unit to check the car while we remained overhead.

Minutes later a police car pulled up. I turned the volume on the police radio up a little higher.

'We have the car!' I heard over the radio.

The baby was still sound asleep in the back seat, totally unaware that it had been taken for a joyride in a stolen car. Relief. I was happy that my last job in the air ended in success.

•

At the end of my shift I stood at my clothing locker and started emptying it into a cardboard box. The top shelf was layered with mementos from thirteen years at the Air Wing. Everything had a memory attached to it. My favourite was an old photograph of me winch training over Port Phillip Bay with a training aid that we named after a yacht that went missing in 1990 and was never found – *Great Expectations*. It was a three-dimensional wooden cross that was painted fluorescent orange and bound with nylon rope. We used to throw the cross into the water from the helicopter, then try to retrieve it with a grappling hook attached to the winch cable. The photograph must have been taken around 1993. I couldn't believe how young I was back then. If I hadn't known better, I'd have thought it was a photograph of a work experience kid who had smuggled himself on board the helicopter.

Piece by piece I placed everything into the cardboard box – more old photographs and the broken winch cable, of course. I stopped for a minute and had a quick look through my two flight log books. The first ever entries in perfect handwriting, blue pen for the text and red for the ruled lines and borders. One flight per line with a small note detailing the type of job. The entries for one particular month caught my eye – fatal accident, overdose, pursuit, another fatal accident. Every flight was claimed, no matter how long. It was a stark contrast to the most recent entries, hastily scribbled onto the page with most flights not important enough to warrant any detail at all. Some not even entered. I closed my locker door. It was empty now except for a couple of well-worn flight suits I left hanging on the rail. I walked through the hangar saying my goodbyes to those who were rostered on that day, then grabbed my box and walked out of the hangar for the very last time.

The following weeks were terrible. I was a lost soul. In leaving Victoria Police, I also lost my identity. Being a copper and member of Victoria Police was not only what I did, but it was who I was.

30

GOVERNMENT HOUSE

I had just finished what turned out to be – in comparison to my Victoria Police training – mind-numbingly dull training with the Federal Police. I was now waiting to be sent overseas when I got the letter from the Royal Humane Society of Australasia. I'd never heard of them until I read the gold-embossed letter informing me that our crew was being awarded bravery medals for the rescue of Ron Palmer. Ray, the pilot, and Brendan, the winch operator, were being awarded a bronze medal while I was being awarded a silver medal – the difference between them remaining in the helicopter and me hanging on the cable. I headed straight to my computer and googled the Royal Humane Society. It was the oldest philanthropic organisation in Australia and had been recognising bravery for over a century. It was quite an honour.

A few weeks later, an invitation to the award ceremony at Government House in Melbourne arrived in the mail. I had always wanted to see the inside of Government House and now I was an invited guest. When the day rolled around, Susan and I attended the ceremony. I was dressed in a borrowed AFP dress uniform because the only uniform I'd been issued so far was a peacekeeping uniform of military-style pants, standard blue police shirt and heavy leather boots – certainly not befitting an occasion such as this.

As we passed through the large iron gates at Government House and drove along the driveway to the main residence, I felt like I was on the set of *Downton Abbey*. The white gravel driveway crunched under the car tyres; the trimmed lawns and manicured gardens framed the magnificent white mansion. The flagpole pitched on top of the tower was missing its yellow governor's pennant – he was not at home – which explained why the presentation was to be made by Lady Southey, AC, the Lieutenant-Governor of Victoria.

We followed the strategically placed signs to the State Drawing Room, where we were met at the door by an aide in military dress uniform. My name was marked off the attendance list, and a small investiture hook was pinned to my right lapel. The aide explained that when it came time for Lady Southey to present the medal, it would be easier to hang it from this hook than to pin it into place.

Stepping into the room, I stopped for a moment to take it all in. Several chandeliers that were bigger than me hung from the high ceiling. The room was filled with century-old oil paintings, ornate silverware and carved mahogany furniture – all of it polished to a high shine. The furniture was covered in gold-embossed linens and everything seemed to be in pairs. There were two fireplaces, two couches and twin coffee tables either side of a bay window, each of them adorned with the very same lamp. Even the oversized chaise longue had its identical twin on the opposite side of the room. The scale of the grandeur dwarfed us. The room had been prepared for guests. The grand piano and Victorian mahogany furniture had all been pushed aside to make room for rows of blue-cloth-covered chairs with tubular frames, more shopping centre food court than governor's residence.

Susan and I sat together, where we were told. Ray and Brendan arrived shortly after and were directed to sit in the vacant seats next to us. There was a booklet with all our names in it and what we had done to deserve our awards. I surreptitiously looked around, curious to see the other people in my position, trying to match people with names. Dressed in uniform, it would have been easy to spot the three of us, even though mine was a Federal Police uniform and the odd one out.

The master of ceremonies was the Society's secretary, Mr Colin Bannister. He was made for the role. He was dressed in a fine tailored suit and vest, his silver moustache chiselled and waxed, and his chest decorated with rows of military ribbons. He read each citation with the execution and precision you would expect from a military man. One by one, the awards were presented, starting with the reading of the award citation – a description of the event that led to the award. At the end of the reading, Bannister called the name of the recipient and the award they were being presented with. One by one, they walked up to Lady Southey to have their award presented to them, while an in-house photographer caught it all on film.

What was most striking was the ordinariness of the heroes who surrounded me. They weren't perfect specimens of human strength and ability. They were regular folk, the kind you see walking into the local cafe or supermarket. They were ordinary people being recognised for extraordinary courage. It was hard to believe what some people had done to receive the same gold-embossed invitation as I did. There was a passer-by who dragged a driver from a burning car and a university lecturer who had disarmed a crazed gunman who had shot dead two students and wounded five others. There was even a posthumous award for a father who had jumped into a swimming hole to save his drowning son. The father couldn't swim but he had died trying. What also struck me was that all these people receiving awards had done so with sheer bravery and without any training.

I felt people looking over at us when Bannister read out our citation. The mention of the words 'police helicopter' was enough to attract everyone's attention. Brendan and Ray wearing their silver wings and me in my borrowed finery stood out like sore thumbs. I felt uncomfortable with the attention. I wanted to disappear under the seat and hide until it was all over. But here, in this grand room, I was a deer in headlights. Bannister began reading the description of the rescue. It was all there in words: the waves, the gasping for air, the near drowning. The words told the story of bravery, but they didn't tell the truth.

I wasn't brave at all. I was terrified. I felt like a failure for being scared. I had let myself down and every other air observer who had come before me.

Under a chandelier bigger than me, I accepted an award that was a lie.

•

After the ceremony everyone was corralled into the courtyard for refreshments and photographs. A newspaper crew weaved their way through the crowd, speaking to each person they found with a shiny new medal pinned to their chest, snapping more photographs, taking notes, then rating each story on their news-worthiness scale. I hoped in vain that three uniformed coppers hiding behind a huge fountain would escape their attention. A journalist made a beeline straight for us. In typical copper mode, we answered her questions with the fewest words possible. Her story was published in the *Herald Sun* the following day along with a photo of the three of us. My smile was forced.

When I got home I opened the medal case and had a quick look inside. It was solid silver and must have been worth a pretty penny. I then closed the case and shoved it into the drawer of my bedside table. I never gave the medal much thought after that.

31

KUKUM TILL WE DIE

A wall of hot and humid air met me at the aircraft door and by the time I reached the bottom of the stairs my uniform shirt was soaked through with sweat. Welcome to Honiara, Solomon Islands. It was March 2006.

I walked across the tarmac, stopping in line for the mandatory handshake from the AFP commander before entering the customs hall, expecting some relief from the heat. There wasn't any. I collected my bag and threw it into the back of a waiting four-wheel drive for the short trip to GBR – that's short for Guadalcanal Beach Resort. I still laugh every time I hear the word 'resort' associated with the AFP base in Honiara.

I spent the afternoon sweating while listening to briefings on local procedures and customs, then we were shown our ITSA. ITSA seemed to stand for International Temporary Subtropical Accommodation – but no one really knew exactly what it stood for. It was just a fancy title for a low-cost accommodation block made from galvanised steel beams, insulated aluminium sheeting and plywood. Each room contained two beds, a shared desk and a temperamental air conditioner. It was where I would sleep for the next four months.

The first opportunity to call Susan and tell her all about the fancy resort I was staying in came later that night. Three telephones were mounted on the wall outside the main dining room. While I sat at one, litres of sweat poured from my skin. Partners weren't allowed on this deployment, for safety reasons, which was probably a good thing as Susan would have hated the humidity.

I was assigned to work as a projects officer for the manager of police special operations. It sounded great when I first heard it, but I was stuck at a desk and working office hours most of the time. It was the first time in my working life that I had ever driven an office desk. But there was an upside. Unlike most coppers on base, I had my own computer, my own chair that I could adjust in all the right places and somewhere to put my coffee mug. I no longer had to search through a bunch of grubby ones stacked three high in a sink waiting to be washed. It was kind of novel at first, but got boring quickly.

My two days off per week were usually spent getting to know the island a little better. Outside the township of Honiara, it was an untouched island paradise. There were plenty of hidden beaches that you could spend hours lying on without seeing another soul, or shipwrecks you could explore with a snorkel and pair of fins. It was hard to believe that only a few years ago the island was the scene of fierce tribal fighting, not to mention some of the most significant battles of World War II.

•

Halfway through my four-month deployment, the Solomon Islands government elections were held. No one really knew how the locals would handle the outcome if the government changed as a result. They were the first elections to be held since the Australian-led assistance mission started in 2003. And the government had been in caretaker mode since the elected prime minister Allan Kemakeza's term ended in 2005.

Everything seemed to be running smoothly on voting day. The result saw Kemakeza's party lose a number of seats, but he retained his own seat and the leadership. He then quickly resigned and his deputy, Snyder Rini, took over the top job. The locals believed that Kemakeza's resignation and the appointment of Rini were fixed and funded by local Chinese businesses.

Within hours the locals had gathered in numbers at Government House to voice their anger. Things quickly spiralled out of control and by mid-afternoon the angry mob of protesters had made its way to the city centre, torched a police car, set rubbish bins alight and started looting shops.

Just after lunch I was called out of my office and asked to head across Honiara to pick up a senior member of the AFP from his residence and bring him back to the safety of our base. I was handed the keys to a brand-new Toyota HiLux four-wheel drive that only a few hours earlier had its blue-and-white checked banding stuck down its sides and a set of red and blue flashing lights mounted on its roof. It was to be gifted to the Royal Solomon Islands Police Force, or RSIPF, but I needed it first.

By the time I walked into our equipment room to grab some gear it had been almost emptied. The racks were bare apart from an odd riot helmet that looked like a war relic painted dark blue, and a few ballistic vests – all extra small. But they were better than nothing.

The main highway into town was unusually quiet. There were signs that the rioters had already swarmed through. Rubbish was scattered over the road. A few shops had their front windows smashed and some of their stock was scattered out front on the footpath, the looters dropping their bounty in a rush to clear out before the coppers turned up. Every public bin had either been rolled into the centre of the road or set alight, filling the street with black smoke. But the looters must have found somewhere else to wreak havoc, as they were nowhere to be seen.

I continued through town and picked up my important passenger. By the time I had driven back into town half an hour later, the angry crowd was back in the main street and slowly making its way towards Chinatown. They targeted all the Chinese-owned businesses along the way, smashing their front windows and walking out with whatever they could carry.

We couldn't get past the crowd, so I parked the HiLux and jumped out. A group of coppers were about to start tracking the trail of rubbish and broken glass left by the swarm of looters, so I joined them and handed the keys of my HiLux to another copper, Ian Jowers, who was staying behind. He would take care of my passenger. Ian was better known to everyone as Zimmer, on account of his age and that he would be the first of us to need a Zimmer frame.

Tracking the looters was like following the path of a tornado. They turned off the highway and crossed over an old single-lane wooden bridge, one of only two ways in and out of Chinatown. By the time the sun went down, the crowd had set almost every building in Chinatown ablaze.

Our commanders considered it far too dangerous for us to cross the old bridge and head in to battle the rioters. They were probably right – we were outnumbered and lacked decent equipment. But in true copper form, I was disappointed that they didn't let us give it a red-hot crack. Instead, we stood at the old bridge for most of the night, questioning our commander's decision while we watched Chinatown burn to the ground.

I left Chinatown soon after midnight and made my way to the Solomon Islands Police Headquarters (HQ) at the western end of town for a briefing from our commander. I hadn't been there long when I was asked to help evacuate injured coppers from HQ back to GBR for medical treatment.

We were to drive to GBR in a convoy of three Toyota troop carriers, each carrying two injured coppers. I was assigned to the second troop carrier with a crew that had already made a few evacuation runs. By all accounts they were no Sunday drive.

I jumped into the back cabin along with John Upton. Uppers was also from Victoria Police and had joined the AFP the same day as me. We had two injured coppers with us, both lying down on the bench seats that ran along either side of the cabin. Uppers had two old plastic riot shields in the cabin already. On his previous runs he held them up against the cabin windows, just in case the glass didn't hold up to the rocks being thrown at them along the way. I tried to find two shields for me, but all I could scrounge up was one that looked like it had been scavenged from a trash compactor and secretly put back into service.

Up front we had a driver and a spotter, both wearing ballistic helmets with protective visors. They were strapped into their seats and ready to go. It was almost three in the morning when I set off on my first run – my crew's fifth.

Uppers told our injured passengers to keep their heads down as we entered the township of Honiara, while the driver and spotter lowered their ballistic visors and sank down into their seats, their heads only just poking above the dashboard. Uppers and I grabbed our riot shields and pressed them hard against the troop carrier's side windows. Our driver started swerving around obstacles placed on the roadway, while his spotter called them out over the police radio, giving the troop carrier behind us some advance warning.

Angry locals stepped out from the shadows and started throwing large rocks and pieces of wood – anything they could pick up was turned into an improvised missile. The sound of each one of them striking the metal panels on the troop carrier's side echoed through the cabin. It was like driving in a storm of cricket-ball-sized hail. A few well-aimed shots hit our side windows. Uppers and I braced ourselves as we saw each of them coming, expecting any one of them to burst through the window and hit us, or at least shower us with broken glass.

We got through unscathed. We were lucky.

As we left the township of Honiara behind, the barrage of missiles stopped and we lowered our shields. A minute later we were passing Chinatown. It seemed as though every building was still ablaze. I looked over towards the old wooden bridge – the coppers were still standing there, watching Chinatown burn.

King George Market was ahead of us and we were expecting more trouble there. It wasn't your standard garden-variety marketplace. There were no large steel awnings and trestle tables packed with colourful tropical produce. This market had a dozen or so stalls made from old wooden fruit boxes lined up along the side of the road, among the town rubbish. The awnings, where they existed, were made of thatched coconut palm fronds held up by a few sticks and twine. Flies usually outnumbered customers and the only produce for sale was individual cigarettes removed from their packets, coconuts if you couldn't be bothered collecting them off the side of the road yourself, the odd can of Coca-Cola, and betel nut – the local version of chewing tobacco. Betel nut was supposed to increase a person's energy levels and produce a high when it was chewed. But all it seemed to really do was turn teeth and gums blood red and produce copious amounts of saliva of the same colour. Splatters of dried blood-coloured spit outnumbered cigarette butts on the streets and footpaths around town.

As we approached the market I could see that the locals had created a debris field on the highway using everything from household rubbish to old fencing palings. They had even dragged an old refrigerator and ironing board out onto the road, obviously to slow us down and give them a better chance of hitting us. But we didn't slow.

We hit the troop carrier's top speed and the rocks started to fly just as we passed the first stall. There was no lighting around the market so I looked ahead through the front windscreen. I could see each of the locals stepping out from the side of the road and into the beam of our headlights, just long enough to launch one of their missiles at us, before disappearing back into the shadows.

Another local then appeared in the headlights. He looked to be carrying something long. A length of wood, maybe? His throwing arm was bent back over his shoulder as if he was going to launch a javelin. I saw a glint as whatever it was caught the light from our headlights. It was a metal star picket.

'Star picket!' our spotter called.

We all braced ourselves. It was airborne. It hit the metal frame between the two cabin windows with a deafening boom, right between Uppers and me. If it had hit a window, both the glass and our riot shields wouldn't have stood a chance. One of us would have been impaled. That was close.

We tore down the road that led to GBR – normally speed restricted – but not tonight. The guards manning GBR's front gate opened them up for us as we slowed to turn into the driveway. The staff at the medical centre were waiting for us as we pulled up out front. The driver kept the troop carrier's engine running while Uppers and I off-loaded our injured passengers. We climbed back into the cabin – there were more injured waiting for us back at HQ.

On our return to HQ, the locals gave us the same reception we received at King George Market and in Honiara. We were thankful that there were only two injured coppers left to evacuate back to GBR.

But on this run to GBR, aims had improved. The locals were a little cockier, stepping out further onto the road to maximise their chances of hitting us.

Again, Uppers told our injured passengers to keep their heads down as we entered the township of Honiara. We covered the windows with our plastic riot shields as the locals threw everything they had at us. We got through relatively unscathed, but the worst was yet to come – King George Market. Our driver accelerated. The heavy troop carrier moaned as it gathered speed.

'Market approaching, guys!' the spotter yelled.

I looked out the front windscreen and could see that more rubbish had been added to the debris field, as well as a barrier made out of timber and tree branches that crossed the road. Every gap between the branches and wood was packed tight with rubbish, which had been set alight at one end.

Our driver didn't slow down. Locals stepped out onto the road, this time getting within metres of our troop carrier. Their bombardment was relentless as our driver lined up the centre of the barrier, then hit it square on. A loud thud resonated through the cabin, the sound of a metal star picket strategically placed in the barrier to pierce the steel belly of the troop carrier. Logs and burning embers scattered across the road and the cabin filled with smoke. We were through and the disappointed locals withdrew into the dark to reload for their next target: the troop carrier coming up behind us.

Just as we passed through the market, we began to slow down. I looked out front and saw that our escort car had also slowed. Just as I was about to question why they had reduced speed, a call came over the police radio. A rock had come through their windscreen and hit the driver in the head. Pulling over and changing drivers would have left them exposed to the angry locals, hell-bent on doing coppers serious harm. Somehow the passengers managed to keep the bleeding under control and the driver miraculously steered the car towards GBR. When we approached GBR's front entrance the guards walked out to the gate, then opened it as our convoy turned into the drive. The second the bumper bar of the last troop carrier passed through the gate, it was closed. And locked.

The escort car in front pulled up at the medical centre and we pulled in behind it. Again, the medical staff were waiting. They helped the driver out of the car – he was a Kiwi copper, one of a dozen or so Kiwi coppers deployed to the Solomon Islands. I'd seen enough head injuries in my time to know that he was lucky to be alive, let alone conscious.

We didn't go back out that night. We couldn't have even if we'd wanted to – our troop carrier had taken a beating. Along with all the dints and scratches covering every inch of every panel, all four tyres were punctured. Later, in the morning, Zimmer handed back the keys to the Toyota HiLux. They were the only thing left to show for that car, except for a burnt-out shell left on the side of the road just outside of Honiara.

•

Rumour was that the crowds were going to hit the streets again the next night. In preparation, the mechanics on base repaired as many of the damaged police cars as they could, with whatever parts and materials they could find. New windscreens would have to be shipped in from Australia, so the broken ones were all removed and replaced with steel-wire mesh screwed directly onto the car's body.

I was teamed up with four other coppers for the night, including Joomby – Graeme Brindley. Joomby and I had a lot in common. He had worked as a helicopter crewman on a Search and Rescue contract for the RAAF prior to joining the Police Force in Western Australia. He then moved over to the Feds a month before I did. I had no idea how he got his nickname, and he didn't volunteer the information.

We were given the keys to a second Toyota HiLux, another brand-new one destined for the Solomon Islands Police. Only this time I made sure someone else signed it out.

All the crews rostered on that night gathered on the floodlit grass behind police headquarters. It was stinking hot as usual and I was dripping with sweat. I had stripped off all the protective gear that I had been issued that night and was lying down on the cool grass, using my ballistics vest as a pillow, trying to get a little rest before the briefing started. There was plenty of banter around our group, including an analysis of the riots so far. As always, the discussion swung around to who was to blame. Not for starting the riots, but for not allowing us to finish them.

At the end of the briefing, right before it was time to head out for the night's entertainment, a representative of the Solomon Islands Government addressed us. During the afternoon, the government had declared an 11 p.m. curfew, so anyone found on the streets after that time was to be arrested. And we had been given all the local powers to do it.

I considered myself reasonably well equipped for the night, as opposed to the night before. My ballistic helmet was in one piece and my vest was at least the correct size, although the riot shields that we were issued were found in an old shipping container at the main police headquarters and looked like they were a hundred years old.

All the crews were assigned a patrol area, and we were to patrol in a convoy. Our convoy was made up of four cars and we were assigned the area covering Chinatown and the shanty suburb of Kukum. Our convoy drove through Honiara on our way to Chinatown. The streets had been abandoned, save the odd stray dog. Smoke from the previous night's fires hung in the air and there was an overpowering smell of food left to rot in the sun.

We drove over the old bridge into Chinatown, then down the main commercial street, Chung Wah Road. There were very few buildings left standing, which meant there was nothing left for the looters. It was hardly worth driving through again. We made our way back out to the main highway and drove a short distance before turning into the suburb of Kukum. It was mostly a residential area, except for a strip of four or five shops nestled among houses. They were all run by locals and, oddly enough, they were all selling the same three products – cigarettes, betel nut and Coca-Cola. Kukum was only a few blocks in from the main highway, so it wouldn't take us long to check.

Our convoy turned onto the shopping strip and we followed, third in line, with one troop carrier behind us. There was no street lighting once we were off the highway, so the leader of the convoy turned on their high beams, lighting up the dirt road and shops on either side. Our lights startled a small group of locals right in the middle of their free shopping spree. They scattered in every direction, careful not to drop their bounty. Some darted back into the shops to get more, despite that fact that a police patrol had just turned up.

We accelerated towards the locals and stopped the car. Our doors flew open and everyone jumped out, armed with expandable batons and antique riot shields, ready to take on the looters. To my amazement, the lead and second car continued through the shopping strip and headed back towards the highway. Perhaps they weren't at the same briefing as us. I couldn't believe what I was seeing. But we were committed.

Even though were were all in uniform, we still identified ourselves as police. Even with the language differences the looters would have understood us. But those who hadn't run away went about their business, collecting any undamaged goods while pretending that we weren't there. In a shop's doorway I saw one local whose arms were full. He kept looking over at me, then to his bounty, then back to me again. I started walking towards him. It was as if he wasn't sure whether he should drop everything and make a run for it, or keep loading himself up.

'Drop it!' I yelled.

He didn't. Instead, he held on extra tight to his goods and started to walk right on past me.

'Drop it!'

He dropped everything. Cans of food and drink fell to the road. He then turned to me and shaped up to take a swing. Clearly, his shopping was worth fighting for. Before he could swing his arm I hit him with the tip of my baton, just above his left knee. His leg collapsed inwards and he dropped to the ground. But he got up again. He looked mad. I wasn't going to wait for him to work out what to do next, so I swapped my baton over to my other hand, grabbed a can of capsicum spray from my belt and off-loaded a cupful of it into his eyes. I was expecting him to drop his head and madly rub his eyes while his sinus ran like a faulty tap. But he didn't. He gently rubbed his eyes like he had just woken up, then stared back at me with a how-dare-you look on his face and started to growl.

I gave him another spray. This time he ran like hell, crossed the road and disappeared into the bushes, probably in search of some cold running water. Joomby had decided that the only way we were going to get the remaining looters under control was to use the OC fogger. It was a fly-spray-sized can of capsicum spray with a pistol grip and a firing trigger, commonly referred to as a 'party pack'. He set the party pack off and aimed it towards the looters, spreading it around like he was trying to put out a fire. The thick cloud of orange-scented mist formed in the air and hovered around us at nose height. The smell of orange zest hit as my nostrils and the back of my throat started to burn.

It was only a light exposure – unlike the one that I had been silly enough to volunteer for during my AFP training, which was supposed to teach me what to expect if I was ever exposed to OC spray accidentally. But instead of spraying the OC in my eyes like a normal exposure, the instructor had soaked a sponge in liquid OC drained straight from the can, then squeezed the sponge over my forehead. The liquid OC filled my eyes and within seconds they clamped shut and my sinuses ran like a fire hydrant. It felt like I had snorted a thousand chillies through my nostrils. The only relief from the intense burning was found at the bottom of a water trough where I forced my eyelids open with my fingers.

By now the troop carrier that was behind us had driven past. The driver was about to turn towards the highway when he spotted a larger crowd of angry rioters around the corner from the shops and heading our way. He tried to do a quick U-turn to drive back out the way he came in, but troop carriers were not known for having a tight turning circle, so he had to nose it into the shops, back up, then turn and drive off. Unfortunately, he backed his rear wheels into a drainage ditch filled with rubbish. He accelerated forwards, trying to drive himself out of the ditch, but his wheels just spun around, adding smoke and the smell of burnt rubber to that of OC spray.

While the troop carrier rocked forwards and back in the ditch, trying to get some purchase on the dirt, the massive driving lights mounted on its front bull bar lit our team up for the world to see, just as the crowd turned the corner. We were sitting ducks.

Rocks fell out of the sky and landed on the ground all around us. As aims improved with practice, it wasn't long before they zeroed in. Rocks crashed against our shields. I heard a distinctive snapping sound above my right ear, then saw the corner of my riot shield break away and fall to the ground.

Joomby ran over to the troop carrier to help the driver, while the rest of us grouped together and held our shields over our heads. The barrage of rocks didn't stop. A rock hit the ballistic helmet of the guy right next to me, leaving a two-inch-long gouge in the side of it, just above his right temple. It left him a little dazed and the rest of us thinking our helmets were not much better than our shields.

Joomby reached in through the troop carrier's open window, turned the driver's steering wheel for him, then told him to back up. The driver accelerated backwards, digging his rear bumper into the back wall of the ditch. Joomby reached in again and turned his wheel in the opposite direction, then yelled at the driver to get out of there.

Joomby ran back to our car, with rocks hitting the ground around him as the troop carrier sped away. We made our way to our car, staying low to the ground, our shields still over our heads, all linked to make one large protective roof. The crowd seemed to have an endless supply of rocks, some large enough to almost knock the shields right out of our hands. We shielded each other as we all scrambled into the car.

'Everyone in?' Joomby yelled.

Rocks started hitting the car roof. We were in a storm of giant hail. A rock hit Joomby's side window, which shattered into tiny pieces of glass. I was last to get in, right behind Joomby. I leant forwards from my seat, over Joomby's right shoulder, and put my riot shield through the window opening and held it up against the door as a makeshift window to give Joomby some protection. The Kiwi copper's injury the night before was still fresh in my memory. A rock hit my shield with a snap. It broke in half, leaving me with the handle and a small piece of perspex. Joomby put the HiLux into reverse and planted the accelerator, backing away from the shops. The engine roared. We had no side mirrors, so whoever was sitting in the front passenger seat opened their door, poked their head out and, looking backwards, attempted to direct Joomby.

'Right hand down!' he yelled.

The passenger was looking towards the back of the car and really meant that he wanted Joomby to reverse to his right – which should have been Joomby's left hand down. Joomby did exactly what he was told, and pulled the steering wheel to the right. A large wooden power pole grated down the right-hand side of car, gouging every panel, and hit my riot shield. I lost my grip, and it fell to the ground.

When he had enough room, Joomby spun the steering wheel around, slammed the gearstick into first and accelerated away. Joomby never saw the giant ditch in front of us until he hit it at full speed. There was an almighty bang. We hit the ditch so hard the back axle twisted out of line. We made it out of Kukum by the skin of our teeth.

●

In the early hours of the morning, when everything had quietened down, we found a place to pull over and rest – a dead-end road off the Kukum highway, overlooking Ironbottom Sound. We all poured out of the HiLux and staggered over to a small grass patch at the end of the road. We removed our helmets and peeled the ballistic vests off our sweat-soaked bodies, dropping them at our feet. One by one we collapsed to the ground with loud sighs of relief.

I lay on the cold grass, my head resting against a pillow made from my helmet and ballistic vest. The vest's ceramic plate was hard as steel, but I wasn't complaining. My shirt was stuck to my skin and there was a cooling breeze coming off the water. My hair reeked of the disinfectant the storeroom clerks had sprayed inside the helmet after the last person had worn it. I knew the smell – Glen 20.

We lay there, recounting the night's events over and over again. With each rendition the rocks got a little bigger and the crowd a little angrier. I could have lain on the grass patch all night.

●

Honiara quickly returned to normal. It was as if the clock had been magically turned back a few days and the riots never happened. The locals had left graffiti messages about their resolve and their love for the overseas coppers on the walls of the buildings that were still standing. The usual 'Fuck the Police' and 'Go Home AFP' were sprayed in brightly coloured spray-paint, probably looted from the hardware store in Chinatown before they burnt it to the ground. There was a more personal message left for a few of us on the wall of the Kukum shops: 'Kukum till we die'.

•

I returned to the Solomon Islands half a dozen times, the last in July 2010. Each time, I stepped off the plane hoping for a deployment that would be more exciting than my first. A trip in December 2006 delivered. I was standing on the tarmac of Henderson Field, the main Solomon Islands airport, waiting for some equipment to arrive on a freighter aircraft. I hadn't spoken to Susan for a few days, so I called her on a satellite phone. She seemed desperate to tell me something. I got the impression that she was waiting for me to ask the right question first. Unfortunately, I was a little slow on the uptake and Susan couldn't wait any longer. 'I'm pregnant!' she said. I might not have been there to see Susan's face when she told me the good news, but I was home for my son Louis' birth.

32

JUST A WALK IN THE PARK

A letter from Government House, Canberra, was waiting for me when I returned home from that first deployment to the Solomon Islands, informing me that Ray, Brendan and I had been awarded a Group Bravery Citation for Ron Palmer's rescue. I had to accept the award in writing before they would make the official announcement and presentation. I accepted it without really knowing much about it. I wasn't sure how 'group bravery' worked – I thought bravery was a personal thing.

A few weeks later I received the official invitation to Government House in Melbourne, where the ceremony would be held.

Having already attended one award ceremony there and feeling a little uneasy about the attention, I decided to attend this one by myself. I was working at the AFP office in the city and when the time came for the ceremony I got up from my desk, put on a suit and tie and quietly left the office as though I was heading out to lunch.

After a short tram ride through town, I was back in Government House sitting in the same food-court-style seats. Brendan and Ray had already received their awards while I was still in the Solomon Islands. I felt just as uncomfortable hearing the same words read out at this ceremony as I had when Colin Bannister at the Royal Humane Society awards had read them several months ago. Again, I felt like a failure for being scared. At the end of the reading, my name was called. I stood up, walked over to Governor David de Kretser, shook his hand, received the award then returned to my seat, eager to head back to the office. Having learned from the last time, and wanting to avoid another photograph in the *Herald Sun*, I snuck out a side exit, forgoing the afternoon tea and denying the waiting media an opportunity to rehash an old story. I knew there were far better stories around me. Back at work, no one was any the wiser.

Later that night, alone, I sat down and opened up the little black jewellery box holding the award. Inside was a beautiful sprig of wattle cast in copper and mounted on a silver plate. A black velour folder held the accompanying certificate that was printed on parchment paper emblazoned with the Australian Coat of Arms. There, in large red lettering, were our three names with the finely written citation and the Governor-General's flowery signature below it. I took a deep breath and started to read.

It was not what I had heard read out at the ceremony only a few hours ago. This account was dramatically different. There was no mention of being catapulted into a raging sea and being forced underwater by heavy waves, or gasping for air, or struggling to get Ron Palmer into a harness. This was a story of a nameless police officer who was merely washed from the deck of a yacht and waited in the water while Palmer swam out to reach him. While fifty feet in the air, he didn't grab Ron's leg to stop him from falling backwards into the ocean. Instead, a harness miraculously caught him by the ankles and he was lifted up and out of the water.

Was this how the Australian Honours and Awards office at Government House in Canberra saw the rescue of Ron Palmer? Where was the panic and the terror and the fact that I had almost drowned, and that the person we were rescuing almost had as well and that there hadn't seemed to be a way out of a rescue where everything was going horribly wrong? As much as I tried to excuse the fact that these were just a bunch of nicely printed words on a piece of parchment written by a harried government staff member, I couldn't.

Struggling with feelings of failure and shame about being scared on the job was one thing, but now, according to Government House, the whole ordeal was nothing more than a walk in the park. It was as if they were trying to erase the very reason why I was suffering.

I wrote a letter to Government House urging them to change the citation. How could they have got it so wrong? They had even read out the citation written by the Humane Society at the ceremony. I received a response from some government official telling me that they had considered my request, but that they would not change it.

And just like that, I transformed from being a regular working copper to a deranged letter writer. In my mind, the citation's words were magnified. 'Swept from the deck' had replaced 'catapulted into the ocean'. *Swept*, like garbage?!

Not surprisingly, Government House did not give a toss about my need for linguistic distinction. I continued to fire letters and emails in their direction and lost track of how many I wrote. While I was lying awake at night, words would pop into my mind. 'I haven't said that yet,' I would mutter as I crawled out of bed, careful not to wake Susan as she had no idea of how I felt and what I was doing late at night. I'd turn on my computer and tap out another letter. I would edit it over and over again. Whatever relief the letters provided was short-lived, fading the moment they hit the bottom of the postbox. It was like a drug – the only way I could feel better again was to shoot off another one. Somehow, I thought that having Government House validate my fear was going to make it all okay. This made perfect sense to me.

The barrage of letters finally came to a halt when I was politely told by the Official Secretary to the Governor-General that what they had written was accurate and supported by Brendan's, Ray's and Ron Palmer's statements. The matter was considered closed. I hadn't read their statements and wondered how they could be so different from mine. Regardless of what the secretary's letter said, it wasn't closed for me. The feeling of failure continued whirling around in my head, keeping me awake at night.

Weeks later, I realised I had not had a full night's sleep in ages. One night, after a few hours of tossing and turning in bed, I got up and rummaged through the bottom drawer of my bedside table and found the black jewellery box that held the award. I walked into my study and dragged the certificate out of a stack of old work documents, placed them both inside a large padded envelope and mailed them back to Canberra the following day.

If I didn't have the award, then none of this really happened.

Now the matter was closed.

•

Some years later I found out why the Official Secretary to the Governor-General was so adamant that their version of Ron Palmer's rescue was accurate. It turns out that Brendan and Ray never made sworn statements. What was provided to the Governor-General's office were two statements with Ray's and Brendan's names on them, but written by someone else – someone who wasn't there. I can only guess that it was a way of controlling what details of the rescue were made public, mainly the slightly embarrassing fact that the RCC could not call a satellite phone because of a cost-saving lock placed on the phone to prevent workers making long-distance calls or calls to mobile phones.

Now it all made sense. But it was too late.

33

BLACK SATURDAY

In the summer of 2009 Victoria suffered through days of extreme temperatures and hot, dry winds. The state was one giant tinderbox and conditions were perfect for it to ignite into flames. And it did. On 7 February, hundreds of bushfires ignited all over the state in what would become known as Black Saturday – the worst bushfires ever recorded in Victoria. A total of 173 people died and over two thousand homes were lost.

The AFP bosses in Canberra had committed sixty of us to the search-and-recovery effort. We loaded up a four-wheel drive with as much gear as we could squeeze into it – ropes, harnesses, chainsaws and a well-equipped first-aid kit – then drove to our first assignment in the township of Churchill, south-east of Melbourne. The fires had reduced Churchill to ash – nothing was left standing and it was our main job to search the rubble for bodies.

•

The first property we went to had been devastated by fire only two days prior. Paddocks on both sides of what was left of a house were all burnt away, leaving nothing but dirt and a fine coating of black soot. They were dotted with cow carcasses singed smooth and puffed up like giant balloons, their legs poking out, all knobbly and rigid. The trees surrounding the place were now thin black trunks with short stumps where the branches used to be. Some were still smouldering.

We started our search through the rubble and waded through a layer of ash, lifting up each blackened beam and rusty sheet of iron as we went. A brick fireplace was still standing proud, but everything else around it had collapsed. Panels of corrugated iron roofing had twisted in the intense heat, and rust had already started to take hold. Thick wooden beams that once supported the roof had all been eaten away by fire.

There were a few handle-less pots and pans all melted out of shape, and crisp white china plates cleaned by the fire were scattered around where the kitchen once stood. Twisted metal wires that were once the inner springs of mattresses marked each bedroom, which we spent a little more time searching.

I covered my nose with my hand trying to filter out the stench of burnt and rotten meat, but it was too strong. With no cows or sheep carcasses in sight, it was hard not to think that its source was a burnt body or two buried underneath the rubble, but there was not enough left of anything to be sure.

After searching the property, we tied some blue-and-white checked crime scene tape around the letterbox, to let the incoming police crews know that this place had been searched. Later on, teams would come in with all the proper protective gear and go through the property with rakes and sieves. They would have a far better chance of finding human remains than we would.

We moved down the road to the next house but were soon told we were needed in the township of Marysville, three hours north of Melbourne. We finished searching the house, before having a quick dinner and a shower. There was no escaping that smell. It was in my hair and on my skin. It had stuck to my uniform like tar and stayed with me even after scrubbing myself until I was red under steaming hot water.

We packed up our four-wheel drive and started the six-hour trip to Marysville via Melbourne to replenish some of our gear. Shortly after 11 p.m. we poked our heads into the Alexandra Police Station, about forty kilometres north of Marysville – the command centre for the Marysville fires. We were met with huge sighs of relief from the local police commanders. Finally, their crews could head home for some respite. *Lucky for some*, I thought.

We relieved crews at roadblocks around Marysville to stop anyone who didn't belong entering the town. While most of Australia was rallying behind those devastated by the fires, others saw an opportunity to profit and had begun looting evacuated houses.

Eventually, after nearly thirty hours straight, our heads went down on clean, white pillows in a small hotel just outside of Alexandra. A break before the work ahead.

•

The local fire station in Marysville was one of the only buildings still standing. It had become a makeshift base for the Victoria Police Search and Rescue squad who were running the search operations for missing people around Marysville. Propped up against one wall was a large whiteboard covered with scribble explaining call signs and tracking the sectors where units were already out searching. The Search and Rescue guys were hunched over a paper map spread out over a trestle table. I recognised them and they certainly knew me, although they all had a look of confusion, no doubt wondering why I was wearing Federal Police patches on my overalls.

Their main search priority was to locate a couple who had been reported missing. James Gormley, an avid environmental campaigner, had taken his girlfriend, Julie Wallace-Mitchell, to Marysville a few days before the fire for their first romantic getaway. The last anyone had heard from them was at the height of the fires, when Julie had telephoned her mother saying that they were surrounded by fire – the phone then cut out.

The Air Wing was sending up a helicopter to help search for them and the Search and Rescue guys were right in the middle of discussing who they could brief and send up in the helicopter to run the search. I was the perfect solution. Another member of the AFP, Leigh Hunter, and I were briefed on the search. Leigh had also worked in Victoria Police as a police prosecutor before he took a job with the AFP. This work was the polar opposite of standing in the Magistrate's Court prosecuting speeding fines and drunk and disorderly cases. We made our way down to the local football oval and waited beside a drum of jet fuel. It had to be for the helicopter, and the crew would land right next to it. The crew would have arranged for a local fuel supplier to drop off the drum when they were tasked to head up this way. It was how the Air Wing was able to operate in remote areas for extended periods. Some country police stations also held drums of jet fuel and the local coppers would deliver them on request – in exchange for a ride in the helicopter, of course.

I could hear the sound of the helicopter approaching. It wasn't the normal whine of the Dauphin but the much quieter single-engine Squirrel. It slowed down as it approached the oval then entered a wide right-hand orbit, sizing up the landing area. It descended into the centre of the oval, stopping in a hover only a few metres above the ground, then turned around and headed straight for the drum – the closer they got to it, the smaller the distance they had to push the drum before refuelling.

I was keen to see who was going to step out of the cockpit once it landed. I had only left the Air Wing three years before so the chances were good that I would know at least one of the two crew. As the rotor blades started to slow the left side door swung open and out stepped the air observer, all six-foot-four of him. It could only be Brooksy – also known as Michael Brooks. I am sure that Brooksy was only in the Police Force for a bit of fun and the Air Wing provided it. He was extremely talented with his hands and spent much of his spare time building aeroplanes in his garage – real ones. He was followed by the pilot, Dermot Oakley. Although Dermot was an air observer, he also held a commercial helicopter pilot's licence, allowing him to move over to the pilot seat when the Air Wing was short of a pilot. It was good to see them both. We rolled the drum over to the helicopter, tested it for water contamination and then attached a hand-wound pump and hose to it. We were ready to pump its contents into the Squirrel's fuel tank, but not before I caught up on all current Air Wing gossip. Familiar topics were covered, in much the same way as we would have done years ago while sitting on the vinyl couch in the Air Ambulance office back at the Air Wing hangar. I was updated on the flying ability of more recently appointed pilots, which old-school air observers were still left on the roster and, of course, who was performing and more importantly, who wasn't. While we talked, Leigh manually pumped all two hundred litres of fuel out of the drum, obviously preferring to exercise his arms and shoulders over interrupting important gossip between old friends.

I jumped into the back seat of the Squirrel. The cushy leather-covered seat was as comfortable as I remembered it. I sat up and reached underneath me for the seatbelt, always done up across the seat cushion to stop it flying out the cabin when the door was open. I did my seatbelt up firmly, not too tight, then moved forwards to make sure I could reach the intercom volume control between the two front seats. I slid the door all the way back, waiting for the click on the catch that locked it open. I turned around and grabbed my headset, which was hanging on a hook on the back wall like I had only put it there yesterday. I put it on and tested the microphone and intercom volume, without a pause.

'All set in the back, Derm,' I said.

'Thanks, Cam.'

It was as though I had never left.

As Dermot started the engine I heard the familiar buzz through my headset, then felt the helicopter rock gently as the rotors started to turn. Everything around me was incredibly familiar. I was back where I belonged and for the very first time I questioned why I had left the Air Wing. *How could I have lost interest in doing this?* I thought to myself.

•

Below us, the town of Marysville had been wiped from the landscape. The surrounding hills, normally covered in eucalyptus trees, were now mounds of ash and burnt-out tree trunks that looked like thousands of giant grey and black needles pointing up from the ground. Any trees not totally consumed by fire were covered with burnt leaves, reddish-brown ones, like tiny pieces of rusted metal.

There was some pressure to find the missing couple, hopefully alive, so that there could be one good story to come out of these fires. The roadway that led from Marysville up to the Lake Mountain alpine area, a cross-country skier's utopia, was our first search area. In summer it should be full of hikers and sightseers.

Dermot tracked the helicopter sideways, crab crawling along one side of the roadway, slowly following the road as we climbed to the top. We would get two bites of the cherry that way – Dermot and Leigh, who were seated on the right side of the helicopter, would check the track and surroundings as we flew over the top, then Brooksy and I, who were seated on the left side, would check the same area as it appeared underneath us.

We arrived at the top of the mountain and saw that the usually packed car park was abandoned. There was no sign of the missing couple. We turned around and flew back along the roadway, this time concentrating on the opposite side of the road.

A call came through on the police radio. A ground unit had found the missing couple's car burnt out on Ghost Point Track, not far out of Marysville. I glanced down at my map – the track was just over the next hill.

'Head south over the next hill, Derm,' I said.

Dermot nosed the Squirrel forwards, increasing speed, then started to climb. As the top of the hill disappeared underneath us, Ghost Point Track appeared. The burnt-out shell of a car was sitting in the middle of it, doors wide open. Two coppers on the ground were checking inside for the remains of our missing tourists. As we got closer, we found what they were looking for. What looked like burnt debris from a distance was actually the bodies of James Gormley and Julie Wallace-Mitchell. One of them was only metres behind the car, the other further along the track.

There were benefits to being in the air, removed from some of the ghastly sights and smells that the street coppers had to put up with. But sometimes you saw things that could only be seen from above. This was one of those occasions.

It was obvious that the couple had turned off the main dirt road and onto Ghost Point Track in an attempt to outrun the fire. They would have had no idea that the track they took curved back around to the main dirt road, putting them right in the path of the oncoming fire again. Their only chance was to make it back to the main dirt road, but a fallen tree blocked their escape route and, with the fire behind them, they could not turn back. The fire raced up the valley and over the track, consuming everything in its path. James and Julie got out of their car and tried to run from the flames.

Within seconds, one of them succumbed to the intense heat and fell to the ground only metres from their car. The other made it one hundred metres along the track before collapsing.

Both lay on the track, face up, arms out by their sides. The gravel around their arms and heads was wiped clear as they thrashed around in pain until all that remained were snow angel impressions in the gravel.

34

COCAINE

It was March 2011 and a few things had changed since I had been deployed to the Black Saturday fires in 2009. Susan had given birth to our daughter, Adele, who was now a feisty sixteen-month-old. Louis was a three-and-a-half-year-old tornado on two legs, destroying everything within his reach. And I was on deployment to Christchurch, New Zealand, leaving Susan and the kids at home for two weeks.

In February, the city had been devastated by a 6.2 magnitude earthquake that killed 185 people. The AFP was sent there to help in the relief effort and to boost the number of police in the town. Prior to flying out, I had seen some of the damage on the local television news services, most of which centred around the Canterbury Television Building and the Pyne Gould Building where the majority of people had been killed, or the iconic Christ Church Cathedral, the town's centrepiece.

In reality, the damage to Christchurch was far greater and more widespread. A third of the city must have been reduced to ruins. Blocks of buildings had either completely collapsed or were beyond repair, buses and cars had been crushed by falling debris, and old churches fared badly – nearly a dozen of them were damaged. One glass-clad building in the middle of town looked almost untouched, apart from single panes of glass that had been removed from each floor. It was from these windows that the fire brigade had evacuated the building after the elevators and stairwells collapsed in a pile of rubble. I thought the stairwell of a multistorey building was the safest place to be during a major earthquake – that's if you couldn't get the hell out of there. Wrong.

Outside the city, whole suburbs were uninhabitable because of a phenomenon called 'liquefaction' where, just beneath the surface, solid ground becomes liquefied after extreme vibrations separate soil and water to create a quicksand-like sludge that swallows any weight above it. On top of that, there were aftershocks that caused further damage – some were close to the magnitude of the earthquake that they followed. They certainly kept me on my toes.

I stepped off the plane from Christchurch and into a job as an investigator on a crime team in Melbourne. The contrast between the two environments couldn't have been sharper. Procedures had changed considerably since I last investigated a crime. That, coupled with the fact that I had also changed police forces and was now dealing with Commonwealth crimes and legislation, meant I was a fish out of water. I almost wished I was back in Christchurch, where I felt a little more at home dodging aftershocks.

The investigators in the crime team I was working in were conscientious and were keen to take any job that was offered – the bigger the better. So, when a job came in notifying us that around two hundred million dollars in almost pure, uncut cocaine had been smuggled into Melbourne, the team grabbed it. The cocaine was compressed into one-kilogram blocks and hidden inside eight shipping crates that contained a ride-on mower each. The mowers arrived in Melbourne on board a container ship that originated in Brazil and had stopped briefly in Hong Kong.

While the rest of the team was busy performing some weird computer magic to find out who was bringing in the shipment, I was helping our forensics team. I was opening up the blocks of cocaine with a surgical scalpel, removing every last gram of the white powder and placing it into evidence bags – all 270 blocks.

The shipping crates were then repacked with 270 blocks of another white substance that was no more illegal than icing sugar. The crates were then transported to a warehouse facility in Laverton, as per the consignee's instructions. With the crates stored away and waiting for the owner to come and collect them, the team began looking for a volunteer to sit at the warehouse, posing as a warehouse worker. Because I had been out of mainstream policing for so long, most of the processes my team were following to establish who was importing the drugs went well over my head. So, I volunteered.

•

The fluorescent orange work shirt I was handed looked like it was fresh from its packaging. I figured anyone coming to collect the crate would be a little suspicious of the guy with the brand-new shirt. So I took the shirt into our car park and rubbed it into the dirtiest corner I could find, covering it in a layer of black grime. I then rolled it up and sat on it while I drove out to the Laverton warehouse. By the time I arrived the shirt looked well-worn. I was going to fit in.

After two days at the warehouse, I received a phone call from the team telling me that a young Chinese male going by the name of Wilson was the main suspect for importing the cocaine. It seemed like a strange choice of fake name for a Chinese guy. I figured he had just watched the movie *Castaway* before being asked to come up with a name, and that the main character's best friend, a volleyball, was as good a name as any.

Wilson had contacted the warehouse a few times prior to his shipment's arrival and had paid for its storage in advance using cash. It was only a matter of time before he came to pick up his goods. The plan was not to arrest him on the spot but to follow him and his cocaine to whoever his buyer was.

It was day four when Wilson came out to the warehouse, unannounced, asking to inspect his shipment. It was good timing, because it was also the day that the other employees at the warehouse were complaining to the boss that the new guy did nothing but sit around on the telephone all day.

Wilson stood at the counter asking the office staff if he could inspect his shipment. Before they blew the whole job, I decided to cut in and take over.

'I'll take you to it, mate,' I said.

He nodded. Wilson was only a little fella. The team told me that he was around thirty years old, but to me he didn't look a day over sixteen. If I had to tackle him to the ground and handcuff him I probably could have done it with one hand tied behind my back.

I took him through the warehouse and pointed out a grey shipping container. Any grey container would have been good enough as long as it was sitting on top of another and too difficult for anyone to reach. I told him that I was more than happy to move all the containers around and put his outside in the driveway so he could look inside, if he was prepared to wait the two hours it would take me to do it. Wilson was not interested in staying around that long and was certainly not willing to have his container out in the open where he could be seen inspecting it. I was more than happy to leave it there as I had no idea how to move containers around anyway. He then jumped in a waiting taxi and left.

The following day, Wilson called the warehouse and I spoke with him on the phone. He sounded happy to hear it was me – the guy who only yesterday was prepared to move all the containers around for him. Wilson told me that he had rented his own storage unit just a few miles away at Kennards Self Storage in Port Melbourne and wanted four of his eight crates delivered there tomorrow. He also said that he had no idea how to operate a forklift and wanted help to move the crates into his unit. I told Wilson that I was driving the delivery truck and could squeeze his delivery in tomorrow and that I'd also help him off-load his crates and put them into the unit. He couldn't have been happier.

The following day I rented a truck from the local rental company, covered their logo on the door with a sticker from the warehouse and then loaded the four crates on the back. The other employees watched on, happy to see that the new guy was finally doing some work. I tied the crates down just like a real delivery guy would do, then jumped on board and headed for Kennards. The Kennards building was in sight, just past the West Gate Bridge. I was starting to think that driving a large delivery truck was easy going, and I could see myself getting used to it, until I took a wrong turn and ended up down a narrow dead-end road. I slowed the truck down and began a three-point turn that ended up a few more points more than I expected. I had almost turned the truck around when I heard an almighty bang come from behind me. The truck stopped. I had backed into a power pole.

I looked up and out from the windscreen. The powerlines overhead were swinging so violently they almost made contact with each other. Only I could be in the middle of delivering 271 kilograms of imitation cocaine to a Chinese drug syndicate and cut the power to half of Melbourne in the process. So I did what any other self-respecting drug courier would do – I looked around for potential witnesses, then drove off, straight to Kennards. I had a delivery to make!

•

Wilson was waiting patiently for me inside Kennards. As I backed the truck into the building he waved his hands around, trying to give me some instructions on reversing. He looked excited to see his delivery arrive and had a grin on his face like he was about to be handed his firstborn baby.

Then, one by one, each crate was taken off the truck with a forklift and put inside his storage unit. As the last crate was being lifted off the truck, one of the metal forks broke through the bottom of the wooden crate. It tipped to one side, almost falling to the ground. Splinters of timber dropped to the floor. Wilson froze with fright. He probably didn't know whether he should try to save the crate or make a run for it and save himself.

I pushed the crate back onto the forks. 'It's okay, Wilson. It says on my paperwork that they are mowers, they're built tough.' He still looked worried – I had nearly dropped his baby.

With the last crate inside his storage unit, Wilson closed the roller door and padlocked it shut, putting the key in his shirt pocket. He paid for the delivery in cash, of course. I was in the middle of writing him a real receipt – to make the delivery official – when he reached into his jeans pocket and took out a crisp fifty-dollar note and handed it to me as a tip.

I had a little chuckle to myself and thought of a tip I could give him in return – make sure you pack a toothbrush tonight. What I would have given to say it out loud.

With the delivery done, it was now up to the rest of the team to weave their magic. And they did.

•

Later that day, Wilson was contacted by Pak Lau, another Chinese national, and instructed to split up the shipment into smaller lots and get them ready for distribution. He then locked himself inside the storage unit and got stuck into the crates with a jemmy, removing all the blocks of compressed icing sugar and placing them into cardboard boxes. The first delivery, to an unknown purchaser, of sixty kilograms was moved into a second storage unit close by, also rented by Wilson.

He then met the buyer in a park in Port Melbourne, where he handed over the key to the storage unit containing the sixty kilograms and the after-hours access code to enter the Kennards building. The buyer was nothing more than a twenty-year-old patsy acting on behalf of someone a lot higher up the supply chain who didn't want to get their hands dirty. Once the patsy had taken possession of the icing sugar, the team decided to close the job down and make the arrests. With the shipment being split up into smaller lots and heading in different directions, they risked losing the three offenders they already had in the bag.

The patsy was the first. He was arrested in an apartment in the centre of Melbourne with sixty kilograms of icing sugar neatly packed into a suitcase, along with 230 thousand dollars in cash, ready to head back to his boss in Sydney.

Pak Lau and Wilson (whose real name was Yiu Yim) were arrested later that evening, also in the city, preparing to off-load another part of the shipment.

Eventually they all pleaded guilty, saving taxpayers the cost of a lengthy trial. Lau was sentenced to twenty years' jail, Yim nineteen and the patsy eleven.

•

That wasn't the last time I saw Wilson. Some years later I had to go to Port Phillip Prison, just outside of Melbourne, to interview an inmate. While I was there I ran into my younger brother, Scott. He had followed in Dad's footsteps and had also become a prison officer. After my interview, Scott invited me to the prison officer's cafeteria for lunch. I felt a little uneasy having my food made and served by prisoners, wondering if they had added a little something to the food knowing who was going to be putting it in their mouth. But Scott assured me that the kitchen prisoners were trustworthy – as trustworthy as a person serving a prison sentence can be.

With my meal in hand I walked over to the coffee machine. There he was, Wilson, making the prison guards their espressos. He recognised me straightaway.

He made an awful coffee, but I supposed he had plenty of time ahead of him to perfect his craft.

35

CHRISTMAS ISLAND

In 2014 our managers were struggling to find a volunteer to spend six weeks on Christmas Island at the island's Immigration Detention Centre. The job involved interviewing refugees to try to identify the Indonesian-based people smugglers packing asylum seekers on board old wooden fishing boats. These boats were barely capable of staying afloat and smugglers were sending them into the Indian Ocean, bound for Australia.

I had spent the last two years travelling all over Australia as part of a team chasing people smugglers, and had just returned home from Malaysia after extraditing one smuggler back to Australia. I had never been to Christmas Island, but when they came around to my desk and asked, I volunteered to go. I was sure Susan would be okay with not having me around the house for six weeks, once I told her.

A mate, Ben Condon, volunteered as well. Ben had also served with Victoria Police before he took up a job with the AFP. But his interest in the island wasn't the same as mine –

he was keen on the exceptional fishing it offered. We stayed overnight in Perth before we had to jump on the six-hour flight over the Indian Ocean to the island. Most people would spend the night discussing how they were going to occupy themselves for six weeks. We spent the night writing an online review on the Dr Pepper braised pork ribs and European beer we devoured at a local restaurant, and discussing how we were going to smuggle Ben's overweight fishing gear onto the plane. With some creative repacking, we managed to share the load without maxing out our baggage limit, except for his seven-foot-long fishing rod tube. That, we just couldn't hide.

•

As we approached Christmas Island, I looked out the aircraft window and saw bright blue skies above us and a blanket of thick cloud covering the ocean below. Somewhere down there was the island, a tiny tip of an underwater mountain poking a few hundred feet out of the ocean.

I had heard stories about the island's runway and that it should be treated with the upmost respect. It sat on a slight hill and ended abruptly at the edge of a cliff overlooking the ocean – not the type of runway that you would like to overshoot because of bad brakes or a major tailwind. I didn't imagine that an airport so far away from the Australian mainland would have all the latest equipment to aid a landing in bad weather, either. The standard was probably the same as that of some of the small country airports I used to fly into on the helicopter – and I hoped that we had some experienced pilots sitting up front in the cockpit.

We suddenly hit a pocket of turbulence as we descended into the layer of cloud. I felt my body jump off my seat, forced back down by the seatbelt. Instinctively, I reached for my secret handle, but it wasn't there. I jammed my legs under the seat and grabbed hold of the armrests. I looked out of the window and saw patches of cloud flash past and the tips of the aircraft's metal wings flexing like soft rubber. My heart raced out of control and I struggled to breathe. My hands and legs clamped on to the seat even tighter.

The sound of the aircraft's engines faded. I could no longer hear people talking or the other usual cabin sounds. Instead, the sounds of the tiniest rattle or of metal rubbing against metal became abnormally loud, almost deafening – like they were only millimetres from my ears.

I had no idea what was happening to me. I started to panic.

Ben was fascinated with the aircraft's moving map display on the entertainment screen in front of him. I didn't want him to know that I was in a state of panic, so I had my well-practised game face on. He had no idea what was happening to me.

I could picture the pilot reading the approach plate for Christmas Island. To the uninitiated, an approach plate looks like the trigonometry diagrams that used to confuse the hell out of me at high school – a bunch of lines, half circles and angles – but for pilots it contains all the information needed to find the runway in shit weather and land on it.

I was now soaking in a pool of my own sweat and could picture the pilots in the cockpit struggling to land the plane, constantly moving focus from one navigation instrument to the other – the vertical speed indicator, altimeter, artificial horizon and the automatic direction finder – while trying to monitor the engines and hydraulics. When we were a few hundred feet off the ground they aborted the landing because they couldn't see the runway, and climbed away to try it all over again.

I looked over towards Ben. His entertainment screen was covered in a mass of red lines indicating our aircraft's track, as though some out-of-control kid had attacked it with a red marker. I was in such a panic, I hadn't realised that the pilots had already made several attempts to land. I began thinking that they were putting themselves under pressure to continue on with the flight and land regardless – a recipe for disaster. I managed to pry one hand off the armrest and open the overhead air vent, directing the flow of fresh cold air onto my face. I concentrated on my breathing, trying to slow it down.

The captain then addressed the passengers over the intercom. The crew had finally given into the bad weather and decided to return to Perth. But with so many attempts to land at Christmas Island we were now low on fuel. That meant a diversion to Port Hedland to top up the tanks – we had another seven hours of flying ahead of us.

I sat at the edge of my seat for the entire flight to Port Hedland, expecting another pocket of turbulence to hit us at any second. My breathing and heart rate only started returning to normal when I spotted the lights of all the small towns along the coast of Australia. I then focused on the land ahead, each minute in the air representing another few miles closer to land.

We commenced our descent north of Perth, which was partially covered by low-level fog. Building and street lights were barely visible. As we flew closer to the city the fog seemed to get thicker and the street lights on the ground began to disappear. I looked out the window and searched for the airport just south of the city. I could see the main roads leading towards it from the city but couldn't see the telltale signs of an airport, like the flashing white control tower light or the blinking strobes and coloured runway markers.

The aircraft banked left and I heard the hydraulic noise from the landing gear being lowered and snapping down and locked. Then came the winding noise of wing flaps being extended. We climbed slightly before the pilot pushed the aircraft's nose forwards and pulled back on the engine power. There were small adjustments to our track and we rocked gently left and right to line up with the centre of the runway.

I felt the aircraft settle. We must have been only feet above the runway. It was almost that time when the pilot usually reduces the engine speed and puts the wheels on the ground. I looked out the window – I could just make out the faint glow of a street light beside the airport through thick grey fog. I thought that if I couldn't see the street lights then there was no way the pilot could see the runway.

The engines roared. I was pushed back into my seat and the aircraft's nose lifted. We were airborne again for another attempt at landing. I took a deep breath.

It wasn't long before I heard the landing gear lock into place for the second time. Fog still covered the ground and if the pilot couldn't land this time we would probably have to head to another airport. I felt the aircraft settle. I looked out the window again. I still couldn't see the ground through the thick fog.

My heart rate started to climb again. I grabbed the seat with my legs and held on tight to the armrests. In only a few more seconds I would feel the wheels touch the ground and this nightmare flight would be over.

We touched down and I was thrown forwards in my seat as the pilot braked heavily. We had landed. The relief was instantaneous. It was the same relief I had felt when I saw city lights on the horizon in front of the helicopter after pushing through miles of shitty weather.

I leant over to Ben.

'The pilot must have been desperate to land – he probably had a hot date lined up,' I said, my joke covering up the fact I had been scared shitless.

I walked into my hotel room sometime before midnight, dropped my bag behind the door and lay face down on the bed. The room was dark and deadly quiet.

I was only moments from falling asleep when moving images of the Ron Palmer incident began to play. I thought I had put that all behind me. But the motion-picture reel kept on playing and it wouldn't stop.

I opened the hotel room minibar in the hope of finding something to wash it all away. The icy cold beer looked inviting, but I opted for a scalding hot shower instead. It didn't work and sleep evaded me. I should have had the beer.

•

After two days of flying my feet were finally touching Christmas Island soil. And on seeing from the air the downhill slope on the runway and the drop to the ocean at the other end, I was happy that yesterday's pilots hadn't tried their luck and landed in the shit weather.

After work there was very little to do on the island. The rest of the team occupied their time by exercising before and after their shifts, while Ben kept himself busy trying to rob the island of its fishing stocks. I had lost interest in doing anything other than spending quiet time alone. I rarely left my room, except to go to work or on nights when Ben and I would walk to the local convenience store to pick up a late-night snack, but I'd return to the solace of my room soon after.

As I learned on that last night in Perth, the quiet brought back the bad memories of Ron Palmer's rescue. Flashbacks of the rescue haunted me day and night.

I left the island six weeks later, exhausted and desperate for sleep.

36

FRIDAY AFTERNOON DRINKS

After Christmas Island, I returned to the AFP office in Melbourne. I had a jury trial about to start for one of two other cocaine smugglers I had arrested and charged during a short secondment to the Serious and Organised Crime team back in 2013. I also found out that I was being transferred to the AFP's Joint Counter Terrorism team. The workload there was intense and, with the public's fear of terrorism heightened after the Lindt Café siege in Sydney only six months earlier, there were no signs that the intensity was going to subside anytime soon. Being busy did nothing for my insomnia, but it did keep the flashbacks at bay and it wasn't long before they were behind me.

I spent the next few weeks stuck in a routine. Each morning I'd walk into the office, greet colleagues, check my emails and put on a tie – although it usually took me a few attempts to get the knot and the length to my liking. After a quick piccolo latte at the cafe across the road, I'd walk to the County Court of Victoria, only a short distance from the office. I was the informant and the one who had arrested the smuggler. As the informant I had to attend the trial, which meant I spent the day sitting in the courtroom, listening to my case against the smuggler presented to a jury.

The smuggler turned unsuspecting gamblers into drug mules by feeding their gambling addictions with injections of cash until their debts were beyond their means. The only way they could repay their gambling debt was to travel to Vietnam and smuggle the cocaine into Australia strapped to their bodies or stuffed into condoms and inserted up their rectums – an interesting case by anyone's standard.

I listened as each witness was sworn in and gave their evidence, then answered the barrage of questions fired at them by the lawyers representing the Crown and the smuggler. At the end of the two-week trial both lawyers presented their case to the jury. It was their last chance to convince the jury to return a favourable verdict before they retired to consider their decision. The next day the jury returned with their verdict – guilty. The smuggler's sentence was to be handed down in a few weeks.

The night before the sentencing I was lying in bed, on the verge of sleep, when the sound of my breathing filled my ears. My chest rose and fell as my lungs filled and emptied. I exhaled and my chest dropped. Then there was silence. Nothing.

I was back underwater, but only for a second. I couldn't breathe. I gasped in panic and air filled my lungs. I had stopped breathing.

The most frightening thing was that I was in no-man's land, somewhere between sleep and wakefulness. I didn't know whether my body had forgotten to breathe, or if I was dreaming. I then lay in bed wide awake, with Susan sound asleep next to me, fearing that if I fell asleep my body might forget to breathe again and I wouldn't be awake to remind it.

Eventually I was drained of all energy and had no choice but to sleep. I closed my eyes just as the sun was about to rise.

Later that morning, while Susan slept, I dragged myself into a scalding hot shower, hoping to replace the flashbacks of Ron Palmer's rescue with the pain of boiling hot water burning my skin. I stepped out of the shower with steam rising from my shoulders. An image of Tony Waddell flashed before me. He was still standing in the cabin of the wrecked helicopter, holding on to the door and looking up to the sky. I hadn't given the death of Tony Waddell and his two companions a second thought in years. I thought I had put it that all to bed.

•

When I walked into the office, I greeted my colleagues, checked my emails and tied the perfect tie knot – my first in a long time. After a quick coffee, I made my way around to the County Court – it was time for my smuggler to hear her sentence. I sat behind the Crown prosecutor while the defendant stood in the dock and listened to the judge. She didn't show any emotion when she was told that she was going to spend the next twelve years in jail. I too gave her sentencing very little thought.

Afterwards, I headed to the Metropolitan Hotel for some Friday afternoon drinks with a mate, Gavin Ryan, a detective from the Victoria Police Sexual Offences Squad. He had also had a court success. He had charged a business executive for raping a young woman in a hotel while she slept. The executive was convicted and sentenced to five years in prison. It is a pity that rape is an offence under state legislation and not federal, because then it would attract longer prison sentences, like drug smuggling offences do. Even so, Gavin got a conviction, and it was worth celebrating. The beers kept lining up and we kept drinking them.

I was just starting to hit my drinking stride when Susan called and reminded me that Louis, now eight years old, had a basketball match on and that I should be there – I was the coach of his basketball team, after all. After a futile attempt to persuade Susan to take my place as coach, I agreed to come home. Just to make sure, Susan said she would drive to Chatham Railway Station with the kids and pick me up.

As a consolation prize, Gavin arranged to meet me at a wine bar a little closer to home after Louis' basketball match had finished. An offer I couldn't refuse. I polished off what was left of my beer and headed for the underground platform at Flagstaff Railway Station, only a short walk from the hotel.

If I hurried I would be able to catch the 5.15 to Chatham.

37

5.15 TO CHATHAM

Friday, 17 July 2015

The 5.15 p.m. train to Chatham was right on time. As it began to slow, I walked along the platform. Just like I did every working day, I tried to line myself up so I'd be standing in front of the doors when the train came to a stop. Today, my timing was out. Dammit. I shuffled sideways with the crowd towards the open doors and was funnelled onto the train.

I always aim to get the seats at the end of the carriage right next to the doors. They are the only seats that back up to the windows so I don't have anybody sitting behind me. From this position, I have a perfect view of every passenger on the carriage. It's a cop thing – a good view of all the passengers and an exit nearby if you need one in a hurry. I sat down as people filled the empty seats around me.

Once the doors closed and the train started to glide out of the station, I scanned the crowd. Skipping over the people in suits, I was drawn to hoodies, scruffy people, unshaven people – anything outside the normal Friday afternoon post-work crowd. I was always on the lookout for passengers most likely to cause trouble. Trains seemed to attract more of those types than any other form of public transport. I reckon I have seen them all, from the self-appointed preacher reciting passages from the Bible to the disgusting old guy with an inappropriate interest in young girls.

A few weeks earlier one of these creeps had walked past an entire carriage of empty seats just so he could sit next to an attractive young woman who was sitting alone. She shuffled over to the edge of her seat to create some space between her and the man. While she was tapping away on her phone, I watched him leering over her. He had 'predator' written all over him and made the hairs on the back of my neck stand up. I could only imagine how he was making her feel. I moved to sit opposite the creep, ready to intervene if he tried anything. When the young woman stood up to get off the train, I stood beside her until she stepped out of the carriage and onto the platform. The creep didn't move.

The usual Friday afternoon crowd ebbed and flowed. Passengers stepping off at stations were immediately replaced by those getting on, so I had to keep scanning the crowd. Coppers can never leave the job behind.

A gaggle of rowdy private school students jumped on at Glenferrie Station. As usual, they all gathered in the doorway and slipped their oversized school bags off their shoulders, dropping them onto the floor. I have never known a group of students to be quiet and this one was no different. I untangled my headphones and searched through my playlist for a tune I could lose myself in. Scrolling on my phone, the bright yellow album colour of *Short Note* by Matt Finish caught my eye. It was a favourite of mine, so I set it to repeat and turned the volume up, then sat back for the twenty-minute ride to Chatham Station.

I jolted awake and opened my eyes in fright. I must have dozed off. Had I had missed my stop? Ripping the headphones from my ears, I frantically looked out the window, hoping I would recognise where I was, but all I could see was a blur of trees and graffiti-covered walls flashing past. None of it looked familiar. I looked around the carriage. Half the passengers had disappeared. Even the noisy school kids had gone.

Shit! I could be anywhere.

Then it happened. I was overcome, flooded, by an indefinable grief. Rolling like a tidal wave, it enveloped me and I felt like my world was coming to an end. My heart started to pound, and a tremble started deep inside me that rocked my body. My breathing accelerated out of control but at the same time I was struggling for air. Tears sprang up in my eyes, stinging, filling my vision, rolling down my cheeks.

Suddenly, everything was loud. Subtle noises that I hadn't noticed before were now going off like alarms inside my head, like bolts of electricity sending me into a state of high alert – the clacking of the train's wheels on the tracks, someone rustling plastic, music leaking out from headphones. Everything roared. My filter was broken. I dropped my head and pressed the palms of my hands hard against my ears. I had to stop the noise.

What the hell is happening?

My brain was in total confusion. I had no idea where this crazy thing was coming from. I was still upright, so I couldn't be dying. I made a superhuman effort to slow my breathing. *Breathe in. Breathe out. Breathe in. Breathe out.* My pounding heart and breathing started to slow and the tears stopped. Nonetheless, I was left in a state of high alert. I scanned the carriage for threats, ready to pounce.

An announcement came over the speaker: 'Now arriving at Camberwell.'

I hadn't gone past my stop and Chatham was only a few stations away.

As the train moved out of the station a second wave of grief hit me. My heart pounded and I struggled to breathe again. Once again, the tears flowed and the trembling started. I dropped my head and covered my face with my hands. I couldn't look up. The passengers on the train must have been staring at the grown man trembling and sobbing like a child.

What the hell was happening to me?

Another announcement. A tinny voice. Super loud. 'Now arriving at Chatham.'

The train slowed as passengers shuffled for the doors, waiting for them to open. I lifted and turned my head, just enough to look out the window, still hiding my face from the passengers. I recognised the familiar Chatham Station platform and ticket machine under a small shelter. As the train slowed to a stop, I went to stand but I couldn't move.

This was my station and I was going to miss it. The warning tone sounded, signalling that the doors were about to close. I reacted without thinking. I leaped towards the doors, hiding my tears behind my hands. The doors caught me like a trap. I forced my way out of the carriage and onto the platform.

The train accelerated away. I stayed on the platform, trembling uncontrollably. Crying. Confused. I had no idea what to do next. People brushed past me as they headed for the station's pedestrian ramp. As the last person passed by me, I turned and followed them down the ramp, still shaking and distraught.

Susan was parked in the street. Louis and Adele, now six, were in the back with their windows down, waiting for me to appear. Through the open windows they waved madly and called out 'Dadda! Dadda!' as I walked down the ramp and onto the street. They always act like they haven't seen me in months, but today their delight was short-lived. They must have realised something was wrong. They sat back in their seats and went silent.

I walked across the road and around to the passenger-side door. Susan leant over and opened it for me. I stood there, not entirely sure if I should get in the car or not.

'What's wrong, Cam?' she asked.

The bombardment of noise continued – the click of heels on the footpath, the roar of cars driving past, the smashing sound of another train roaring into the station. I heard everything like it was inside my head.

'I can't do this anymore,' I said in a shaking voice.

'Do what?' Susan sounded puzzled. She had no idea what was happening.

I didn't have an answer. I just stood there with tears running down my face, struggling to breathe, as Louis and Adele sat quietly in their seats watching their dad fall apart.

While I couldn't put it into words for my wife and kids, I knew exactly what had gone wrong. In fact, I knew the day, the hour, the minute my world turned upside down. I knew exactly where it had happened – in the middle of Bass Strait.

You never forget the day you almost drowned. The memory had come calling, knocking on the door of my mind with skeletal fingers, demanding to be let in. Demanding to be heard.

38

DIAGNOSIS

Susan dropped the kids at a friend's place – I guess she didn't want them to see what was happening to their dad. Then she drove me home. When we pulled into the driveway of our house I just sat in the car in tears, shaking and having trouble breathing. I couldn't get out. There seemed to be this enormous barrier between the car and our front door, and I couldn't walk through it.

My neighbour, Neil Murchie, came over as soon as he found out that something was wrong. I don't remember much about that night, but I do remember Neil sitting in the car with me while Susan started making phone calls to the AFP and Victoria Police welfare for help. Somehow Neil managed to convince me to open the car door, step out and walk into the house – something I thought at the time was utterly impossible.

One of the people Susan called that night was Nadia Crescias, a friend of hers. Nadia is a psychiatric nurse and, luckily for me, she had the night off. She dropped everything and came straight over to the house. I hadn't met Nadia before and this wasn't my preferred way to be introduced to one of Susan's friends, but I wasn't in any condition to argue. I remember Nadia sitting next to me on the end of my bed, calming me down, explaining to me what was happening. If it wasn't for Nadia I would have spent that night in a psychiatric ward, away from Susan and the kids. That would have been my worst nightmare.

I'm not sure how Susan and I would have got through that night without Nadia and Neil. They stayed in the house with us until I settled down. I fell asleep within seconds of my head hitting the pillow – it was the first solid night's sleep I'd had in months.

•

The following morning, Susan drove me to our family doctor's consulting rooms. I sat silently in the passenger seat as she drove. I could only imagine what she was thinking. Julie's rooms weren't like standard ones. You could easily mistake her for being a paediatrician instead of a general practitioner, with every square inch of the walls covered in brightly coloured photographs, stuffed toys and tiny figurines.

I walked in with Susan, trying to hold my shit together – at least until I could explain to Julie what had happened on the train.

'What's wrong, Cam?' she asked.

Her question was enough. I burst into tears as I told her about the breaking down on the train, the sleepless nights and the flashbacks that were haunting me. Susan was shocked, hearing what was happening to me for the very first time.

Julie had the perfect amount of empathy, but also wasn't one for fluffing around with words. She preferred to get straight to the point and fix the problem.

'I think I know what's wrong, Cam.' Her voice was kind and calm as she explained that I was suffering from PTSD – or post-traumatic stress disorder.

'I think your work has finally caught up with you,' she said.

I nodded, not really understanding what she was saying.

'It's going to take a while to get better, Cam, but we'll get there. I think it is time to rest. Later on we can consider whether or not to continue with work.'

It took me a few seconds to understand exactly what Julie was saying. Then it hit me – my police career had just ended. I didn't know what to say. Being a copper was the only job I'd ever had. I didn't know how to do anything else. I was losing my identity all over again, just like when I had left the Air Wing.

Julie gave me a month off work, a prescription for some serious sedatives and a referral to a psychologist. Afterwards, Susan and I headed to a cafe we knew nearby. I sat on a seat along a large bench in the centre of the cafe. It wasn't my usual seat – mine in the back corner was taken. I had taken my first sip of coffee when the world's volume was suddenly turned up.

Noises around me exploded inside my head, just like on the train – a chair being pushed back from a table without being lifted, a patron dragging his feet as he walked, a metal teaspoon striking the side of a glass as someone stirred their coffee, someone else plunging their knife deep into their food like they were trying to saw through bone.

My heart raced out of control as I prepared for the sound of the knife scratching the china plate – it might as well have been fingernails on a chalkboard. It was fight time – I had to stop the noise.

Susan was quick enough to notice me boiling over. 'We should go, Cam,' she said.

I ran out of the cafe, my heart rate through the roof and my breathing out of control. Every muscle in my body had tensed up and I was overheating – I was just about ready to explode. Instead, I burst into tears.

•

After Julie declared me unfit to return to work, I spent the next month at home hardly ever venturing too far away from the house. The local shopping strip and cafe were my limits. But I would end up drained of energy from battling with all the stimuli – people talking, loud footsteps, noisy eaters. What little patience I had left was used up just in time for Louis and Adele to come home from school. Unlike at the shops, I couldn't walk away if they got too loud and my reactions had far greater consequences. It wasn't long before their voices were raised, just like all kids, and very quickly the volume passed my incredibly low threshold.

It wasn't like there was a build-up of anxiety. For me it was as if there was only a two-stage switch – off and overloaded. I would lose control in an instant and explode into yelling, louder and more frightening than ever before. Both the kids would jump in fear and run for the sanctuary of their bedrooms. On one occasion I found Adele sitting in the corner of her bedroom, sobbing and hugging her legs that were pulled up tight against her chest. She refused to come out of her room until Susan got home.

As if Louis and Adele hadn't put up with enough already.

I'd walk away feeling like an arsehole, and rightly so. But no matter how much I apologised to them or explained what was wrong with me, the damage was done. The bad experiences were now embedded in their little memory banks, just like some traumas were embedded in mine.

Somehow I don't think they'll forget. My biggest fear now is that when Louis and Adele become adults and are asked what their childhood was like, the only thing they'll remember with any clarity is their dad scaring them when he yelled.

My worsening temper and shrinking patience were not just unleashed on Louis and Adele, though. Susan copped it the worst, usually over something trivial that under normal circumstances wouldn't even be worth mentioning. I consider myself immensely lucky that Susan decided to stick by my side, where others might not have.

I took Julie's advice and saw a psychologist, and was soon swallowing a handful of pills, one or two per symptom: anxiety, depression, insomnia and hyper-arousal, just to name a few. Most of the medication I was taking had side effects that were almost as bad as the symptoms they were trying to suppress. Some days I felt like my stomach was full of nothing else but tablets.

With the help of both the psychologist and a psychiatrist I learned a few techniques to help manage the symptoms of PTSD. What seemed to work for me was sticking to a tried and tested routine, nothing too strenuous on the brain – get out of bed, shower, get dressed, go to the local cafe for a coffee or three, then return home for an afternoon nap. I had to turn myself into a recluse of sorts until I could tolerate environments that were full of triggers, like crowds, social gatherings, kids' weekend sports and even family meals. And I had no idea how long that would take. When I did get the courage to step outside my routine, and things went right, I almost felt normal. But every now and then I was reminded that PTSD is always there.

39

LAVERS HILL

The Great Ocean Road is 250 kilometres of bitumen that snakes along the rugged south-west coast of Victoria, treacherous to the ships of yesteryear – many lie wrecked on the jagged rocks below. Beyond the moody dark sapphire sea is Bass Strait and the Southern Ocean.

Susan and I were driving along the road, on the way to a family holiday on Kangaroo Island. I was still on sick leave from work. It was the first time we had gone away since I had been diagnosed the year before and a family holiday was really going to test how my treatment was going. The kids were in the back seat, occupied by the DVD player, watching *Jurassic Park* or *Monsters, Inc.*, depending on whose turn it was to pick the movie. The drone of either served two purposes – first, it kept them quiet, and second, them being quiet kept me from blowing my stack.

A few hours into the drive, we were in the middle of the Otway Ranges and Susan slowed the car to negotiate a T intersection in the road. In a profound moment of deja vu – like I was transported back in time – the helicopter was sitting on the large grass median strip that surrounded the intersection. Its cabin doors were open.

I blinked my eyes and turned to Susan. I was back in the present. I shook my head and took a deep breath.

'I've been here before,' I said.

We passed a sign that said Lavers Hill and moments later we drove through the town. It was a typical small country town with a general store, a few old weatherboard buildings and a community hall. That's about it. If you weren't paying attention you would blink and miss it. Nothing there seemed to jog my memory.

Several kilometres later, we entered a sweeping right-hand bend with a slight downhill slope. The car increased in speed. Tall trees and thick forest undergrowth lined both sides of the road, blocking the view of oncoming traffic. My eyes locked on a galvanised steel barrier on the opposite side of the road, just one of many we had passed. But this one was different. It was sitting in the shadow of a large tree with shredded bark peeling off its trunk.

In a flash, everything came flooding back.

•

We landed the helicopter on the large grass median strip at the T intersection on the outskirts of Lavers Hill. It was 2004 and I was working with the paramedic Mark 'Rakka' Lamb. A motorcycle had collided with a car and Rakka and I had been driven from the helicopter to the accident site by the local volunteer ambulance officer.

When we got to the scene, the motorcycle rider was lying on the road next to that galvanised steel barrier, his mangled motorcycle resting against the large tree. The other volunteer ambulance officer was kneeling next to him, supporting his neck. Rakka went straight to work while I set up the Propaq monitor and connected its leads and oxygen sensor to the rider. The volunteer then stood back and recited the mechanics of the crash and the rider's condition. He had been hit head-on by a car travelling in the opposite direction. The force of the collision threw him through the air and onto the road barrier.

The rider was barely conscious and in a great deal of pain. I could see the shattered end of his femur poking out of his leg. I assumed that he had a major neck and chest injury as well, but they were the least of his worries. His breathing was shallow and he was probably not getting enough oxygen.

Rakka asked the rider his name. His responses were short and delivered with a strong American accent.

'Henry. Henry Skokowski,' he said.

Rakka and I worked on autopilot to do everything we could to get Henry stable enough to fly back to The Alfred Hospital trauma centre in Melbourne. Rakka lifted Henry's arm and began tapping his skin, searching for a vein. I got the IV line ready then reached into the drug case and drew up two syringes, one of Pancuronium, the other Suxamethonium – or Panc and Suxs if you're in a hurry. Rakka called out a needle gauge.

'Fourteen-gauge, Cam,' he said.

I quickly grabbed the needle out of the drug case, tore open the packet and held it out. Rakka drew the needle from its protective tube and gently inserted it through Henry's skin before pulling it out, leaving a paper-thin plastic cannula in his vein.

I secured the cannula with tape and connected up the IV line, then started the flow of fluids.

Henry took a deep, painful breath and struggled to say something to Rakka. I watched my partner lean forwards to catch the words.

'Don't let me die,' Henry whispered.

'We're just going to give you something for the pain. Then put you to sleep for a while, okay? You'll probably feel a little dizzy, but then you'll fall asleep,' Rakka said.

Henry didn't answer. He had used up all his energy for those last few words.

I handed the laryngoscope to Rakka and he then gave me the go-ahead to inject the drugs. One at a time, I connected the syringes to a valve on the IV line and slowly squeezed the drugs into the fluid. We both watched and waited. Seconds later Henry's arms went limp and his whole body relaxed. The drugs did their job to sedate and paralyse him. He would no longer feel any pain but would not be able to breathe on his own.

Rakka gently tilted Henry's head back, lowered his jaw and fed the laryngoscope blade past his tongue. He then fed a long plastic endotracheal tube past his vocal cords and into his airway. Rakka inflated a small balloon at the end of the tube with a syringe of air, locking the tube in place and stopping it from coming out. Then he listened to Henry's chest with his stethoscope. Everything sounded as it should.

I attached the bag from the Laerdal mask to the end of the tube and gave it a squeeze. Oxygen-enriched air filled Henry's lungs. His chest rose and fell. One squeeze was one breath. He was now getting oxygen.

With the lifesaving interventions done, we got Henry ready to fly, fitting a neck brace and placing him on a rigid spinal board. Everything else could wait until we were back in the helicopter and in the air. Rakka checked him over one more time before declaring him stable enough to move. With the help of the volunteers, we lifted Henry onto the stretcher and loaded him into the road ambulance for the short trip back to the helicopter. All the while I was filling his lungs with air with every squeeze of the Laerdal bag.

Our pilot was waiting with the side door of the helicopter open and the loading frame extended to take the stretcher. I then jumped in the back with Rakka, just in case things went horribly wrong while the pilot started the helicopter.

We climbed straight up to gain enough altitude to clear the trees and powerlines surrounding the intersection. The pilot tilted the helicopter's nose forwards and we began the seventy-minute flight to The Alfred Hospital.

Ten minutes after take-off, Henry stopped breathing, then his heart stopped. Rakka leant over him, placed his right hand on his chest and started one-handed chest compressions. With his other hand he held on to the cabin's centre pillar to stop himself from falling over. He yelled out the drugs he wanted to get Henry's heart going again. I scrambled to the drug kit and drew up the syringes. When I moved back to Henry I saw sweat dripping down Rakka's face from the exertion of CPR. The hot sun beating through the cabin window didn't help. I injected the drugs into the IV line, opened up the line and forced the drugs through Henry's veins. Our monitor told us that his heart was pumping again. With relief, Rakka stopped CPR and wiped his soaking brow with his sleeve.

An hour later, The Alfred Hospital helipad appeared in the distance. Rakka had been on constant watch, checking Henry's heart rate, blood pressure, oxygen level and fluid consumption at regular intervals – writing them down so the emergency room doctors could see his progress.

The helicopter slowed and started its descent towards the helipad.

Henry stopped breathing and his heart stopped again. Rakka started CPR and I administered more drugs. This time our interventions couldn't get him back. By the time our wheels touched down on the helipad, Henry was dead.

It turned out that Henry Skokowski was indeed American and was in Australia on holidays. The guy that drove onto the wrong side of the Great Ocean Road and hit Henry head-on, then drove off and left him for dead, was also American. The driver had just flown into Melbourne and had been drinking on the plane. The police eventually tracked him down and charged him with culpable driving and leaving the scene of an accident. He served three years in jail. Hardly enough of a sentence for what he did to Henry and his family.

EPILOGUE

Henry Skokowski whispering the words 'Don't let me die' while he lay on the roadside at Lavers Hill is now another flashback I struggle with. Just like being underwater and nearly drowning, or seeing Tony Waddell standing upright in the cabin of that wrecked helicopter. Over time, more flashbacks have surfaced. I now see images of snow angels in the gravel, and rocks falling from the sky. I can even hear the sound of Robert Baulch drowning in his own vomit and can taste the sea water from Lindsay Dack's mouth.

It doesn't take much to trigger a flashback. Seeing a major car accident reported on the evening news or hearing the sound of a distant siren is more than enough. But they don't always need triggers. Flashbacks can appear unprovoked and unannounced, so they are impossible to avoid. Having PTSD is like spending your days walking through a minefield, wondering if you'll step on something that will trigger another memory and expose it forever. Or worse, trigger whatever it was that I experienced on the train to Chatham.

•

Late one night, more than twelve months after I was diagnosed, Susan and the kids had already gone to bed and I was on the couch watching some mindless television when I became overcome with grief. I knew what was coming. Just like on the train. The rate of my breathing increased immediately and my body started to shake. I managed to drag myself to the bedroom and sit on the edge of the bed. Susan was still awake.

'It's back,' I said.

'What's back, Cam?'

I didn't answer. Seconds later I was curled up in the foetal position with all my joints locked into place. I moved my hands towards my mouth and tried to pry my jaw open with my fingers – a futile attempt to get more air into my lungs.

Susan called an ambulance.

After being locked into place for so long, my muscles started to cramp. The pain was excruciating and all I could do was lie there and moan.

The ambulance turned up in no time at all – or at least it felt like it. I heard two paramedics walk into the bedroom. I tried to look at them, but I couldn't open my eyes. I could hear Susan explaining that I had PTSD. I had never felt so hopeless in my life, lying on my bed, curled up in a ball and unable to speak, paramedics leaning over the top of me, just like I used to do to others.

It was a short ride to Box Hill Hospital. Along the way, my breathing slowed and my muscles started to relax. I heard the reversing alarm as the ambulance backed up to the hospital's emergency door and the driver slamming their doors shut. Seconds later, the rear door opened. The driver reached in and grabbed hold of the end of my stretcher. I heard the familiar clicking of metal as my stretcher was pulled out of the ambulance and its legs dropped and locked into position. Sounds I had heard a hundred times before.

Once inside the hospital, I was given some sedatives to calm me down. I spent the next few hours being interviewed by the psychiatric registrar, trying to justify to her why I should be sent home and not admitted to the ward. Only when the registrar was satisfied that I wasn't going to self-harm was I allowed to go home.

•

It has taken some time and nearly two years of proper treatment, but I realise now that the way I dealt with all the trauma I witnessed on the job was not the right way, if there is a right way. Work for me was a separate life, one that I hid away from those on the outside. It was a life that was devoid of all emotion and feeling – they just got in the way. I suppose that's why police forces recruit people like me in the first place, because of our ability to cope in the face of serious trauma, to put it all behind us and move on. I was immensely proud of my ability to handle trauma. The greater and more extreme it was, the better I seemed to perform.

Then came the rescue of Ron Palmer and my near-drowning – the moment when, finally, I couldn't block out my emotions anymore. What I felt more than anything was fear, and fear was unacceptable to me. That was the first domino to fall. The second domino fell during the nightmare flight to Christmas Island. Then the flashbacks started, then even more emotions – feelings that I had blocked out for years came rushing to the surface like molten lava. Turns out the navy-blue flight suit wasn't the suit of armour that I had always thought it was. I wasn't ten feet tall and I certainly wasn't bulletproof – no one is.

I never returned to work after my breakdown on the train. Doctors have since told me that I will never go back to policing, after thirty-four years' service. They say it's time for me to rest, that maybe one day I can work part time in a job where there's a little less action. I am not sure what that will be – I've only ever had one job. This is certainly not how I wanted my police career to end. I was hoping to retire like everyone else, with a gold watch and a pension. Perhaps it just wasn't meant to be.

I wouldn't wish PTSD on my worst enemy, but for all those who are going through the same battle – focus on your successes. My policing career – like every other copper's – is made up of a long list of people who have lived without fear and violence, have been able to watch their children grow up or even grown up to have their own children – all because of my commitment to my job. The shame is not that I now have PTSD, but that it took PTSD to make me realise the good that I had done.

•

As for my lucky cigar? It sits in the bottom drawer of my bedside table. It's starting to show its age, with its aluminium tube covered in dents and scratches. Every now and then I will come across it when I'm looking through my drawer for something else. Each time I take the cigar out of its tube, pass it beneath my nose and enjoy that fantastic aroma of tobacco and Spanish cedar. Then I put it away again.

It kept me safe for so long. And I'm still here, so perhaps it still carries a little luck.

ACRONYMS

ADF	automatic direction finder
AH	artificial horizon
AFP	Australian Federal Police
ALT	pressure altimeter
ASI	air speed indicator
CFA	Country Fire Authority
D24	Victoria Police communications centre
GBR	Guadalcanal Beach Resort
ECG	electrocardiograph
HQ	Solomon Islands Police Headquarters
HSI	horizontal situation indicator
HUET	Helicopter Underwater Escape Training
ICU	Intensive Care Unit
ITSA	International Temporary Subtropical Accommodation
IV	intravenous line
MICA	Mobile Intensive Care Ambulance
PTSD	post-traumatic stress disorder
RAAF	Royal Australian Air Force
RADALT	radar altimeter
RCC	Rescue Coordination Centre
RSIPF	Royal Solomon Islands Police Force
SOG	Special Operations Group

RESOURCES

Australian resources

Lifeline – lifeline.org.au

Beyond Blue – beyondblue.org.au

Black Dog Institute – blackdoginstitute.org.au

Sane Australia – sane.org

Head to Health – headtohealth.gov.au

New Zealand resources

Lifeline Aotearoa – lifeline.org.nz

Mental Health Foundation of New Zealand –
mentalhealth.org.nz

Anxiety New Zealand Trust – anxiety.org.nz

The National Depression Initiative – depression.org.nz

ACKNOWLEDGEMENTS

PTSD is an insidious illness. It destroys one's very self and takes a huge emotional toll on those closest to you. My wife, Susan, stood by my side through all of it. I could not have been easy to live with, and I am sure there were times when Susan considered packing my bags and leaving them at the front door for me to find. Without her unwavering support, this book would never have been written.

My two children, Louis and Adele, have only ever heard stories of their dad working in a police uniform, or in the big blue-and-white police helicopter that flies over our house sometimes. But now they live with a dad who suffers as a result of that work. I hope that one day they will read this book and maybe even forgive me for what I have put them through.

Back in 1992, I walked into the Air Wing mess room and was surprised to see a blonde woman sitting at the table. I originally thought that one of the crew had a new girlfriend and was planning on taking her for a fly – not that that ever happened, of course. It was actually Vikki Petraitis, an accomplished author of true crime who had managed to get approval to fly around with us for the shift in search of material for her book *Victims, Crimes and Investigators*. It was another twenty-three years before we met again, not long before I was diagnosed with PTSD.

When Vikki found out that I was using writing as self-administered exposure therapy, she encouraged me to make it a little more formal and turn it into a book. Vikki had a unique ability to find the inspiration when I had run out and the words when they had escaped me.

The owners of the Red Brick Cafe in Surrey Hills, Chris Kabay and Bruce Facey, managed to keep up with my demand for coffee while I sat in the back corner of their cafe madly tapping away at my laptop. When I failed to show up for my morning coffee some days they would call me, just to check if I was okay. And as it turned out, Chris was a fine editor as well – although maybe a little picky!

The fear of having someone read and critique my work is something that took me considerable time to overcome. Initially, I only sent two friends, Ann and Grant Spurrell, a single chapter to read. I just wasn't prepared to risk exposing more than a few thousand words to criticism – especially if they found my work was better suited to wrapping up fish and chips. Friends like Rachel Holt, Barb Kristoff, David Mills and Keith O'Toole followed, and with their help I became comfortable enough to hand my work over to anyone who was prepared to read it, including publishers.

Finally, I consider myself extremely lucky to have Hachette Australia as my publisher. Sophie Hamley, the non-fiction publisher at Hachette, nurtured me through the publishing process and answered all my ridiculous questions in a language that even I could understand. Rebecca Allen, my editor, seemed to know exactly what I wanted to achieve with each and every chapter, sometimes even before I did, and then helped me get them there.

And thanks also to the rest of the team. Christina Pagliaro, my copyeditor, and Rod Morrison, my proof reader, who both probably wished that I had paid a little more attention in English class at high school. Layla Saadeldine, Hachette's Production Controller, who kept everyone, including me, on a tight schedule. Graeme Jones for his text design and Luke Causby for his impressive cover design.